DIPLOMA IN FRONT OFFICE THE COMPLETE SYLLABUS

DR ANSHUMALI PANDEY

ISBN 979-888591504-5

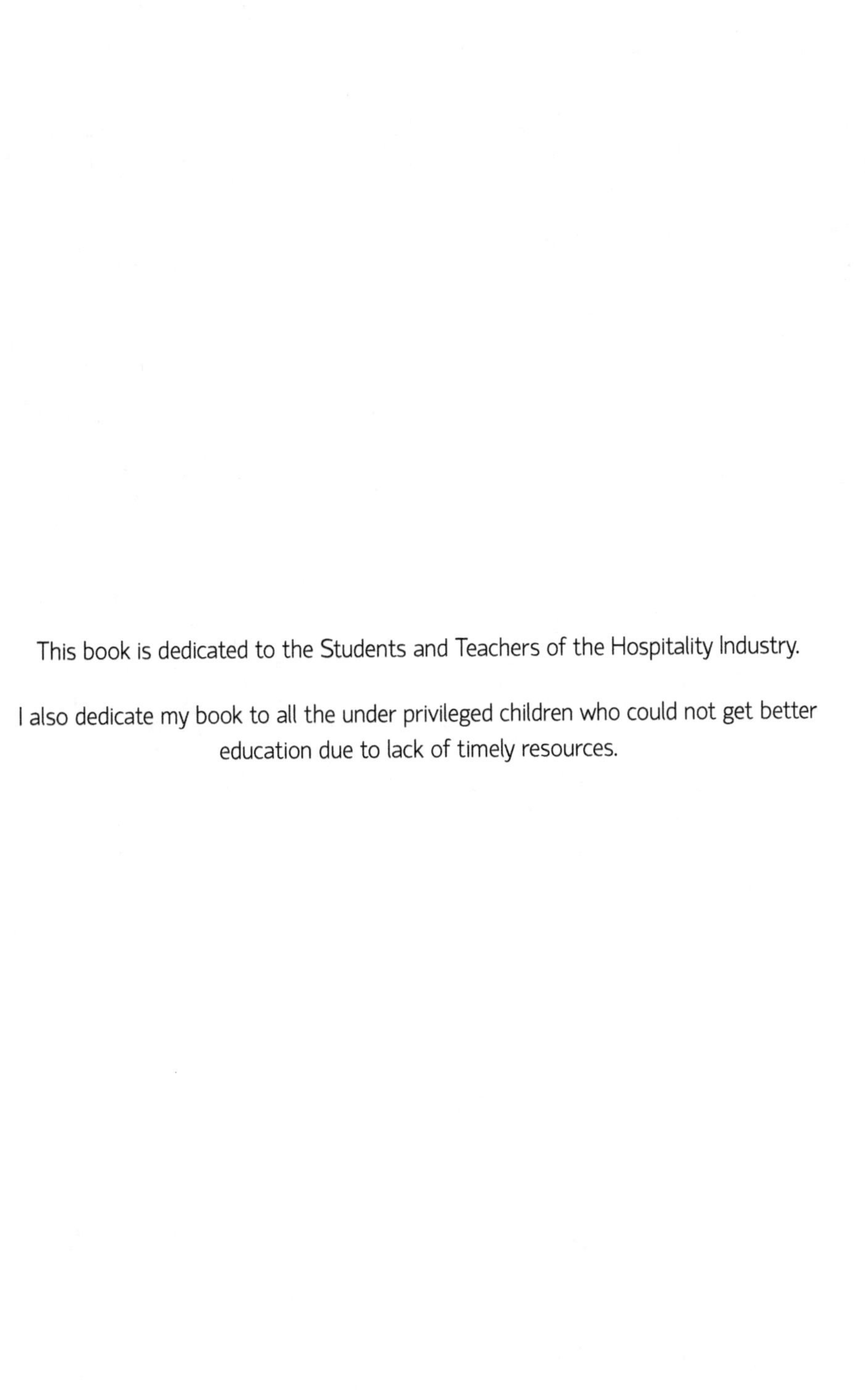

This book is dedicated to the Students and Teachers of the Hospitality Industry.

I also dedicate my book to all the under privileged children who could not get better education due to lack of timely resources.

Contents

Contents

Foreword

Irrespective of whether you get a formal college education or not, books consisting of all the basic elements of Front Office is always a great help in establishing and running a commercial residential outlet.

The scale of investment and type of outlet may vary but the fundamentals of Front Office Management are always based on Hygiene, Nutrition, Cost, Customer satisfaction, and Honesty. These fundamentals do not change for a sustainable Residential Business, food business, or any business for that matter.

This book "Diploma in Front Office, The Complete Syllabus" is written with an aim to help the Students, the Teachers, and all those would be chefs and managers who could not get a formal education in the field of Commercial Hotel Management.

The Complete Syllabus indicates the Theory component of the Diploma in Front Office course as prescribed in the syllabus of various AICTE, UGC approved Government Universities and the National Council for Hotel Management & Catering Technology.

There is always scope for further reading and the limit is endless. However in my experience if the readers could follow the concepts from this book and focus on more and more practical training and practice, it will give them an edge and will save time.

Best wishes...

Dr. Anshumali Pandey
Author

Part A: Front Office Operations

Front Office Operations

Unit 1: Introduction to Tourism, Travel and Hotel Industry

(***Topics Covered:*** *Introduction to tourism, travel and hotel industry and their inter-relationship. Interdependency of tourism, travel and hospitality industry. Acronyms and terminology of hotel industry. Classification of hotel. Supplementary accommodations.*)

INTRODUCTION TO TOURISM, HOSPITALITY AND HOTEL INDUSTRY:

TOURISM

Tourism is an activity performed by bonafide travellers. Tourism can also be defined in terms of product as sum of three components, i.e. attraction of the destination, the facilities of the destination and the accessibility of destination.

TOURIST

People who travel for a variety of reasons and are out from their area for more than 24hours for various reasons such as business, conferences, pleasure/leisure, pilgrim activity, medical, studies etc.

Various categories of tourists are:

- Domestic: Tourist coming from different parts within the country.
- International: Tourist coming from different parts of the globe.
- Inbound: Tourist coming from other countries to our country.
- Outbound: Tourist going from our country to other countries.

COMPONENTS OF TOURISM:

Tourism industry comprises of numerous components, some of which are travel sector to accommodation sector to sightseeing facilities and other facilities. Classifying it into different sectors helps in the functioning as well as defines the employment opportunity.

Tourism industry comprises of the following components:

- <u>Accommodation Operations:</u> It includes:-

Hotels, Motels, Resorts, Supplementary accommodation, Timeshare, Other types of hotels

- <u>Transportation Services:</u> It includes:-

Ships, Airlines, Railways, Limousines, Coaches, Cabs etc.

- <u>Food & Beverage Outlets:</u> It includes:

Restaurants, Vending machines, Cafeteria, Snacks bar, Bar, Fast food outlets etc.

- <u>Retail stores:</u> It includes:-

Gift shops, Handicraft shops, Shopping Malls, Super markets etc.

- <u>Activities:</u> It includes:-

Recreation, Entertainment, Festivals, Fairs and mela, Shows, Ethnic festivals, Seasonal festivals, Meetings, Exhibition, etc.

<u>HOSPITALITY INDUSTRY AND TOURISM:</u>

Tourism refers to all that industry which provides all necessary and essential services to tourist, one of the basic and first important facility which a tourist need is Accommodation. At that point of time the origin of hotel industry took place.

The term HOTEL was used in England in about 1760. Hotel according to British can be defined a place where bonafide traveller can receive food and shelter, provided he is in a position to pay for it and is in fit condition to be received.

A hotel can also be defined as an establishment where primary business is to sell rooms to the travellers and which may furnish various other services such as food, beverage, laundry etc.

<u>Interdependency of tourism, travel and hospitality industry:</u>

Before we look at the connection between hospitality and tourism, let's review exactly what the hospitality industry is. Well, the hospitality industry is an industry that offers services to us that go beyond our basic needs and generally require extra income to purchase. These services include things like accommodations, restaurants, transportation, and leisure activities. So, every time a traveller stays in a hotel, grabs dinner at a nice restaurant, hires a tour guide, or flies on an airplane, he/she is supporting the hospitality industry.

Now, let's take a look at what tourism consists of. When a traveller travels somewhere for pleasure, he/she is taking part in tourism. Tourism is the act of visiting places for enjoyment purposes. Tourism happens when tourists travel to different places with the intention of participating in leisure activities.

The hospitality industry consists of hotels, restaurants, transportation, and leisure activities. Many times when we purchase these services, we do so while we are travelling. Thus, every time we travel to a new country for pleasure and stay at a hotel, we are purchasing a service in the hospitality industry. Every time we fly to a destination, we are purchasing a service from the hospitality industry. And every time we grab a bite to eat at a local restaurant, or hires a tour guide to show us the local sites, we are again purchasing a service in the hospitality industry. Therefore, when a traveller travels and becomes a tourist, he looks to the hospitality industry to fulfil a place to stay, eat, travel, and participate in fun activities. In basic terms, the hospitality industry provides the services needed for tourism.

<u>Acronyms and terminology of hotel industry:</u>

1. **<u>ACCOUNT AGING:-</u>**A method for tracking past due accounts according to the date the charges originated.

1. **<u>AGEING STATEMENT: -</u>**A statement which shows how old the unpaid account has become.

3. **<u>ACCOUNTANCY CYCLE:-</u>**A period from when a financial transaction occurs to the time it is reconciled and is shown on the financial report of

the company.

4. **ALLOWANCE:-**The amount which is reduced from the folio as an adjustment against improper, unsatisfactory or no service to the guest. It may also because of posting error.

5. **AUDIT TRAIL:-**It is documented history of transactions.

6. **BACK OFFICE:-**It is also called as <u>Back Of the House</u>. It is branch of front office department which is responsible for all managerial activities and maintaining ongoing status of the business of the hotel.

7. **BAG PULL:-**The process of bringing down the luggage of the group members from their rooms to lobby on the day of departure of the group just before the departure.

8. **BLANKET RESERVATION:-**A block of rooms held for a particular group with individual members requesting assignments from that block i.e. a unit that has been reserved for a specific arrival date but not for specific guest, sometimes also referred as blocked room.

9. **BLOCK:-** An agreed upon number of rooms set aside for members of group planning to stay at hotel.

10. **BOUNCED RESERVATION:-** Sometimes due to some error in planning a guest with reservation may be refused accommodation. This situation is called as bounced reservation. They are also called as <u>Walking of the guest</u>.

11. **BUCKET:-**it is specially designed collapsible rack which is normally kept on the cashier's counter top for holding the guest folio. It is also called as <u>cashier's well</u>or <u>folio tray</u>or <u>Tub</u>.

12. **BUMPED RESERVATION:-**Refusal of accommodation to a guest holding confirmed reservation and subsequently putting him in some other hotel.

13. **CALL ACCOUNTING SYSTEM:-**A device linked to the hotel telephone system that accurately accounts for guest telephone calls by identifying each phone number dialed from guest room telephones and tracking charges.

14. **CARD KEY:-**An electronic or magnetic small plastic card used in electronic locking system that operates through a master control console at front desk which is wired to every guest room door. They are also called as magnetic or electronic card.

15. **CASH BANK: -**An amount of money given to a cashier at the start of work shift so that he or she can handle the various transactions that occur.

16. **CHARGE BACK:-**Sometimes the credit card company refuses the payment of voucher signed by the customer which is sent by the hotel. The given situation is called as charge back.

17. **CITY ACCOUNT:-**A non guest account is called as City account.

18. **CORKAGE:-**It refers to the charges made by a licensed establishment for providing service equipments, bottle openers, soda etc. to customers who bring their own alcoholic beverage for consumption in the hotel.

19. **CUT-OFF-DATE:-**The date by which the confirmations should come otherwise after this date the block of these rooms are released for general sale.

20. **DELINQUENT ACCOUNT:-**A city ledger account that has not been settled within a reasonable collection period, usually 90 days.

21. **DEMI PENSION:-**Other name of this MAP, Modified American Plan. They are also called as half Pension. In this system room tariff includes Room rent, English breakfast and one major meal i.e. either lunch or dinner.

22. **DENIAL CODE:-**A code generated by an online credit card verification service, indicating that the requested transaction has not been approved.

23. **DOUBLE UP:-**when a room is occupied by two unrelated guests, it is called as double up.

24. **DOWNGRADE:-**Moving the guest's reservation to a lower quality room is called as downgrade.

25. **DUE OUT:-**Guests expected to check out on a given day who have not yet done so.

26. **DUE BACK:-**A situation that occurs when a cashier pays out more than he or she receives, the difference is due back to cashiers cash bank.

27. **EARLY BIRD:-**A term used in fully automatic system of Night Auditing and referring to mainly creating and distribution of reports. It is also called as Flash.

28. **END OF THE DAY:-**An arbitrary stopping point for the business day.

29. **EXPRESS CHECK OUT:-**A pre departure activity that involves the production and early morning distribution of guest folios for guests expected to check out that morning.

30. **FLEX TIME:-**A program of flexible work hours that allows employees to vary their times of starting and ending work.

31. **FLOOR LIMIT:-**A limit assigned to hotels by credit card companies indicating the maximum amount in credit card charges the hotel is permitted to accept from a card member without special authorization.

32. **FOLIO:-** A statement of all transactions affecting the balance of single account.

33. **FORFEITED DEPOSIT:-**The amount that the guest has paid as advance for booking a room, may be forfeited whole or some in case of his no-show and is called as Retention charge in that case.

34. **FRANKING MACHINE:-**A machine which is used for printing postage stamp value on the envelope.

35. **<u>FRONT OF THE HOUSE:-</u>** those part of front office department with which the guest come in direct contact.

36. **<u>FULL DAY:-</u>** It is way of measuring a chargeable day for accounting purpose for a guest. For example it will be three meals for an American plan hotel and no meals and only overnight stay for European hotels.

37. **<u>GARNI HOTELS:-</u>**A hotel which has no food and beverage service facility.

38. **<u>GLOBAL DISTRIBUTION SYSTEM:-</u>**A distribution channel for reservations that provides worldwide distribution of hotel reservation information and allows the selling of hotel reservations around the world, usually accomplished by connecting the hotel company reservation system with an airline reservation system.

39. **<u>GRAVEYARD SHIFT:-</u>**A work shift which begins from midnight.

40. **<u>GATEWAY CITY:-</u>**A city located in an area that makes them the first practical stop for an International Flight Coming in to a country.

41. **<u>HOUSE COUNT:-</u>** Total number of guest is staying in the hotel at a particular time.

42. **<u>HOUSE LIMIT:-</u>**A credit limit established by hotel.

43. **<u>HUBBART FORMULA:-</u>**A formulae developed by Ray Hubbart for determining room rate keeping in consideration operating expenses, room sales, and pre desired return on investment (ROI).

44. **<u>HURDLE RATE:-</u>**The minimum retail price below which the room cannot be sold.

45. **<u>IDLE TIME:-</u>**it is also called as <u>hidden rest</u>. This is period that must be allowed during duty when a person does not work.

46. **<u>IN BALANCE:-</u>**A term describing the state of accounts when the totals of debit amounts and credit amounts are equal.

47. **INCIDENTAL ACCOUNT:-**Charges which are guest's own responsibility, which is not paid by the company or tour operators.

48. **INTER SELL AGENCY:-**A reservation system that handles reservation for many products such as airlines, car rentals and hotels etc.

49. **KEY CARD:-**Sometimes used as identification card given to a guest, but usually contains general information facility, catering outlets, location of the hotel etc., which is given by the receptionist at the time of check in.

50. **KEYING:-**Coding system used in an advertisement to identify the response from the media.

51. **LATE CHECK OUT:-**A guest who with the permission of the hotel checks out of the hotel after the check out time, without paying any extra charge.

52. **LATE CHARGES:-**The amount of any purchase informed by any point of sale cashier to the main cashier after the departure of guest and which remains outstanding.

    They are also the charges which hotel imposes to a guest who does not leave at check out time and wants to stay for few extra hours.

53. **LEAD TIME:-**The time between when a reservation is made and when the guest is due to arrive.

54. **LEDGER:-** A grouping of accounts.

55. **LOCK OUT:-**When a guest is not allowed access to the room usually due to an unpaid bill.

56. **MARKET MIX:-**The distribution in percentage of the hotel guest into various categories such as tourist, businessman etc.

57. **NET CASH RECEIPT:-**The amount of cash and checks in the cashier's drawer minus the amount of initial cash bank.

58. <u>NO- SHOW:-</u>A guest who made a room reservation but did not register or cancel.

59. <u>OFF:-</u>It means that the room is off the list of rooms available for sale due to some reason. Also called as <u>Red Slip Room</u>.

60. <u>OPTION DATE:-</u>It is the designated date by which the prospective guest is required to confirm his booking.

61. <u>OUT OF BALANCE:-</u>A term used to describe the state of accounts when the totals of debit amounts and credit amounts do not equal.

62. <u>OVERAGE:-</u>An imbalance that occurs when the total of cash and checks in cash register drawer is greater than the initial cash bank plus net cash receipts.

63. <u>OVERBOOKING:-</u>A situation in which hotel books more room than available.

64. <u>OVERDUE ACCOUNT:-</u>A city ledger account that is unpaid beyond the current billing period, usually between 30 and 90 days.

65. <u>OVERFLOW FACILITY:-</u>A property selected to receive central system reservation requests after room availabilities in the system's participating properties within a geographic region has been exhausted.

66. <u>OVERSTAY GUEST:-</u>A Guest who stays after his or her stated departure date.

67. <u>PAID IN ADVANCE:-</u>A guest who pays his or her room charges in cash during registration. PIA guests are often denied in house credit facility.

68. <u>PAIDOUT:-</u>Cash disbursed by the hotel on behalf of a guest and charged to the guest's account as a cash advance.

69. <u>PRODUCT LIFE CYCLE:-</u>It is a concept which says that all products have a point of growth, maturity and decline due to change and competition.

70. **RACK RATE:-** The maximum retail price of the room is called as Rack Rate.

71. **RACK SLIP:-**A paper slip which is adjusted in racks such as reservation rack, room rack and information rack.

72. **RATE CUTTING:-**Reducing room tariff to attract more business.

73. **RED BOOK:-**A hard bound register used in diary system in non automated method of registration.

74. **RELEASE DATE:-**Rooms may be allocated to agents for sale who may deal with them without reference to the hotel. The release date is the point at which the control of the sale rests to the hotel. Usually 24 to 48 hours before each sale date.

75. **RETENTION CHARGE:-**These are the charges which may be collected from guest for making guaranteed reservation in the hotel and when does not turn up on the scheduled date due to reasons best known to him.

76. **ROUTING:-**The process where credits/debits incurred by one account are manually or automatically transferred to another account.

77. **ROOM COUNT:-**The number of occupied rooms in a hotel.

78. **ROOMING:-**A procedure of escorting the guest and carrying of his luggage to the assigned room by the bell boy.

79. **RUN OF THE HOUSE:-**Room assignment based on room availability at the time of check in.

80. **SEAMLESS CONNECTIVITY:-**the ability of travel agencies to book reservations directly into hotel reservation systems as well as verify room availability and rates.

81. **SHOULDER PERIOD:-**A mid price season between peak and off season.

82. **<u>SHORTAGE:-</u>**an imbalance that occurs when the total of cash and checks in a cash register drawer is less than the initial bank plus net cash receipts.

83. **<u>SIBERIA:-</u>**A term normally used for inferior quality rooms , such as near the staircase etc. guest must be informed about its situation and condition before selling it.

84. **<u>SKIPPER:-</u>**A guest who leaves the hotel without settling his bill.

85. **<u>SLEEP OUT:-</u>**A sold room where the guest did not stay during the night.

86. **<u>SLEEPER:-</u>**Room available for sale but not sold out.

87. **<u>SLIPPAGE:-</u>**The term used when analyzing the group room performance. It is difference between what is contracted and what actually arrives.

88. **<u>SPLIT FOLIO:-</u>**Folio in which guest's charges is separated into two or more folios.

89. **<u>STAY OVER:-</u>**A room status term indicates that the guest is not checking out today and will remain at least one more night.

90. **<u>STOP OVER GUEST:-</u>**They are also called as <u>layover guest</u>. This refers to the guest who en route from one destination to another stops in between on a third destination and breaks his journey. This is generally on airlines expenses.

91. **<u>SUPPLEMENTAL TRANSCRIPT:-</u>**A detailed report of all non guests account that indicates each charge transaction that affected a non guest account that day, used as a worksheet to detect posting errors.

92. **<u>TRAFFIC SHEET:-</u>**A telephone department control sheet usually used for long distance calls.

93. **<u>TRANSPOSITION ERROR:-</u>**also called as transcription error and is caused by wrong recording of sequence of digits for example 289 is written as 298.

94. **TURN AWAY:-**To refuse accommodation to walk in guest, because the rooms are not available. They are also called as <u>Displacement</u>.

95. **TURN DOWN:-**An evening service provided by housekeeper where she prepares the bed for night use.

96. **TURN IN:-**The cash deposited by the departmental cashier with general cashier at the end of the day.

97. **TIPSY GUEST:-**A drunkard guest who may misbehave with the staff.

98. **UNDER BOOKING:-**An erroneous belief that all the rooms are sold while in fact they are not.

99. **UNDERSTAY:-**A guest who checks out before his scheduled date of departure.

100. **VPO: -**Visitors Paid Out. If small Payments are made by front desk on the behalf of guest such as taxi fare, cinema tickets etc., then a voucher is prepared called as Visitors paid out voucher which is signed by guest and later settled at the time of departure.

101. **VOUCHER:-**The signed bills of the guest which is settled at the time of departure of the guest.

102. **WALK OUT:-**A skipper guest is also called as walk out guest.

103. **WALK IN:-**A guest who comes to the hotel without prior reservation. They are also called as <u>Chance guest</u>or <u>Off Street Guest</u>.

104. **WALKING:-**Due to lack of availability of rooms, once the accommodation is refused to a guest who is holding reservation are called as Walking of the guest. They are also called as <u>Bounced Reservation.</u>

105. **WASH FACTOR:-**Deletions of unnecessary group rooms from a group block.

106. **<u>WATCH DOWN</u>:-**Blocking fewer rooms than the number requested by the group, based on group history.

107. **<u>WHO</u>:-**An unidentified guest in a room that is vacant as per front desk record.

108. **<u>YIELD</u>:-**The ratio actual rooms revenue to the potential room revenue.

109. **<u>ZEROING OUT</u>:-**At the time of departure bringing the account balance to zero.

FRONT OFFICE ABBREVIATIONS

1. AHMA - American Hotel & Motel Association
2. AH&LA – American Hotel & Lodging Association
3. AH&LEI – American hotel & lodging Educational Institute
4. A.M - Antemeridian
5. CCTV - Closed Circuit Tele Vision
6. CVGR - Company Volume Guaranteed Rate
7. CIP - Commercially Important Person
8. DG - Distinguished Guest
9. DNA - Did Not Arrive
10. DND – Do Not Disturb
11. DNS - Did Not Stay
12. DSS - Decision Support system
13. ECO - Express Check Out
14. EDC - Electronic Data Capturing
15. EDP - Electronic Data Processing
16. EPBX - Electronic Private Branch Exchange
17. EPABX - Electronic Private Automatic Branch Exchange
18. FERA - Foreign Exchange Regulation Act
19. FIT - Free Individual Traveller/ Free independent traveller
20. FFIT - Foreign Free Independent Traveller
21. FHRAI - Federation of Hotels & Restaurant Association Of India
22. FF&E - Furniture, Fixture & Equipment
23. FRRO - Foreigner's Regional Registration Office
24. GDS - Global Distribution System
25. GIT - Group Inclusive Tour

26. HIS - Hotel Information System
27. HAI - Hotel Association of India
28. HLP - Heat Light & Power
29. HRACC - Hotel & Restaurant Approval & Classification Committee
30. IATA - International Air Transport Association
31. IATO - Indian Association of Tour Operation
32. IHRA - International Hotel & restaurant Associates
33. ISD - International Subscribers Dialling
34. MAP - Modified American plan
35. MCO - Miscellaneous Charge
36. MIS - Management Information System
37. MLS - Minimum Length of Stay
38. MOD - Managers on Duty
39. NTA - Not to be allotted
40. OOO - Out of order
41. PPPN - per person per night
42. PIA - Paid in advance
43. PRPN - Per room per night
44. POS - Point of Sale
45. PSO - Passengers service order
46. RNA - Room not assigned
47. SITS - Special Interest Tours
48. STD - Subscriber Trunk Dialling
49. SOP - Standard Operating Procedures
50. SPATT - Special Attention Guest
51. TQM - Total Quality Management
52. TAAI - Travel Agents Association of India
53. UFTAA - Universal Federation of Travel Agent Association
54. VIP - Very Important Person
55. VPO - Visitors Paid Out
56. VR - Vacant & Ready
57. WATS - Wide Area Telephone Services
58. WTO - World Travel Organization
59. WATA - World Association of Travel Agents.

CRITERIA FOR CLASSIFICATION OF HOTEL:

- **Standard classification** includes 1 Star, 2 Star, 3 Star, 4 Star, 5 Star, 5 Star Delux, Heritage properties
- **Size** includes small, medium, large & very large.
- **Location** includes Downtown (City Centre), sub urban, Airport (Transit), Resort, Motel, Flotel.
- **Clientele** includes commercial, transit, B&B, Timeshare, Casino, Convention, Motel.
- **Duration of stay** includes commercial, resort, semi residential, residential hotels.
- **Level of services** includes budget, mid market, up market hotels.
- **Ownership** includes proprietary, franchise, management contract, time share, condominiums.
- **Alternate accommodation** includes sarai, dharamshala, lodge, daak bunglows, yatri niwas, circuit house, youth hostels.

STANDARD CLASSIFICATION

The Indian hotel industry follows the star rating system, which indicates the number and standards of facility offered to them. The classification is done by central government committee called HRACC, Hotel & Restaurant approval and classification committee who inspects and assesses the hotel based on the facilities and services offered. The HRACC includes the chairman and other members chosen from the government and industry association such as:

FHRAI- Federation of Hotel & Restaurant association of India.

HAI- Hotels association in India.

IATO- Indian association of Tour operations.

TAAI- Travel agent association of India.

IHM- Institute of Hotel Management.

In case of Heritage category the representative of Indian Heritage Hotel Association (IHHA) is included in the committee. The committee visits the hotel and evaluates the facilities and services of the hotel before the grade is awarded.

ONE STAR HOTELS:

These properties are generally small and independently owned, with the family atmosphere. There may be a limited range of facilities and the meals may be fairly simple.F&B service may not be served or some bathroom may not have attached bath or shower. However maintenance cleanliness and comfort would be of an acceptable standard.

<u>TWO STAR HOTELS</u>:

In this class hotels will typically be small to medium sized and offer more extensive facilities than one star hotels. Guests can expect comfortable, well equipped over night accommodation with attached bath. Reception and other staff will aim for more professional presentation.

<u>THREE STAR HOTELS</u>:

At this level hotels are usually of size to support higher staffing levels as well as a significantly a higher quality and range of facilities.

Reception and other public areas will be more spacious and the restaurant will normally also cater to non resident also.All bedrooms will have attached bath and shower and offer good standard.

<u>FOUR STAR HOTELS</u>:

Expectation at this level includes a degree of luxury as well as qualities and the furnishings, decor, and equipment in every area of hotel. Bedroom will also usually offer more space. They will be well designed with coordinated furnishing and decor. There will be high staff to guest ratio with provision of standard service. 24 hours room service, laundry and dry-cleaning services. The restaurant will demonstrate a serious approach to its cuisine.

<u>FIVE STAR HOTELS</u>:

These offer spacious and luxurious accommodations throughout the hotel matching the best international standards, the interior design should impress with its quality and attention to detail comfort and elegance. The furnishing should be in immaculate. The service should be formal, well supervised and flawless in its attention to guests needs. The restaurant will demonstrate a high level of technical state. The staff will be knowledgeable, helpful and well versed in all aspects of customer care, combining efficiency courtesy.

<u>HERITAGE HOTELS</u>:

The properties set in small forts, palaces or havelies. They have added new dimension to cultural tourism. In a heritage hotel a visitor is offered rooms that have their own history, is served with traditional cuisine, is entertained by folk artists, can participate in activities that allow a glimpse into the heritage of the region.

Heritage hotel are further subdivided into:

- Heritage (1935-1950)
- Classic (1920-1935)

- Grand (before 1920)

CLASSIFICATION ON THE BASIS OF SIZE:
SMALL HOTELS:
Less than 100 rooms (International Standards)
Less than 25 rooms (Indian Standards)
MEDIUM HOTELS:
100-300 rooms (International Standards)
25-100 rooms (Indian Standards)
LARGE HOTELS:
400-600 rooms (International Standards)
100-300 rooms (Indian Standards)
VERY LARGE HOTELS:
600-1000 rooms (International Standards)
More than 300 rooms (Indian Standards)
CLASSIFICATION ON THE BASIS OF LOCATION:
DOWNTOWN HOTEL:
This type of hotel is located in the centre of a city or within a short distance from business centre, theatres , shopping areas, public offices etc.

They are generally preferred by business clientele. Guest here stay for shorter duration and room rents are higher.

SUB URBAN HOTEL:
Providing similar facilities as the downtown hotel, they are set in suburban areas. Such hotels are ideal for people who prefers quite surroundings.

The room rate being moderate, the length of guest stay may increase.

RESORT:
Hotels that is located at tourist destinations with calm, pollution free and natural ambience. The room rates may vary from moderate to high depending upon the services like golf course, pool, health club, water sports, trekking etc.

AIRPORT HOTELS:
These are situated in the vicinity nearby the transit position, offering all services of commercial hotel and are generally used by the passengers.

MOTEL:
These are located on highways and provide modest facilities to road travellers. Facilities like Garages, parking for individuals and refuelling stations may be provided.

FLOTEL:

These types of lodging facilities float on the surface of water. They may be built on top of rafts or semi sub-merssible platforms.

CLASSIFICATION ON THE BASIS OF CLIENTELE:

COMMERCIAL HOTEL

Commercial hotels are situated in heart of the city. They are also known as business class or downtown property. Generally duration of stay is few days only and weekend business is slack. They must have services like facilities to meet the basic business demands, swimming pool, speciality restaurants, bar, disco, 24 hour room service, health club etc.

CASINO HOTEL

The focus in this type of hotels is on gambling and provision of casino. Casino hotels are not seen in India but are very popular in America, particularly Las-Vegas. These are high class hotels with luxurious rooms and other top class services and amenities.

B&B HOTEL

Bed and breakfast hotels are also known as B&B inns. These are the lodging establishments that provide room with breakfast ranging from continental to full breakfast. They are located along commercial and holiday routes and in rural and resort areas.

SUITE HOTELS

It is new concept in which the guestrooms of the hotel are with living room or parlour. These rooms sometimes have small kitchenette, a refrigerator and a sink for washing the dishes. The clientele for these hotels are business people, vacationers and professional such as lawyers etc. People are more attracted to such hotels as they get two rooms instead of one and can work and entertain in an area which is separate from bed room.

CONFERENCE HOTELS

Hotels which are specially designed to accommodate group meetings. Full service hotels of this category offer overnight stay facilities to the conference delegates to make meeting a success. Swimming pool, fitness centre, jogging facilities and may be spas are also provided. They may usually operate on special tariff for group such as an all inclusive tariff which include room, meals, meeting room, audio visual etc.

CLASSIFICATION ON THE BASIS OF DURATION OF GUEST STAY:

COMMERCIAL HOTEL

RESORT

SEMI RESIDENTIAL HOTELS:

These hotels provide accommodation to guests on weekly or monthly basis like residential hotels as well as on per day basis like transient hotels. Reduced rates are provided to long staying guests. Transient guests who want to take the advantage of reduced rates for longer stay also come to such establishments.

RESIDENTIAL HOTELS:

Residential hotels are also often called as apartment hotels or apartment house. Room in a residential hotel are sold on a monthly or yearly basis. Rooms may be furnished or unfurnished, single or en suite. Almost all residential hotels operate a restaurant, offer telephone service, laundry and valet service. Advance rents are usually collected while other charges are billed weekly.

These types of hotels normally operate on European plan. Recent development in this area includes cooperative hotels and Condominiums in which the tenants own the apartment and pay the management a fee for maintenance. When the rooms are not occupied by the owner the management often has the right to rent them on temporary basis, so that the hotel will contain both resident and transient guests. They are also called en pension. Such establishments are very popular in U.S and Europe. Long staying guests generally stay from months to year and rent may be paid per week or per month. Facilities provided are less than the commercial hotels.

CLASSIFICATION ON THE BASIS OF LEVELS OF SERVICES:

BUDGET HOTELS:

These are the hotels which provide basic guest rooms to stay at an economical rate with limited F&B service facility.

MID MARKET:

These hotels are often also called as mid range service providers hotels. In these hotels rooms are having basic amenities, telephone EPBX, In room dining and other such facilities are being provided. The room rates are moderate.

UP MARKET:

These class of hotels are also considered as luxury class hotels. Almost all the services are being covered in these types of hotels; rooms are of high class with all the imported and expensive furnishings. In room dining round the clock, coffee shop, other F&B Outlets, Laundry services, Spa, health club, Gym, Business centre, swimming pool etc are the facilities and services provided in these type of hotels.

CLASSIFICATION ON THE BASIS OF OWNERSHIP:

INDEPENDENT HOTEL

These hotels are on ownership basis and do not have any affiliation or contract through any other property, and also do not have any tie-up with any other hotels with regards to policy, procedures and other financial obligations. The advantage in this type of hotel is that they need not maintain a particular image and they are not bound to maintain any set targets, but can adopt the changing trends. They work as an autonomous body.

MANAGEMENT CONTRACT

Another type of organization which operates properties owned by individuals or partners are management contract hotels. The contract is entered on long term basis between the owner and the operator and usually as per the contract.

- Owner retains the legal and financial responsibilities.
- Operator pays for operating expenses and recovers from the owner and agreed upon fees.
- Owner is responsible for paying taxes, insurance and debts.

CHAIN

There are many single owned hotels, yet more and more hotels and motels are now getting affiliated to each other. This gives them advantage of large central organization providing reservation system, management aids, financial strength, manpower specialities, merchandise and promotional help. When two or more operations belonging to same organizations run, they are considered to form a chain. E.g. Sheraton, Hilton, Holiday inn etc.

REFFERAL CHAINS

A referral chain is made up of independently owned and operated hotel and motel and provides shared advertisement, joint reservation system and standardized quality, but there is no shared managements or financial functions.

FRANCHISE

The word franchise means that one company ties up with another company, taking help of the other company to run the business. It is the method of distribution where by one property that has developed a particular pattern for doing business gives the benefit to other properties. The most important benefit is of belonging to one already known group. Franchise is a system in which the franchise owner grants another the right or privilege to merchandise a product or service for a specified return.

Management Franchise: full management and reservation support is offered in this type of franchise.

Marketing Franchise: here marketing support for reservation is offered but the management is run by owner itself.

Name Franchise: only the brand name of the franchise company is used and no support is offered.

Joint Venture: here two companies come together and jointly invest on a project. One company may have strong brand value where the other partner is all to contribute the required capital.

ALTERNATE or SUPPLEMENTARY ACCOMODATION:

This consists of all types of accommodation other than the conventional hotel type. This can be described as premises which offer accommodation but not the extra services of the hotel. It is a very economical type of accommodation.

Main distinguishing features are:

- The standard of comfort is modest in comparison to the hotels.
- The accommodation is sold at a very low price.
- They have informal atmosphere and freedom regarding dress code.
- There is more emphasis on recreation, entertainment and sports.

Supplementary accommodation a very important role in total available tourist accommodation in the country. It caters to both domestic and international tourists.

Types of supplementary accommodations:

- Sarais / Ddharamshalas (Inns)
- Youth hostels. E.g. YMCA
- Camping sites.
- Circuit house/ Dak bunglows- govt. accommodation
- Tourist bunglows
- Travellers lodges/forest lodges
- Dormitories
- Paying guest accommodation
- Rotels (hotels on the wheels) e.g. Palace on wheels
- Flotels (hotels on water) e.g. Houseboats.

CHAPTER TWO

Unit 2: An Overview of Room Division

*(**Topics Covered**: Prologue with room division department and its sub-departments. Standard layout of front office department and its sections. Organization structure of hotel with special reference to front office department. Duties and responsibilities of front office employees. Personality traits of front office employees. Front office equipment (non-automated, semi-automated & fully automated). Coordination of front office with other departments and sections.)*

Room Division:

The room division comprises departments and personnel essential to providing the services guest expect during a hotel stay. In most hotels, the rooms division generates more revenue than all other divisions combined. The front office is one department within the rooms division. Others are housekeeping, uniformed services, and the concierge. In some properties, the reservations and switchboard or telephone functions are separate departments within the rooms division. Figure at previous page shows a sample organization chart for the rooms division of a large hotel.

<u>Prologue with room division department and its sub-departments (front office, uniformed service and housekeeping) and their sections:</u>

The Front Office

This is the most visible department in a hotel. Front office personnel have more contact with guest than do staff in most other departments. The front desk is usually the focal point of activity for the front desk to register; to receive room assignments, to inquire about available services, facilities, and the control center for guest requests concerning housekeeping or engineering issues. Foreign guest use the front desk to exchange currency, find a translator, or request other special assistance. In addition, it may also be base of operations during an emergency, such as a fire or a guest injury. The functions of the front office are to:

1. Sell guestrooms, register guests, and assign guestrooms.

2. Process future room reservations, when there is no reservation department or when the reservation department is closed.

3. Coordinate guest services.

4. Provide information about the hotel, the surrounding community, and any attractions or events of interest to guest.

5. Maintain accurate room status information. Maintain guest and monitor credit limits.

6. Produce guest account statements and complete proper financial settlement.

Uniformed Service

Employees who work in the uniformed service department of the hotel generally provide the most personalized guest service. Given the high degree of attention awarded guest by this department, some properties refer to uniformed service simply as guest service. Among the primary positions within the uniformed service department are:

1. Bell attendant – persons who provide baggage service between the lobby area and the guestroom.

2. Door attendants – persons who provide curb-side baggage service and traffic control at the hotel entrance.

3. Valet parking attendants-persons who provide parking service for guest's vehicles.

4. Transportation personnel – persons who provide transportation service for guests.

5. Concierges – person who assist guest by making restaurant reservations, arranging for transportation, and getting for tickets for theater, sporting, or other special events, and so on.

Bell Attendants: many guests arrive at a hotel with heavy baggage or several pieces of luggage. Guest receives help handling this luggage from probably the best-known employee among the uniformed service staff: the bell attendant. Bell attendant should be clearly selected. Since most hotels have carts for transporting baggage, the physical ability to actually carry the baggage is not a critical job qualification. More important, bell attendants should have strong oral communication skills and display genuine interest in ach guest. Depending on the size and complexity of the hotel, bell attendants may be counted on to:

1. Transport guest luggage to and from guestrooms.

2. Familiarize guest with the hotel's facilities and services, safety features, as well as the guestroom and any in-room amenities.

3. Provide a secure area for guest requiring temporary luggage storage.

4. Provide information on hotel services and facilities, as well as group functions.

5. Deliver mail, packages, messages, and special amenities to guestrooms.

6. Pick up and deliver guest laundry and dry cleaning.

7. Perform light housekeeping services in lobby and entry areas.

8. Help guest load and unload their luggage in the absence of a door attendant.

9. Notify other departments of guest needs, such as housekeeping for a crib or extra towels.

While many of these tasks appear simple, they all require a degree of professionalism. For example to assist a guest with his or her luggage, the belt attendant must know how to properly load a luggage cart. Fragile items must not be placed below heavy items. The cart must also be properly balanced so that it does not tip over or become difficult to steer. It is through informal conversation that bell attendants become key players in the hotel's guest's names. This makes guests feel more welcome and allows the bell attendant to provide more personal service.

Door Attendants

Door attendants play a role similar to bell attendants; they are dedicated to welcoming the guest to the hotel. These employees are generally found in hotels offering world-class or luxury service of the duties door attendants perform include:

1. Opening hotel doors and assisting guest upon arrival.

2. Helping guest load and unload luggage from vehicles.

3. Escorting guests to the hotel registration area.

4. Controlling vehicle traffic flow and safety at the hotel entrance.

5. Hailing taxis, upon request.

6. Performing light housekeeping services in the lobby and entry areas.

Experienced door attendants are capable of handling all these tasks with aplomb. A skilled and experienced door attendant learns the names of the frequent guest. When these guest returns to the hotel, the door attendant is able to greet them by name and can introduce them to other front office staff. Such personal service enhances the reputation of the hotel and provides the guest with as unique experience.

Valet parking attendants

Valet parking is generally available at hotels offering world-class or luxury service. Specially trained employees park guest and visitor automobiles. Thpersonal attention and security of valet parking service is considered both a luxury and a convenience. Guest does not have to worry about finding a parking space, walking to the hotel in inclement weather, or finding their vehicles in the parking lot. Hotels generally charge a higher fee for valet parking, guest are also likely to tip the valet parking attendant.

The uniformed service department is responsible for all vehicles under its care and reports information to the front desk each night so that parking charges can be posted to guest accounts. In addition, when the vehicle entrance to the hotel is busy, valet parking attendants should help keep the area running smoothly by providing traffic control assistance.

Concierges

Even though this guest service position has existed for quite some time, the concierge is perhaps the concierge was the castle doorkeeper. A concierge's job was to ensure that all the castle occupants were secure in their rooms at night. Traveling royalty was often accompanied by a concierge who provided security and traveled ahead of the royal party to finalize food and lodging arrangements. As hotels became more common in Europe, the concierge eventually became apart of the staff that provided personalized guest services. It is not uncommon to find a concierge at a world-class or luxury hotel.

Concierges may provide custom services to hotel guest. Duties include making reservations for dining securing tickets for theater and sporting events; arranging for transportation, and providing information on cultural events and local attractions. Concierges are known for their resourcefulness. Getting tickets to sold out concerts or making last-minute dinner reservations at a crowded restaurant are part of a concierge's responsibility and reputation. Most successful concierges have developed an extensive network of local, regional, and national contacts the concierge has established at restaurants, box office, car rentals offices,, airlines , printers, and other businesses. Some hotels actually encourage concierges to visit appropriate businesses and organizations to establish and strengthen such relationships. Finally, a highly successful concierge should speak several languages.

Housekeeping

Housekeeping is perhaps the most important support department for the front office. Like the front office, housekeeping usually is part of the rooms division of the hotel. In some hotels, however, the housekeeping function is considered an independent hotel division. Effective communication among housekeeping and front office personnel can contribute to guest satisfaction while helping the front office to effectively monitor guestroom status. Housekeeping employees inspect rooms before they are available for sale, clean occupied and vacated rooms, and communicate the status of guestroom until the room has been cleaned, inspected and released by the housekeeping department.

The housekeeping department often employs larger staff than other departments i.e. the rooms division. Normally, an executive housekeeper is in charge of the department, aided by an assistant housekeeper. In larger hotels there can be several assistant housekeepers, each responsible for specific floors, sections, or, in room attendants, lobby and general cleaners, and laundry personnel. Room attendant are assigned to specific sections nof the hotel. Depending on the hotel's service level, average guestroom size, and cleaning tasks, room attendants may clean from 8 to 18 rooms per shift. If the hotel has its own laundry, housekeeping department staff may be charged with cleaning and pressing the property's linens, towels, uniforms, and guest clothing. Housekeeping personnel (usually executive housekeepers) are responsible for maintaining two types of inventories: recycled and non-recycled. Recycled inventories are those items that have a relatively limited useful life but are used repeatedly in housekeeping operations. Theses inventories include such items as linens, uniforms, and guest amenities like irons and hair dryers. Non-recycled inventories are those items that are consumed or worn out during the course of routine housekeeping operations. Non-recycled inventories include cleaning supplies, small equipment items, and guest supplies and personnel grooming items. Guest amenities and m\linens are among the items and conveniences most often requested by guests.

To ensure the speedy, efficient rooming of guest in vacant and inspected room, the housekeeping and front office departments must promptly inform each other of any change in a room' status or availability. Team work between housekeeping and the front office is essential to effective hotel operations. To more familiar housekeeping and front office personnel are with each other's departmental procedures, the smoother the relationships.

Standard layout of front office department and its sections:

Division of labor is the guiding principle for dividing the entire unit into small section on the basis of tasks performed by the employees of the department. The front office department can be divided in to following sections for effective and efficient discharge of the duties of its employees:

§ Reservation

§ Reception

§ Information

§ Cash & bills

§ Travel desk

§ Communication

§ Uniformed services

o Bell Desk

o Concierges

Lobby

According to Oxford dictionary, _lobby is an area just inside a large building, where people can meet and wait'. The hotel lobby is an area furnished with seating arrangements and is used as common place for meeting and waiting by the hotel guests. Lobby is located immediately upon entry into the hotel building. The front office is located within the premises of the lobby. The lobby is an important place in the hotel as it is the first and last point of guest contact with hotel. Hence, a considerable amount of fund is invested by the owner to make the lobby aesthetically appealing to the guest. A well appointed lobby creates the impression about the overall standard of the hotel in the eyes of the guest. The lobby is managed by the lobby manager.

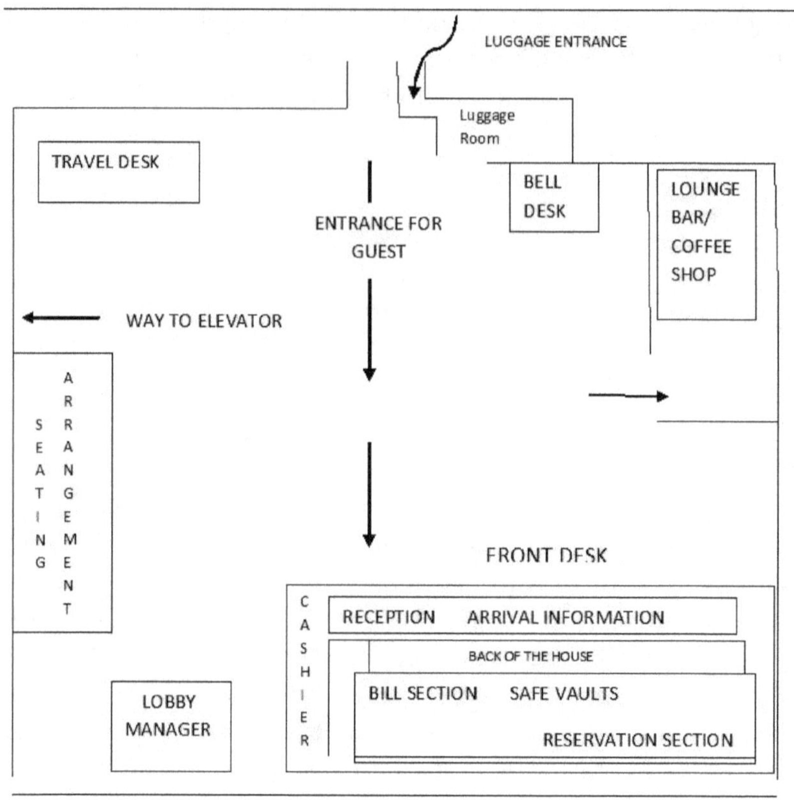

LAYOUT OF FRONT OFFICE DEPARTMENT

<u>Organization structure of hotel with special reference to front office department:</u>

The front office staff organization is deliberately designed to achieve objectives of the organization. It refers to the structure of well defined jobs, each bearing a definite authority, responsibility, and accountability. The organization structure is built upon the following pillars:

- Division of labour
- Span of control

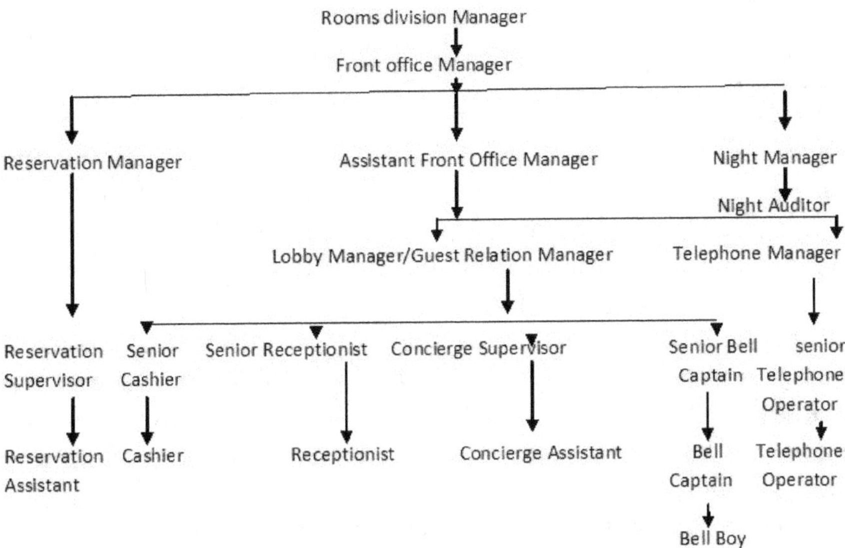

Duties and responsibilities of front office employees:

Guests remain in direct contact with the front office staff throughout their stay at the hotel. As the front office personnel are the first and last point of contact with the guest, they reflect the image of the hotel and hence should carry themselves and behave in a way which fits the vision of the organization.

Following are the qualities of front office personnel which is needed to be efficient on their duties:-

- Pleasing Personality
- Personal Hygiene
- Physical Fitness
- Honesty
- Salesmanship
- Diplomacy
- Good Memory
- Good Communication Skills
- Calmness

- Courteous
- Loyalty
- Punctuality

CONCIERGE:

A concierge is a hotel employee who provides information and personalised services to the guest like dinner reservation, tour and travel arrangements and obtaining tickets for special events in the city. A concierge is often expected to achieve the impossible; dealing with any request a guest may have, relying on the various contacts with various merchants and service providers.

The concept of Concierge came from the day of European royalty. The concierge was the castle door keeper in that time. His duty was to ensure that all castle occupants were safe in their rooms at night. When royal family travels, they often took their concierge with them for security and for making food and lodging facilities.

As the hotel industry grew, concierge became the part of hotel staff to provide personalise services to hotel's guest.

FUNCTION OF CONCIERGE:

Concierge provides following services to the guest:-

- Making reservations for dining in famous restaurants.
- Obtaining tickets for theatres, musical, sporting events etc.
- Arranging for transportation by Limousine, car, coaches, buses, etc.
- Providing information on cultural and social events like photo exhibition, art shows and local places of tourist interest.

BELL BOY:

Bell boys transport the guest luggage at the time of check in and check out. They also escort guests to their rooms and familiarize them with the room facilities and services provided by the hotel.

DUTIES & RESPONSIBILTIES OF BELL BOY:
The major duties and responsibilities of bell boy are:-

- Handles the guest luggage i.e. transport, a guest luggage from lobby to room at the time of check in, and from room to vehicle at the time of departure.
- Put luggage tag at the time of arrival of the guest

- Escort guest to their rooms and familiarize them with the facilities and electronic equipments to be used.
- When collecting luggage at the time of checkout, take a look inside the room in a hospitable manner to ensure everything is at its place.
- Keep the record of left luggage room
- Inform about the suspected scanty baggage guest at the time of check in.
- Help in locating guest in specified area within the hotel premises.
- Delivers mails, packages and messages to guest in their rooms.

Functions of Reservations:

- Receiving reservation requests through various means like telephones, fax, e-mail, sales representatives or central reservation systems.
- Processing reservation request received from all means , on PMS (Property Management System).
- Depending upon the availability of the desired room type and projected sales during and around the requested stay dates, the reservation request may be confirmed, waitlisted or denied
- Updating the room availability status after each reservation transactions.
- Maintaining and updating reservation records.
- Preparing reservation reports for the management.

Functions of Reception:

- Receiving and welcoming guest.
- Completing the registration formalities.
- Assigning the room
- Sending arrival notification slips to the concern departments.

Functions of Cash & Bills (Cashier)

- Opening and maintaining guest folios.
- Posting room charges and guest folios.
- Recording all credit charges in guest folios.
- Maintaining a record of cash received from guest.
- Preparing bills at the time of check out.
- Receiving cash/travellers cheque/cheque/demand draft for account settlement.

- Handling credit/debit/cash cards.
- Organising foreign currency exchange for the settlement of the guest account.

Function of Travel Desk

- Arranging pick up and drop services for guest at the time of their arrival and departure.
- Arranging for the guides who can communicate in guest's language.
- Organising sightseeing tours in and around the city.
- Making travel arrangements like railway and air tickets.

Function of Information Desk

- Answering incoming calls. Directing calls to the guest room through EPBX system.
- Providing information services.
- Processing guest wake up calls.
- Answering enquiries about hotel facilities and events.
- Coordinating emergency communication.

Personality traits of front office employees:

Most often, a front desk employee is the first person with whom a guest comes in contact. The guest starts building the image of the hotel from the physical appearance and personality of the front office personal. The gestures, grooming, and personal presentation of a front desk employee are very important in leaving a good impression in the mind of the guest. The front desk personnel should be well turned out; they should have a pleasant personality, greeting guests with a smiling face and showing interest in their concerns.

Qualities of front office personnel:

Physical Fitness: A front office employee must be physically fit to mange long hours on his feet. During peak business time or shortage of staff they may have to work at long stretches. Front office professionals must bring in physical fitness regimes into their personal lives.

Personal Hygiene: Front office employees should follow the highest standards of personal hygiene. The front office staff is the first point of physical contact to a guest with the hotel. A good sense of hygiene is very important for them as their appearance influences the image of the hotel. The staff need to look their best at all the times.

Pleasant Personality: A front desk employee is the first person whom a guest comes in contact. The gesture, grooming and personal presentation are very important for front office staff for leaving a good impression on guest.

Diplomacy: It is very important characteristic for front office staff. They should be very diplomatic in attending the guest's complaints for hotel or hotel services. If front office employee has to reject a room booking request, he should do that work diplomatically, without upsetting or offending the guest.

Calmness: The front office should be able to remain calm in high pressure situations. In some situations it happens that guest become unsatisfied or angry because of some problem in the services or products offered by the hotel to the guest at that time it is required that the front office staff deal calmly with the guest. The calmness of the front office staff in such situations will help to diffuse the tension and resolve the problem of guest.

Loyalty: The front office staff should be loyal to their job, as well as for the hotel and the management loyalty develops a sense of belongingness among the staff, which reflect in their behaviours with guest.

Good Communication Skill: The front office staff must possess good communication skill because they have to interact with guests at the time of their arrival, during their stay and also at the time of departure. They should be polite, confident and clear in their communication. They should be good in English, if they know a foreign language then that will be an advantage for them.

Salesmanship: They should possess salesmanship quality. They can motivate guest to increase their length of stay. They should be equipped with complete knowledge about hotel.

Good Memory: The front office staff must possess good memory because guests like to be recognized by the hotel staff and addressed by their names. A good memory will help the front office staff to remember and respond to the reservation requests and special preferences of guests. This gives a personalized touch and establishes a lasting relationship with the guest.

Honesty: They should be honest and trustworthy. Honest employees are an asset to an organization and build a good impression of hotel in guest's mind.

Courteousness: During interaction with guest it is important that a front office staff should be courteous and polite. They should never agree with the guest. A smooth resolution of problems teamed with the courteous behaviour of the hotel staff will develop a good will among guest.

<u>Front office equipment (non-automated, semi-automated & fully automated) :</u>

<u>NON AUTOMATED</u>

- Front Desk
- Lobby desk
- Bell desk
- Travel desk
- Page board
- GRC cabinet
- Cashier well/bucket
- Luggage Trolley
- Bell Hop Trolleys
- Luggage net

<u>SEMI AUTOMATED</u>

- Date & time punching machine
- Credit card imprinter
- Telephone
- Telex machine
- Facsimile machine
- Billing and posting machine
- Photocopying machine
- Safe vault

<u>AUTOMATED</u>

- POS machine (Point of Sale), computer system with advance softwares and networking
- Laser Printers
- EPABX System
- EDC machine (Electronic Data Capturing machine)

- Magnetic Strip Reader for Card Key

Coordination of front office with other departments and sections:

The front office department play an important role in delivering quality service to the guest. Front office coordinates with various departments for smooth operations of the hotel. The below listed are the few departments with which Front office department coordinates with:-

HOUSEKEEPING:

The front office and housekeeping departments communicate with each other for the following information:-

Room Status:-

As rooms generate maximum revenue for hotels, the information about hte room status should be updated correctly and frequently. The front office and housekeeping departments must closely coordinated on the room status. The housekeeping department preapares an occupancy report, which is sent to the front office department where it is tallied with room status records of front desk. This helps to :-

- *Updates room status.*
- *Find Sleepers.*
- *To know the exact House Count.*
- *Charge the guest if an extra person has occupied the room.*
- *Coordinates in Guest room change requests.*

Security Concerns:-

The housekeeping personnel should inform the front office about any unusal circumstances that may indicate a violation of security for the hotel guests. Also Front office department informs Housekeeping department about the Scanty Baggage guests to keep an eye, if something security violation of the hotel is taking place. It is the duty of Front office personnel to inform In house or civil authorities to ensure the safety and security of the guests.

Special Arrangements:-

Guests may requests for additional or special amenities during their stay, like extra blanket, towel etc. When such requests are received at front desk, they should be immediately conveyed to the housekeeping department. For special guests the front office may request the housekeeping department to put extra amenities in the guest room like flower arrangement, bath robe etc. The front desk also informs the housekeeping department to make special arrangements for VIPs, SPATT, groups and crews

F&B DEPARTMENT:

Front office department informs the F&B department about the arrival and departure of guests, which helps them to plan their work schedule and staff requirement. It also notifies the F&B department about special food arrangements and parties. The front office department usually send the following information:-

- *The arrival & Departure of the Guests.*
- *Setting of Bars in VIP's room*
- *In house and expected VIP List*
- *The scanty baggage and NO post Status Guest.*
- *Groups and Guests with Bookings of Specific meal Plan.*

Also F&B department shares information related to security concerns found during in room dining. They also inform Front office departments about banquet bookings through Function Prospectus.

ENGINEERING & MAINTENANCE:

The front office department communicates with engineering and maintenance department for the proper upkeep of the equipments and systems installed in the hotel. The front office informs the maintenance department of any repair work required in guest rooms. In case the maintenance activity is required in a room which is occupied by a guest, the two departments work out a schedule so that the maintenance work is carried out in the absence of the guest. But if the extensive work needs to be done, the guest may be requested to change the room.

SECURITY:

The front office informs about scanty baggage and doubtful guests to security department to keep an eye on their rooms. When a guest has security concerns like unlocking of double locked door, fire, robbery, theft and any other emergency, the front desk should explain the emergency procedure to the guest while calling on security personnel to resolve the problem.

ACCOUNTS:

The front office department closely works with accounts department for handling Non guest accounts, back debt accounts, credit card accounts etc.

SALES & MARKETING:

Though nowadays, Front office is having its own team of sales and marketing which closely deals with following:-

- *Guest History*
- *Probable Guests*
- *Offers & Packages*
- *Advertisement of Rooms & Events etc.*

For successful Optimum booking, Sales and marketing department plays an important role for the Hotel.

HUMAN RESOURCE:

Front office coordinates with HR department for the requirement of new staffs, training of existing staffs, and requirement of Industrial & Vocational Trainees etc. On the guidelines regarding Job Specifications received from Front Office department, HR department floats or conducts Interviews for the recruitment of eligible staffs for Front Office Department.

CHAPTER THREE

Unit 3: Functions of different sections of Room Division Department

(Topics Covered: Front office, Reservation, Reception/front desk, Lobby desk, Guest relation desk, Telephone, Business centre, Mail and message section, Cashier desk, Night auditor. Uniformed service, Bell desk, Concierge, Travel desk, Airport representative. Housekeeping, Control desk, Horticulture, Linen and uniform room, Laundry, Room status terminology)

Front Office Operations:

Traditionally front office functions include reservations, registration, room and rate assignment, guest services, room status, maintenance and settlement of guest accounts, and creation of guest history records. The front office develops and maintenances a comprehensive data base of guest information, coordinates guest services, and ensures guest satisfaction. These functions are accomplished by personnel diverse areas of the front office department.

Organization:

Large hotels often organize the front office according, with different employees handling separate areas. This division of duties can enhance the control the front office has over its own operations. Front office personnel can provide more specialized attention if each area is responsible for only one segment of the guest stay. Such a separation of duties may not be practical in small hotel, where it is common for one or two individuals to handle all front desk operations. The front office in a large hotel supports many positions with a considerable separation of duties. These positions typically include, but are not limited to the following:

1. A front desk agent who registers guests and maintains room availability information.

2. A cashier who handles money, post charges, and oversees guest account settlement.

3. A mail and information clerk who takes messages, provides directions to guests, and maintains mail.

4. A telephone operator who manages the switchboard and coordinates wake-up calls.

5. A reservations agent who responds to reservation requests and creates reservation records.

6. A uniformed service agent who handles guest luggage and escorts guests to their rooms.

If a hotel property is computerized, each employee may be restricted to accessing only those computer records pertinent to his or her function.

The front office of a mid-size hotel performs the same functions, but with fewer employees. Staffs are often cross-trained and job duties are typically combined. For example, a front desk agent may also serve as a cashier and mail and information clerk. He or she may also be trained to assume the duties of a switchboard operator and reservations agent in their absence. During busy period, several desk agents may be working at the same time. Although each staff member may be assigned identical duties, the desk agents may informally divide the functions among themselves. For example, one person may decide to register guest and handle the switchboard, another may function as a cashier, and a third may handle reservations and information requests.

Small hotels may have a single front desk agent who performs neatly all the functions with little assistance. If the front desk agent becomes overwhelmed by the workload, the general manager or accountant, if properly trained, may help relieve the burden. In a small property, the generally manager and accountant often become more directly involved with front office operations.

Reservations:

Travelling to a place other than home town urge the need of a safe and comfortable place to stay. Now-a -days peoples are travelling too frequently due to advent of safer and faster modes of transport. Peoples while planning their trips to other places prefer to be sure that they will have a suitable accommodation when they reach at destination. This can be achieved by making an advance booking of the hotel room.

Reservation section of front office department of the hotel is responsible for receiving and processing the reservation queries. Depending upon the level of automation, volume of business, and house customs the procedure of processing reservation queries may differ from hotel to hotel in terms reservations handling, maintenance of reservation records, confirmation, amendments, and cancellation of reservation.

Layout of reservation section:

The location of the reservation section depends upon the size of hotel and volume of business. In a very small hotel the same function can be performed by the front desk. In a large hotel a separate section is needed. If a separate section of reservation is needed then it should be located preferably behind the reception counter and should have a communication door between reception and reservation section.

Function of reservation section:

The reservation section of front office department of hotel performs the function of processing reservation request of the future guest. This section is headed by a Reservation Manager, who is assisted by reservation supervisor and a team of reservation clerks/ assistants. Following are the functions performed by the reservation section:

- Receiving the reservation request
- Processing the reservation request
- Depending upon the availability of desired room type reservation request may be confirmed, waitlisted or denied.
- Updating the room availability status after each reservation transaction like confirmation, amendments and cancellation.
- Maintaining and updating the reservation records
- Preparing reservation reports

Reception:

According to oxford dictionary, ―reception is a place inside the entrance of a hotel or office building where guests or visitors go when they first arrive‖. This section of front office receives and welcomes the guests at their arrival in the hotel. The personnel of this section receive all necessary information about the guest to complete the registration formality. After completing the registration formalities, room is assigned to the guest and bell boy carries the guest luggage and escorts the guest to his room. The entire process should be carried out in professional way in a warmth and friendly atmosphere to create a positive guest impression.

Layout of reception section:

The reception section of the front office of a hotel is located in close proximity of entrance gate of the hotel. The layout of the reception section depends upon the size of hotel and volume of business. The front desk assistant carries out many tasks; hence, the front desk should be designed in a way to assist them in performing those tasks. The front desk may be circular, L-shape, curved or straight depending upon the requirement.

Function of reception section:

The reception section of front office department of hotel performs the function of welcoming the hotel guest. This section is headed by a supervisor and a team of receptionists/ front desk assistants. Following are the functions performed by the reception section:

- Receiving the guests
- Completing the registration formalities
- Assigning the room.
- Sending Arrival notification slips to concerned departments

Information:

As the name suggests this section of the front office provides information to guests. This section is manned by information assistant. In a small hotel the same function may be provided by the receptionist. The need of a separate information desk is felt in hotels having large number of rooms and the traffic of guest is higher.

Function of Information section:

The information section of front office department performs a variety of functions. Some of them are as under:

- Maintaining resident guest rack
- Handling guest room keys
- Handling guest mails, telegrams, fax, courier, parcels etc.
- Provide information to guest regarding hotel facilities, services, city information etc.
- Handling guests messages
- Handling paging

Cash & bills:

Cash and bills section of front office department records all guests' monetary transitions. This section maintains guest's folios and prepares the guest bills at the time of departure of the guest. This section is headed by cashier. This section performs the following tasks:

- Opening and maintaining guest folios
- Posting room charges in the guest folio
- Posting all credit charges in the guest folio
- Posting all cash received from the guest
- Preparing bills at the time of check-out
- Receives the cash, travelers cheques, demand draft for account settlement
- Handles credit cards for settlement of guest account
- Foreign currency exchange

Travel desk:

The travel desk deals with the guest's needs of transportation, air-ticketing, railway reservations etcetera. The hotel may operate the travel desk or it may be outsourced to a external travel agency. The travel desk performs the following tasks:

- Air-port/ railway station pick-up and drop
- Providing vehicles to guest if demanded on the basis of pre-determined charges
- Making railway reservations/cancellations and amendments for guest
- Purchasing air-tickets for the guest
- Arranging the sightseeing tours

Communication:

The communication section maintains a complex communications network. The hotel may have its own privet branch exchange along with Post &Telegraph lines. In olden days all outgoing calls were routed through operator. This was done to make proper accounting of the outgoing calls. Switchboard operators may also place wake-up calls and coordinate emergency communications. Now-a-days due to advancement in technology the guest are able to make outgoing calls without routing the operator. There is computerized call accounting system which charges the guest account if he makes an outgoing calls. The wake-up calls may also be registered on the system which dials the guest extension at registered time and plays pre-recorded message when answered. The telephone operators may also protect guests' privacy-and thereby contribute to the hotel's security program-by not revealing guestroom numbers to any other person. Many hotels also provide guest paging services over the public address system. These systems generally operate through communications section. Recent technological advancement in equipment has considerably decreased the responsibilities and workload of telephone operators.

Bell Desk:

Bell desk is located in a very close proximity of the entrance gate of the hotel. This section is headed by a bell captain. Bell boys and page boys are the team member of the bell desk. They handle the guest luggage from their entry in hotel porch to their rooms at the time of arrival and from their rooms to lobby and then to the guest vehicle at the time of their departure. The bell desk person is the last front desk employee who comes in guest contact at the time of departure of guest. The bell desk performs the following tasks:

- Handling guest luggage
- Locating guest in a specified area of the hotel (paging)
- Posting guest mails.
- Making sundry purchase for the guest
- Keeping guest luggage in left luggage room
- Escorting guest to their rooms
- Educating guest about functions of weather control, using in-house telephone directory.
- Providing information to guest about hotel facilities and services when asked by guest

Uniformed Service:

Employees who work in the uniformed service department of the hotel generally provide the most personalized guest service. Given the high degree of attention awarded guest by this department, some properties refer to uniformed service simply as guest service. Among the primary positions within the uniformed service department are:

1. Bell attendant – persons who provide baggage service between the lobby area and the guestroom.

2. Door attendants – persons who provide curb-side baggage service and traffic control at the hotel entrance.

3. Valet parking attendants-persons who provide parking service for guest's vehicles.

4. Transportation personnel – persons who provide transportation service for guests.

5. Concierges – person who assist guest by making restaurant reservations, arranging for transportation, and getting for tickets for theatre, sporting, or other special events, and so on.

Bell Attendants: many guests arrive at a hotel with heavy baggage or several pieces of luggage. Guest receives help handling this luggage from probably the best-known employee among the uniformed service staff: the bell attendant. Bell attendant should be clearly selected. Since most hotels have carts for transporting baggage, the physical ability to actually carry the baggage is not a critical job qualification. More important, bell attendants should have strong oral communication skills and display genuine interest in ach guest. Depending on the size and complexity of the hotel, bell attendants may be counted on to:

1. Transport guest luggage to and from guestrooms.

2. Familiarize guest with the hotel's facilities and services, safety features, as well as the guestroom and any in-room amenities.

3. Provide a secure area for guest requiring temporary luggage storage.

4. Provide information on hotel services and facilities, as well as group functions.

5. Deliver mail, packages, messages, and special amenities to guestrooms.

6. Pick up and deliver guest laundry and dry cleaning.

7. Perform light housekeeping services in lobby and entry areas.

8. Help guest load and unload their luggage in the absence of a door attendant.

9. Notify other departments of guest needs, such as housekeeping for a crib or extra towels.

While many of these tasks appear simple, they all require a degree of professionalism. For example to assist a guest with his or her luggage, the belt attendant must know how to properly load a luggage cart. Fragile items must not be placed below heavy items. The cart must also be properly balanced so that it does not tip over or become difficult to steer. It is through informal conversation that bell attendants become key players in the hotel's guest's names. This makes guests feel more welcome and allows the bell attendant to provide more personal service.

<u>Door Attendants:</u>

Door attendants play a role similar to bell attendants; they are dedicated to welcoming the guest to the hotel. These employees are generally found in hotels offering world-class or luxury service of the duties door attendants perform include:

1. Opening hotel doors and assisting guest upon arrival.
2. Helping guest load and unload luggage from vehicles.
3. Escorting guests to the hotel registration area.
4. Controlling vehicle traffic flow and safety at the hotel entrance.
5. Hailing taxis, upon request.
6. Performing light housekeeping services in the lobby and entry areas.

Experienced door attendants are capable of handling all these tasks with aplomb. A skilled and experienced door attendant learns the names of the frequent guest. When these guest returns to the hotel, the door attendant is able to greet them by name and can introduce them to other front office staff. Such personal service enhances the reputation of the hotel and provides the guest with as unique experience.

<u>Valet parking attendants:</u>

Valet parking is generally available at hotels offering world-class or luxury service. Specially trained employees park guest and visitor automobiles. The Introduction to Front Office personal attention and security of valet parking service is considered both a luxury and a convenience. Guest does not have to worry about finding a parking space, walking to the hotel in inclement weather, or finding their vehicles in the parking lot. Hotels generally charge a higher fee for valet parking, guest are also likely to tip the valet parking attendant.

The uniformed service department is responsible for all vehicles under its care and reports information to the front desk each night so that parking charges can be posted to guest accounts. In addition, when the vehicle entrance to the hotel is busy, valet parking attendants should help keep the area running smoothly by providing traffic control assistance.

<u>Concierges:</u>

Even though this guest service position has existed for quite some time, the concierge is perhaps the concierge was the castle doorkeeper. A concierge's job was to ensure that all the castle occupants were secure in their rooms at night. Traveling royalty was often accompanied by a concierge who provided security and traveled ahead of the royal party to finalize food and lodging arrangements. As hotels became more common in Europe, the concierge eventually became apart of the staff that provided personalized guest services. It is not uncommon to find a concierge at a world-class or luxury hotel.

Concierges may provide custom services to hotel guest. Duties include making reservations for dining securing tickets for theater and sporting events; arranging for transportation, and providing information on cultural events and local attractions. Concierges are known for their resourcefulness. Getting tickets to sold out concerts or making last-minute dinner reservations at a crowded restaurant are part of a concierge's responsibility and reputation. Most successful concierges have developed an extensive network of local, regional, and national contacts the concierge has established at restaurants, box office, car rentals offices,, airlines , printers, and other businesses. Some hotels actually encourage concierges to visit appropriate businesses and organizations to establish and strengthen such relationships. Finally, a highly successful concierge should speak several languages.

Housekeeping:

Housekeeping is perhaps the most important support department for the front office. Like the front office, housekeeping usually is part of the rooms division of the hotel. In some hotels, however, the housekeeping function is considered an independent hotel division. Effective communication among housekeeping and front office personnel can contribute to guest satisfaction while helping the front office to effectively monitor guestroom status.

Housekeeping employees inspect rooms before they are available for sale, clean occupied and vacated rooms, and communicate the status of guestroom until the room has been cleaned, inspected and released by the housekeeping department.

The housekeeping department often employs larger staff than other departments i.e. the rooms division. Normally, an executive housekeeper is in charge of the Introduction to Front department, aided by an assistant housekeeper. In larger hotels there can be several assistant housekeepers, each responsible for specific floors, sections, or, in room attendants, lobby and general cleaners, and laundry personnel. Room attendant are assigned to specific sections nof the hotel. Depending on the hotel's service level, average guestroom size, and cleaning tasks, room attendants may clean from 8 to 18 rooms per shift. If the hotel has its own laundry, housekeeping department staff may be charged with cleaning and pressing the property's linens, towels, uniforms, and guest clothing.

Housekeeping personnel (usually executive housekeepers) are responsible for maintaining two types of inventories: recycled and non-recycled. Recycled inventories are those items that have a relatively limited useful life but are used repeatedly in housekeeping operations. Theses inventories include such items as linens, uniforms, and guest amenities like irons and hair dryers. Non-recycled inventories are those items that are consumed or worn out during the course of routine housekeeping operations. Non-recycled inventories include cleaning supplies, small equipment items, and guest supplies and personnel grooming items. Guest amenities and linens are among the items and conveniences most often requested by guests.

To ensure the speedy, efficient rooming of guest in vacant and inspected room, the housekeeping and front office departments must promptly inform each other of any change in a room' status or availability. Team work between housekeeping and the front office is essential to effective hotel operations. To more familiar housekeeping and front office personnel are with each other's departmental procedures, the smoother the relationships.

<u>Room status terminology:</u>

1. **OCC - Occupied:** A guest is currently occupied in the room
2. **Stay over:** The guest is not expected to check out today and will remain at least one more night.
3. **On-Change:** The guest has departed, but the room has not yet been cleaned and ready for sale.
4. **DND - Do Not Disturb:** The guest has requested not to be disturbed
5. **Cleaning in progress:** Room attendant is currently cleaning this room.
6. **Sleep-out:** A guest is registered to the room, but the bed has not been used.
7. **On-Queue:** Guest has arrived at the hotel, but the room assigned is not yet ready. In such cases, the room is put on Queue status in-order for the housekeeping staff to prioritise such rooms first.
8. **Skipper:** The guest has left the hotel without making arrangements to settle his or her account.
9. **Vacant and ready:** The room has been cleaned and inspected and is ready for an arriving guest.
10. **Out of Order (OOO):** Rooms kept under out of order are not sellable and these rooms are deducted from the hotel's inventory. A room may

be out-of-order for a variety of reasons, including the need for maintenance, refurbishing and extensive cleaning etc.

11. **Out of Service (OOS):** Rooms kept under out of service are not deducted from the hotel inventory. This is a temporary blocking and reasons may be bulb fuse, TV remote not working, Kettle not working etc. These rooms are not assigned to the guest once these small maintenance issues are fixed.

12. **LO - Lockout:** The room has been locked so that the guest cannot re-enter until he or she is cleared by a hotel official.

13. **DNCO - Did not check out:** The guest made arrangements to settle his or her bills (and thus not a skipper), but has left without informing the front desk.

14. **DO - Due Out:** The room is expected to become vacant after the following guest checks out.

15. **CO - Check-Out:** The guest has settled his or her account, returned the room keys and left the hotel.

16. **LC - Late Check out:** The guest has requested and is being allowed to check out later than the normal/standard departure time of the hotel.

17. **EC - Early Check-in:** Guest has requested for an Early Check-in and is being allowed to check-in earlier than the normal/standard check-in time of the hotel.

18. **VC - Vacant and Clean** - Room is Vacant and Cleaned by the housekeeper.

19. **VD - Vacant and Dirty** - Room is Vacant and Dirty.

20. **VR - Vacant and Ready** - Room is Vacant and Ready for Check-in

21. **OR - Occupied and Ready**

22. **OC - Occupied and Clean** - Room is Occupied and Cleaned by the Housekeeping.

23. **OD - Occupied and Dirty** - Room is Occupied and yet to be cleaned by the housekeeping.

24. **V/C or O/V - Status Unclear** - (Either the room is Vacant and Clean or Occupied or Vacant) need to be verified by the Housekeeping staff.

25. **VCI - Vacant, Cleaned and Inspected** - Room is Vacant, Cleaned and Inspected by the Housekeeping Supervisor.

26. **H/L - Heavy Luggage** - Guest has Heavy or more luggage than usual.

27. **L/L - Light Luggage** - Guest has light or very less luggage.

28. **N/L - No Luggage** - Guest has no luggage also know as Scanty Baggage.

29. **DL - Double Lock** - Guest has put a double lock in the room.

30. **CL - Chain Lock** - Guest has placed a Chain Lock in the room.
31. **HU - House Use** - Room is used by the hotel staff or someone staying from the management team.
32. **NCI - Newly Checked In** - Room was checked in within the last one to two hours.
33. **NS - No Show** - A guest who made a room reservation but did not register or Check-in.
34. **SO - Sleep Out**
35. **SR - Service Refused** - Guest refused to clean the room.
36. **V - Vacant**
37. **MUR - Make-Up Room**

CHAPTER FOUR

Unit 4: Hotel Rooms and Tariff Structure

(Topics Covered: Definition of room and its characteristics, Room taxonomy (Standard, Promoted and Suite Configured Rooms), Definition of room tariff and its fixation basis, Room rate taxonomy (Standard, Special/ Discounted & Promoted Room Rates), Group rates, Discount and allowances.)

Definition of room and its characteristics:

Hotel Room means a room (or suite of conjoined rooms offered as a single accommodation) (i) in a hotel (ii) that is used to provide private sleeping accommodations to paying customers and (iii) that typically includes linen or housekeeping service. A hotel room is usually occupied by transients or travelers who do not enjoy an exclusive right or privilege with respect to the room, but instead merely have an agreement for the private use or possession of the room. A room is a "hotel room" only if the customer has the right to exclude other customers from the room.

Room Taxonomy:

SINGLE ROOM

A single room has one single bed for single occupancy. An additional bed (extra bed) may be added to this room on the request of a guest and charge accordingly. The size of the bed is normally 3ft.X6ft. However the concept of single rooms is vanishing nowadays. Mostly hotels have twin or double rooms and charge of single room if occupied by single person.

DOUBLE ROOM

A double room has one double bed for double occupancy. The extra bed may be added on request and charged accordingly. The size of double bed is generally 4.5ft.X6.5ft.

TRIPLE ROOM

A triple room has three separate single bed and can be occupied by three guests. This type of room is suitable for groups and delicates of meetings and conferences.

QUAD ROOM

A quad room has four separate single beds and can accommodate four persons together in same room.

TWIN ROOM

A twin room has two single bed separated by bed side table. The size of bed is usually 3ft.X6ft.

HOLLYWOOD TWIN

A Hollywood twin has two single beds sharing a common headboard.

DOUBLE DOUBLE ROOM

A double double room has two double beds and is normally preferred by a family or a group, as it can accommodate four persons together.

KING ROOM

A king room has a king sized bed. The size of the bed is 6ft.X6ft. An extra bed can be added to this room and charged accordingly.

QUEEN ROOM

A Queen room has a queen room has queen sized bed. The size of the bed is 5ft.X6ft.

INTERCONNECTED ROOM

An interconnecting room is a room which has a common wall and a door or room which connects the two rooms. This allows the guests to access any of the two rooms without passing through the corridor. These types of rooms are ideal for families and crew members.

ADJOINING ROOM

These rooms share a common wall with one another but are not connected by a door.

ADJACENT ROOM

These rooms are very close to one another but do not share a common wall. These rooms are situated side by side.

STUDIO ROOM

These are the rooms which are called multi utility rooms also. They have furnitures like sofa cum bed, Murphy bed, Closet Bed etc. The furniture is such which is used for sitting purposes during the day time and for sleeping during night time.

PARLOUR ROOM

A parlour has a living room without bed and may have sofa and chairs for sitting. It is generally not used as bedroom.

SUITE ROOM

A suite comprises more than one room. Occasionally, it can also be a single large room with clearly defined sleeping and sitting areas. The decor of such units is of very high standards, aimed to please those guests who can afford the high tariff of the room category.

DUPLEX ROOM

These suites comprises of two rooms situated at different levels or floors which are connected by an internal staircase, the suite is generally used by business guests who wish to use the lower level as an office and meeting place and the upper level room as the bedroom. These types of room are quiet expensive.

EFFICIENCY ROOM

It has an attached kitchenette for guest preferring longer stay. Generally these types of rooms are found in holiday and health resorts where guests stay for longer time.

PENT HOUSE

It is generally located on the topmost floor of the hotel and has an attached open terrace or open sky space. It has very nice decor and furnishings and is among the costliest rooms in the hotel, mostly preferred by celebrities and major political personalities.

LANAI

These are the rooms which has veranda or the balcony which has scenic beauty view may be of hill side or a garden or beach etc.

HOSPITALITY ROOM

These rooms are designed for hotels in-house guest who would need to entertain or meet outside their allotted rooms. Such rooms are generally charged on hourly basis.

CABANA

It is situated away from the main hotel building in the vicinity of a swimming pool or sea beach. It may or may not have hard bed and is generally used for changing room and not as a bed room. These rooms are having bathing facility.

Definition of room tariff and its fixation basis:

The various tariff patterns followed by hotels have come to be identified by the areas where such patterns originated. Hotels charge their guests according to the following plans:-

EUROPEAN PLAN:

The tariff consists of room rent only. All other expenses would be paid by the guest as per the actual use or consumption. The tariff plan is also called as EP.

CONTINENTAL PLAN:

The room tariff includes continental breakfast along with room rent. The tariff plan is also called as CP.

AMERICAN PLAN:

The tariff plan is also called as En-Pension and Full Board Plan. The tariff includes all meals i.e. breakfast, lunch and dinner along with the room rent. The menu for the food & beverages are fixed. The tariff plan is also called as AP.

MODIFIED AMERICAN PLAN:

The tariff plan is also called as Demi-Pension. The tariff includes breakfast and one major meal i.e lunch or dinner along with the room rent. The tariff plan is also called as MAP

BERMUDA PLAN:

The room tariff includes American breakfast along with the room rent. The tariff plan is also called as B&B plan or Bed & Breakfast Plan.

TARIFF

The term tariff means rate and when applied to rooms of a hotel, it means room rates.

Hotel room rates fixation is a difficult task. The combination of all the rates offered at a hotel is called rate structure.

BASIS OF CHARGING:

1. Competition :Rates must be competitive with other hotels of the same standard and providing almost similar services and facilities provided by the other hotels

2. Customer Profile: The category of customers coming to the hotel must also be considered, their social and financial status.

3. Standard of service provided: The standard of service provided by hotels are also one of the important factor while fixing room tariffs.

4. Price cuts for special business: The price cuts make sense only if:

- It is necessary to cut the price in order to get the business
- It does not replace other more profitable business.

1. <u>Locality:</u> The locality in which the hotel is situated gains prominence while fixing room rates. If a hotel is situated in a posh locality where all the shopping approaches to airport and railway station are worthy. The room rates would be comparably higher than those situated at backward and far off locality.
2. <u>The surroundings:</u> Cost of land and building, architecture, construction, surroundings are also being considered.
3. <u>Various amenities:</u>

- *Room service*
- *Air conditioning*
- *Swimming pool*
- *Television*
- *Internet*
- *Pick up and drop service/car rentals*
- *Laundry service*
- *Hot and cold running water*
- *Toiletries/bathroom amenities*
- *Concierge*
- *Restaurant/bar/coffee shop*
- *Cake shop*
- *Banqueting*
- *Lobby*

8. <u>Room location:</u> Location of the rooms also matters a lot. Front rooms and rooms opening to better views.
9. <u>Publicity:</u> The amount of publicity done by a hotel and special budgets prescribed also matters in deciding room rates. This type of expenses has to be adjusted somehow as it has no source of return but is a must in popularising the various services of a hotel.

TARIFF FIXATION:
CHECK IN AND CHECK OUT BASIS:

The most common way of fixation of tariff, the hotel fixes a specific time usually 12 noon. As checkout time which means that the guest charging cycle begins at 12 noon and finish at 12 noon next day for guest staying in the hotel , after 12 noon next day charge may be levied.

24 HOURS BASIS:

In this system the charges of rooms start from the time when the guest checks in and he has to pay for one day. For example; if a guest arriving at 10 AM on a particular day his charges would be till the 10 AM of the next day. This system is good for small and budget hotels.

ON THE BASIS OF COMPETITORS RATE:

Some hotels fix their room tariffs on the basis of what their competitors are charging. This is the most unrealistic method and does not include any consideration of the features and facilities of their own organisation. The hotel which is considered as a guideline is called Price market. This price market is usually a large organisation.

NIGHT BASIS:

In this system the guest is charged with the number of nights which are spent irrespective of time of arrival i.e. if he spent two nights he will be charged for 2 nights with minimum of a day.

DAY CHARGE/DAY RATE:

Sometime a guest may stay in a hotel for few hours only and may not spend the nights, in such a case where guest stays only for six hours. Maximum hotels may charge special discount rate which is usually 50% of the rack rate, this type of rate is called Day rate or Day used rate.

INCLUSIVE/NON INCLUSIVE RATE:

On the basis of meal plan

European plan, American plan, Modified American plan, Bermuda plan, Continental plan.

European plan (non inclusive rate)

Continental plan, American plan, modified American plan, Bermuda plan (Inclusive rate)

EUROPEAN PLAN:

The tariff consists of room rent only. All other expenses would be paid by the guest as per the actual use or consumption. The tariff plan is also called as EP.

CONTINENTAL PLAN:

The room tariff includes continental breakfast along with room rent. The tariff plan is also called as CP.

AMERICAN PLAN:

The tariff includes all meals i.e. breakfast, lunch and dinner along with the room rent. The menu for the food & beverages are fixed. The tariff plan is also called as AP.

MODIFIED AMERICAN PLAN:

The tariff includes breakfast and one major meal i.e lunch or dinner along with the room rent. The tariff plan is also called as MAP

BERMUDA PLAN:

The room tariff includes American breakfast along with the room rent. The tariff plan is also called as B&B plan or Bed & breakfast plan.

RULE OF THUMB APPROACH:

It is one of the very traditional ways of charging rates. In this system 'one rupees' rate is fixed for every 'thousand rupees' spend on room construction cost.

For example;

Amount spend on room construction is Rs. 1,00,000,00 then assumed amount of room rent would be:

Rs1,00,000,00 / 1,000 = Rs. 10000

UPSIDE DOWN METHOD (ASSUMPTION METHOD):

In this method the hotel first estimate its sales volume in terms of money then calculates all the expenses then estimates the room sales. Now from the total sales volume the amount of expenses are deducted to get the desired net profit. On the basis of projected room sales, projected gross sales and projected expenses the room tariff is calculated. This method is always not reliable as it is based heavily on projected figures only. It is the latest methods which are used nowadays in hotel industry.

DIFFERENT TARIFF:

RACK RATE:

It is the price at which a hotel sells its rooms when no discounts of any type are offered to the guest. However typically vary by the type of room. For eg. A rack rate for a hotel best and most popular room will be higher than that of its less popular room. Larger rooms, suite rooms and room with special amenities, views or other features typically have their own unique rack rates

DISCOUNTED RATES:

GROUP RATE:

A published tariff prices given to group operators which is communicable only in retail travel agents, tour operators etc. Generally commissionable at 10% of the published rack rate.

GOVERNMENT RATE:

Usually government employee is given per day allowance for their travelling and accommodation and allowances for food also. Some hotels offer them a rate which give them above facilities within that price.

SEASONAL RATE:

Season and resort hotels which usually have fluctuating demand changes their rates usually as per the season and offer different rates during the season and packages during off season.

CRIB RATE:

A special rate applicable for child below 12 years old of age accompanying their parents.

EXTRA BED RATE:

Generally ¼ of the published room rate.

CREW RATE:

Special rates for airlines crew members. The total number of rooms are taken on consistent and continuous night basis for a period of time, generally for a year.

WEEKDAYS/WEEKEND RATES:

This is one of the another factor on which the rate fixation can be done for example On a hill station where the guest are more during weekends i.e. Friday to Sunday, the rates may be higher and from Monday to Thursday the rates may be lower. Similarly the rates of downtown hotel during weekdays i.e. between Monday to Thursday may be higher and Friday to Sunday may be lower. Traditionally, a hotel location type decides their weekend and weekdays demands level and helps in fixing the tariff accordingly.

MEMBERSHIP RATES:

Some hotels gives spectacular rates to the member of various esteemed organisation such as esteemed clubs etc. These may vary from 50% to complementary on accommodation only. Some rebate may also be given on food and beverage service. This is called industry or membership rates, it is offered to hospitality trade organisation like FHRAI and TAAI etc.

CHAPTER FIVE

Unit 5: Guest Cycle

(Topics Covered: Different Stages of Guest Cycle and involved activities. Equipment under different modes of guest cycle.)

<u>Different Stages of Guest Cycle and involved activities:</u>

The Guest Cycle:

The hotel guests passes through a definite path from reservation to arrival, stay, and departure. They pass from reservation, arrival, registration, allotment of rooms, stay and use of hotel facilities, and finally departure from the hotel. These phases remain the same in case of every guest and constitute the guest cycle.

The four distinct phases of guest cycle are as under:

§ Pre-arrival

§ Arrival

§ Stay

§ Departure

§ After departure

<u>Pre-arrival:</u>

The activities that are carried out before the arrival of the guest forms the pre-arrival phase of the guest cycle. This is the first stage of interaction with the guest. Reservation is the most important pre- arrival activity. The probable guest contacts hotel for reserving a room for their proposed stay in the town. During this phase guest chooses a hotel for stay. The guest choice about a particular hotel is affected by factors like advertisement, recommendations from friends, previous experience with the hotel, reputation, location etc. The prompt reply and tactful handling of a call for reservation request by the reservation assistant can create the good first impression of the hotel in the eye of the future guest. During the reservation process the hotel may ask for advance deposit from the guest. Following activities are carried out in this phase:

- Processing reservation request of the guest.
- Creation of guest folio in case hotel has received any advance payment.
- Blocking the room for the guest.
- Making special arrangements for the guest (if required).

The data collected during the process of reservation can be utilized in future front office and sales activities. A well managed reservation system can maximize the room sales by monitoring room availability and forecasting room revenue.

Arrival:

The guest arrival at the front desk is probably the first instant when hotel may have a face to face interaction with the guest. This is a very critical stage as guests develop their perception regarding standard and services that the hotel can provide to them. During this phase the guest is received and registration process begins. The guest is asked to verify their details already printed in registration card. The registration activity is an agreement between the hotel and the guest. The hotel offers the accommodation product and services to the guest. The guest signifies their assent to pay for the services received. The following activities take place in arrival phase of the guest cycle:

§ Reception and welcome of the guest (aarti, tilak and garlanding/ offering welcome etc)

§ Registration of the guest

§ Room rate and room assignment

§ Dispensing key to the guest

§ Luggage handling of the guest by bell desk

§ Delivering mails if hotel has received mails on behalf of guest.

Stay:

This is the stage of the guest cycle during which the guest actually experiences the facilities and services offered by the hotel. The guest services and facilities which are offered during the stay of the guest are discussed in chapter 9 in detail. Hotel must take care for safe and comfortable stay of the guest. The courteous and helpful behavior of the staff may mask little lack in services. The services and facilities offered during this stage are critically important in attracting repeat business from the same guest. The activities that are carried out during the stay of guest are as under:

§ Creation and maintenance of guest accounts

§ Message handling
§ Key handling
§ Handling guest- mail
§ Guest paging
§ Safety deposit locker
§ Procedures for guest room change
§ Left Luggage Procedure

Departure:

As the maxim goes that all well that ends well. Same is the case with the guest departure. All the drawbacks can be marks by efficient and hassle free check- out procedure. During the departure stage the guest settles their account by making payment to throughpre established mode for the services received from the hotel. A great care should be taken during the departure stage, as it is the last point of guest contact to receive any unpaid bills and to develop loyalty in the guest to patronize the property over and over again. Following transactions take place in departure stage:

§ Preparation and presentation of guest bills
§ Settlement of guest account
§ Luggage handling by the bell desk
§ Left luggage handling in case guest wishes to keep their luggage with the hotel for a short duration of time
§ Sales and marketing activity (future reservation)
§ Bon voyage to guest

After Departure:

This stage of guest cycle is a real challenge to the hotel. It is during this stage that the activities of the hotel will bring back the guest to the hotel. For this it is important that the hotel management creates occasions of contacting guests and keep reminding him about the hotel from time to time. This can be done by sending letters, mailers, and feelers to the guest on his Birthday, His marriage anniversary and other such occasions which may be important for him and his family.

Equipments Used in Front Office:

For carrying out all day to day work many types of equipment are used in front office department. They can be grouped in to following broad categories:

- Manual equipments
- Semi-automated equipments

- Automated equipments

<u>Manual Equipments Used in Front Office:</u>
ROOM RACK:

- The room rack is large front office equipment located just behind the front desk.
- The room rack is a wooden framework designed and contains a metallic array of pockets which contain a large number of room rack slips for showing the reservation and housekeeping status of each guestroom of a property.
- The room rack slip contained in the metallic pockets shows the type of room (Double, Twin, King, Suite), the occupancy status of the guestroom (occupied, Vacant, not cleared) and the name of the guest registered in the guestroom.
- The current occupancy status of the guestrooms is indicated by the coloured strips inserted in the pockets of the room rack.
- It is the joint effort of the front desk and housekeeping to timely update the room rack in order to have an accurate room status position.

INFORMATION RACK:

- The information rack is another important device positioned in the front desk and is used by the front desk agent to track the various in-house guests of the hotel.
- The Information is a revolving device that contains information about the various guests presently registered in the hotel with the name of the guests alphabetically arranged in the rack and the information taken from the upper portion of the folios of the guests.
- The Information contained in the information rack are name of the guest, number and type of room occupied, rate of the guestroom, date of arrival and departure and the billing instructions.

MAIL AND MESSAGE RACK:

- The mail and message rack is a wooden framework containing an array of pigeonholes with each pigeonhole used to store the various mails and messages received for an in-house guest.

- Previously, the mail and message rack used to contain the keys of the guestrooms in the pigeonholes and was thus called the mail, message and key rack
- But nowadays, the mail rack has been isolated from the key rack and has been moved behind scenes to present a more professional appearance and at the same time ensuring the security of the mails and message of the guests of the hotel.

KEY RACK OR KEY DRAWER:

- The key rack or the key drawer is important front office equipment located underneath the counter of the front desk.
- The key rack as the name suggests, is a wooden or metallic framework containing an array of slots used for keeping the keys of the guestrooms in sequential order of the guestrooms present in the hotel.
- This rack is maintained by the front desk in hotels where metal or hard keys are used and is thus essential front desk equipment for such hotels.

FOLIO WELL OR FOLIO BUCKET:

- A folio well or folio bucket is also an important equipment used in the front desk cash section.
- This equipment contains a large number of slots where the folios are arranged sequentially according to the room number.
- The folio well is used by the front office cashier to store and tack the folios of the various registered guests of the hotel and is used to maintain the folios safely for future use and reference.

Semi-Automated Equipments Use in Front Office:
POSTING MACHINE:

- The accounting posting machine is very essential equipment used in the semi-automated front office system for posting the various charges in the accounts of the guests.
- The posting machine is generally used to calculate the totals of the guest accounts, departments and transactions.
- The mechanical features of the accounting posting machine are arranged in such a logical sequence the job of posting the charges into the various

guest accounts becomes very easy.

- The line pick-up keys ensures that the posting machine is not over printing a line as the operator indicates where the accounting posting machine should start the calculation and should start printing.
- There is a key pad in the account posting machine which is used by the cashier or the operator to enter the room numbers of the guests, department key (e.g. room, tax, food) and also the type of transaction (e.g. debit, credit, transfer)

CASH REGISTER:

- The cash register is semi-automated equipment used optionally by the front desk.
- The cash register is generally used by the front desk to record the various sales of sundries at the front desk such as stamps, newspapers, candy etc.
- The various required mechanical features present in the cash register include a key pad, category key (stamps, newspapers, candy) and amount entering key.

WAKE UP DEVICES:

- The wake up device is a very important device used by the front desk or the telephone exchange of non-automated hotels to remind the staffs of awakening the guests at requested times.
- The most famous and common wake- up device is known as the James Remindo timer which is an alarm clock with pull out pins.
- Many hotels also use a simple alarm clock for awakening the guests. The guests' requests for wake up calls are recorded in a wake-up sheet with the information of time, room number and name of the guest.
- In fully automated systems, the telephone exchange automatically places the various requests of the guests for wake –up calls by automatic- voice- recorded wake- up messages. This feature is of great help when many guests have to woken up at the same time on the hotel.

CREDIT CARD IMPRINTER:

- The credit card imprinter is very important equipment used for the purpose of front office accounting.

- The equipment is used especially when the guests present credit cards at the time of their arrival or departure to settle their bill.
- The credit card imprinter makes an imprint of the credit card used by the guest as a method of payment.

TYPEWRITER:

- The typewriter is very important semi-automated equipment used for preparing various documents related to the front office operations and also related to the guests.
- The front office employees use typewriters to prepare guest reservations confirmation letter, to prepare the registration card of the guest and also to conduct the other word processing jobs of the department.

Automated Equipments Used in Front Office:
CREDIT CARD VALIDATOR :

Computerized telephone system which allows the proper billings of the outgoing calls of the guests. The credit card validator is automated front office equipment used by the front office cashier to check the validity of the credit card presented by the guest as mode of payment at the time of arrival or departure of the guest.

- This equipment is a computer terminal linked to a credit card data bank, which holds information concerning the validity of the credit card of the guest.
- The credit card equipment assures the hotel management that the guest has credit balance high enough to cover the projected charges and it also verifies that the card presented by the guest is not a stolen property.

TIME STAMPING MACHINE:

- The time stamping is a mechanical or an electronic device which is used extensively by the front office of a hotel, records the check-in check-out time of the guests, delivery time of any mail or message for the in-house guests.
- This device imprints the date and time on a piece of paper either electronically or mechanically and is thus important equipment for carrying out the operations of the front office leading to guest

satisfaction.

FAX MACHINES:

- The full form of FAX machines is Facsimile, important electronic equipment.
- This a facsimile reproduction equipment that operates through telephone lines and are used extensively by the front office to receive and send official documents important from point of view of the guest or the hotel management at large.
- While sending a fax message, the operator dials the destination fax machine number and then sends the fax message by inserting the message page in the machine.
- It is important that the destination fax machine should be switched on when the fax message is sent from the hotel.

CALL ACCOUNTING SYSTEM:

- A call accounting system is a fully
- This type of automated telephone system has been introduced in a large number of hotels nowadays due to the reason for providing improved services to the guest.
- The call accounting system is called APBX or Automated Private Branch Exchange and is used in the hotel telephone exchange section of the front office department to automatically trace and bill the outgoing calls made by the guests during their stay at the hotel.

COMPUTER:

- All the automated hotels around the world are excessively using computers for the day to day operations, administrations and management.
- Computers are also widely used in the front office departments of the hotels for the purpose of reservations, registration, accounting and auditing.
- Computers are efficient to operate and are extremely user friendly and thus help the employees to store and retrieve important data of the guest from time to time to carry out the various guest services.

CHAPTER SIX

Unit 6: Reservation

(Topics Covered: Definition and importance of reservation, Modes and Sources of reservation, Tool and process of reservation, System of reservation, Manual (Card and Hotel Diary), Semi-automated (Whitney , computerized), Fully automated (CRS and GDS). Types of reservation (on different basis), Guaranteed vs. Non-guaranteed, Transient vs. Group. Reservation amendment/modification and cancellation policy, Reservation Network/Channel (CRS), Affiliated reservation network, Non-affiliated reservation/referral group, Reservation supply chain (online companies)- Expedia, Make My Trip, Travel Related Services. Reservation terminology and documentation.

<u>Definition and importance of reservation:</u>

Reservation of the hotel accommodation is one of the important responsibilities of the front office department. A potential guest contacts a hotel for availability of the desired type of accommodation and any allied services that the hotel offers. The front office department needs to react to the enquiry of the guests.

For a guest, reservation increases the chances of a better deal for assured accommodation on arrival. For a hotel, reservation can enable a better management of guest experience during usual as well as peak seasons. Reservation procedure varies depending on the size and brand of the hotel and the reservation system employed.

Importance of a Reservation System:

Profitable business ventures rely on effective marketing principles, which include reviewing people who are in need of hotel products and services, determining their needs, developing products and services that meet their needs, and making a profit on the sale of those products and services.

A well-organized reservation system allows hotels to ensure a steady flow of guests into their properties. Hotel chains offer their members the ability to fill 30 percent or more of available rooms on a nightly basis. Independent hoteliers have the onerous responsibility of creating exciting marketing programs to capture room business. Easy access to a hotel's data bank of rooms helps in fulfilling the customers' needs as well as in reaching a targeted daily occupancy rate, average daily rate, yield percentage, and Rev-PAR. A reservation system represents the primary means of producing positive cash flow and a favourable income statement.

<u>Modes and Sources of reservation:</u>

MODES OF RESERVATION:

A. *Verbal (Telephone, in person)*
B. *Written (Letters, emails, fax etc.)*

<u>VERBAL MODE:</u>

Reservations requests may also be made through oral communication i.e. in person or on telephone. The advantage of oral communication is that it is fast, convenient, and generates immediate response or feedback, and one can get the complete information and clear any doubts through oral communication. The disadvantage is that it does not provide a permanent record.

<u>WRITTEN MODE:</u>

The reservation request which is made in written are considered as written mode. The different written mode of reservation request includes letter, fax, e-mail etc. The advantages of written mode of reservations are that they are clear and provide a written record for the hotel, which can be referred to in case of any miscommunication or confusion.

Sources of Reservations:

People travel for various reasons such as personal as well as for MICE. There are various

sources from whom the requests of reservation pour in:

· **Direct Request from Guests:** The prospective guests can approach individually

to the hotel for reservation of accommodation mostly when they are single travelers

or family travellers.

· **Request from Travel Agent:** They can approach the hotel for booking accommodations for group travellers.

· **Request from Corporate Agent**: An organization can request a hotel to reserve

accommodations for their employees, clients, or visitors.

· **Request from Airlines**: The airlines can reserve accommodations for their

working staff for routine stay as well as in case of flight cancellations.

· **Request from Institutions**: Various SMERF or NGO institutions request to

reserve hotels for sports people, delegations of embassies, or performing-art

program groups, workshop groups, and alike who travel to different location.

SYSTEMS OF RESERVATION:

- *Non automatic (Manual)*

  - *Cardex system*
  - *Card system*
  - *Diary system*

- *Semi Automatic*

  - *Whitney System*

- *Automatic (Fully)*

  - *Computer reservation system*
  - *Central reservation system*
  - *Instant reservation system*

CARDEX SYSTEM:

The basic concept of this system is like the library cardex system. The system consists of a rack which is readily available in various sizes in the market.

These racks consists of 12 drawers (1 for each month) , in each drawer there are 31 cardex sheet which can be arranged overlapping each other with a transparent plastic sheet covering them. The sheets are arranged in such a way that the bottom part of each sheet showing the date and day is visible for the entire span of 1 month. In this respect the reservation request with in the lead period of 1 year shall be entered in the cardex sheet as per the date of the arrival.

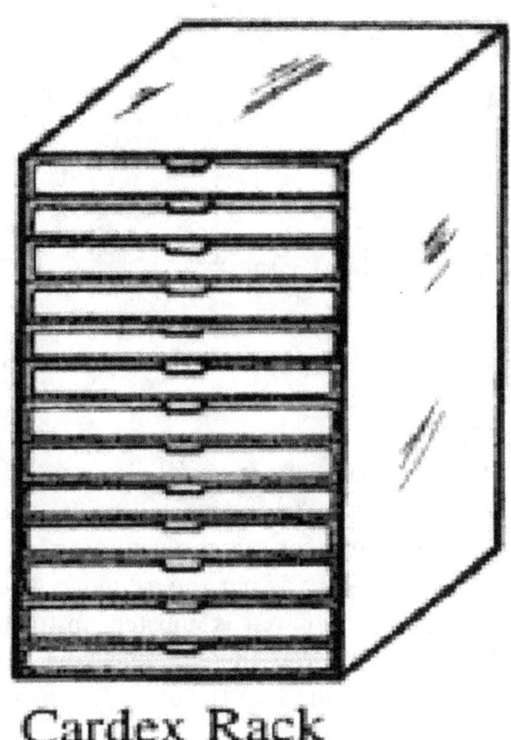

Cardex Rack

CARD SYSTEM:

In this system four compartments metal rack carrier for placing the reservation can be used. The design varies from hotel to hotel, reservation card are arranged in the rack in date wise order. Current month in 1 rack following months in other rack follows by the following year and the expired card are kept in the last rack.

In this system of reservation the request made by the guest are recorded on a reservation card form. Different colour card are used to identify different prospective guest. Next the card is placed in the respective place in the rack in alphabetic sequence. Racks are arranged in date wise order , current month racks and racks for following month containing 31 metal dividers , these dividers divides the mentioned dates. Next rack is having 12 dividers for the months of next year as well.

Card Rack System (Old but very effective)

DIARY SYSTEM:

The system is known as diary system because a diary is used for the forms. In this system the hotel maintains a diary in which the name of the guest is written on diary page as per the date of arrival. One page of the diary is mentioned with a date as per the calendar. Thus the entire guest from whom reservation is required is enlisted on to the respective page of the diary date wise. Thus preparing and checking of the movement list become easier. The tools required for the diary system are:

- *RSB(Room Status Board)*
- *ALC(Advance letting Chart)*
- *Room reservation form*
- *Hotel diary/ Booking Diary*

SAMPLE FORMAT OF BOOKING DIARY

S.No.	NAME	PAX	ARRIVAL TIME	ADVANCE	DATE OF DEPARTURE	BOOKING DATE	BOOKED BY	SIGN OF RESERVATION ASST.	ROOM NO. ALLOTED	REMARKS

ADVANCE LETTING CHART:

This is also called as advance reservation chart or conventional chart. This is a tool by which the room availability position can be known against the requested period of a particular month. Reservation section maintains one ALC for each month separately. They are kept in file in special order. ALC used by small hotels because of some disadvantages. The main disadvantage being the types of room cannot be located easily on the chart. Rooms being allotted in advance on the ALC do not allow the management of the hotel to make any alteration in the planning. ALC should be updated with pencil only.

Hotel APVS

Month .... Year ....

Room No	Date	1	2	3	4	5	6	7	8	9	10	11	12	13	14	15
	Room type	S	M	T	W	TH	F	SA	S	M	T	W	TH	F	SA	S
101	S.B.															
102	D.B.															
103	T.B.			Mr./Mrs.						Mr. / Mrs.						
104	Dup															
105	CAB					Mr./Mrs.										
106	DB							Mr./Mrs.								
107	SUITE		Mr./Mrs.													

Advance Letting Chart

DENSITY CHART:

Density chart are also known as density control chart. This is a tool by which the room availability position can be known against the requested period of particular month. Reservation section maintains one DCC for each month separately. They are kept in a file in serial order. Density chart has got many advantages in respect to ALC and is used by hotels of any size. Density control chart should be updated with pencil only.

Hotel APVS

Month .... Year ....

Room Type	Date	1	2	3	4	5	6	7	8	9	10	11	12	13	14	15	16	17	18
	Room No	S	M	T	W	TH	F	SA	A	M	T	W	TH	F	SA	S	M	T	W
Single Bed	101			X	X	X	X									X			
	106							X	X	X									
	105				X	X				X	X	X							
Double Bed	108							X	X	X									
	101		X	X	X	X													
	109				X	X				X	X	X	X	X			X		
Twin Bed	112							X	X										
	115			X	X					X	X	X	X						
	103					X	X												
Duplin	110							X	X	X									
	115										X	X	X	X					
	114		X												X	X	X	X	X

Density Chart Sample

ROOM RESERVATION FORM (RR FORM):

This is a tool which is optional in the procedure of room reservation in some system of reservation in the hotels. This is a tool by which the reservation assistant can record all necessary and relevant information regarding the prospective guest for the purpose of processing the reservation request.

HOTEL APVS
ROOM RESERVATION FORM

DATE_______________

NAME____

ADDRESS:____

PHONE EMAIL:____

RESERVE : ☐   AMMEND: ☐   CANCEL: ☐

FROM:___________________   ARRIVAL TIME:________________________

TO:___________________   DEPARTURE TIME:______________________

RATE:__________________   PLAN:_____________________________

BOOKED BY:____

ADDRESS:____

LETTER/FAX/TELEPHONE NO. :_________________ DATED:___________

DEPOSIT:_________________________VIDE RECEIPT NO.:_____________

BILLING INSTRUCTIONS:_______________________________________

REMARKS IF ANY:____

CONFIRMATION REQUIRED :_____________________YES/NO

REPLY SENT ON/BY:____

SIGNATURE OF RESERVATION ASSISTANT

SEMI AUTOMATED SYSTEM OF RESERVATION:
WHITNEY SYSTEM OF RESERVATION:

Whitney system of reservation is developed by American Whitney Duplicating and Check Company in 1970. This system consist of racks mounted vertically on wall and standard size slips called whitney slips or Shannon slips which is being filled in by the staff and put it into the slots of the whitney racks. The slips are colour coded to identify the guest type like FIT, GIT etc.

A whitney system racks consists of a total of forty three racks out of which thirty one racks are kept for the current month (one for each day), eleven racks for the next eleven months of the year, and one rack for the for the next year. The thirty one racks are arranged as per the date of the month.

Sample colour coding followed in most of the hotels are white coloured slips for FIT guests, Yellow coloured slips for GIT guests, pink colour for airlines crews and blue coloured slips for VIP guests.

DATE OF ARRIVAL	NAME OF GUEST	ROOM TYPE	RATE	DATE OF DEPARTURE
MODE OF RESERVATION	RESERVED BY	DATE RECEIVED		
AGENCY (If any)				
Billing Instruction			Confirmation Date	

SAMPLE FORMAT OF WHITNEY SLIP

AUTOMATED & FULLY AUTOMATED SYSTEM OF RESERVATION:

Though the information stored in the automatic system is same as in manual system, but it has already changed the speed and accuracy in making reservations. The processing of reservation request does not require manual study of density chart or advance letting chart. The reservation assistant can check the availability of rooms by clicking on a link on the computer. In this system, the reservation information is feed into the electronic format of the reservation form, and the information is transferred to the central server where the room status is updated automatically.

When a reservation assistant receives a reservation request, he/she checks whether the room is available or not using this system. If the request is accepted, the system automatically blocks the room for the desired duration of time and removes the room from the availability records. The automated system saves the trouble of manually updating the records. It also generates electronic confirmation letters that are sent to the guest's email addresses or postal addresses.

The system is also equipped to automatically generate reports like occupancy records or forecasts. CRS (Centralised reservation system) and GDS (Global Distribution System) are the examples of automated system.

An automated system itself is having different generations or units, in the beginning of automated generation we were having <u>computerised reservation system,</u> the main reason of using this system was that it was very efficient and time saving and at the same time it is very effective system. Hotels which operate on computer usually are fully dependent on the system, as there is very little paper work, very little filing work as well as the system is time saver.

The main features that the computer reservation system should cover are as follows:

- *In receiving queries*
- *Displaying room status and maintaining guest history.*
- *Few computers are programmed in such a way that they do possess decision making capability.*
- *It displays occupancy status and efficiently makes amendments or cancellations.*
- *It generates various reports and list and hence reducing extra paper work and workload.*

The other example of fully automated system is CRS (Centralised reservation system) which is generally used by the hotel chains. A chain of hotels which has a CRO system has reservation office in different cities although they may have no unit operating in that city. All the units are connected with this centralised reservation system. There are two basic types of central reservation system, they are **Affiliate network** and **Non affiliate network.**

An affiliate network is a hotel chains network where all the individual units of chain are linked through the central network.

A non affiliate reservation system connects non chain properties and enables independent hotel operators to get the benefit of reservation which the units of chain get and this system also take care of advertising of the properties.

Few CRS networks used in India are Amadeus- Hires, Abacus- Hotel net, Galileo- Room Master, Team four hospitality- Resnet and Utell world reservations (GDS).

INSTANT RESERVATION AND SELF RESERVATION:

It is basically a division or unit of a chain of hotels where the reservation for any of its properties are taken instantly. Though this system is modernised by the development of computer and networking. Now a guest can find self check in kiosk at the hotel lobby and can also do the booking of the other units of the same hotel chain from that kiosk.

Types of reservation (on different basis):

<u>TENTATIVE RESERVATION/WAITLISTED RESERVATION:</u>

When a request from prospective guest is received for some future day arrival and the hotel blocks the room for the guest provisionally in the hotel records such as charts, diaries, racks or computers and sends a letter of offer to the prospective guest.

The offer has a cut off date by which the guest should send his confirmation which may be in the form of letter, guarantee by company credit card and deposit etc. Once the hotel receives the confirmation through any mode about the guest confirmation, the reservation changes to confirmed or guaranteed reservation and are updated accordingly

<u>GUARANTEED RESERVATION:</u>

In this type of reservation the prospective guest confirms his arrival by giving guarantee to the hotel of his arrival by following ways:

- *<u>ADVANCE PAYMENT OR DEPOSIT GUARANTEE:</u>*

In this case the hotel request the prospective guest to either send the complete deposit or partial deposit and on receiving that makes the booking for the prospective guest. In this case if the guest does not arrive on the arrival date the room is not released for about 24 hrs or on the basis of hotel policy, the hotel can always forfeit the advance received from the guest in case of his no show.

- *<u>CREDIT CARD GUARANTEE:</u>*

It is the case where a prospective guest makes booking and gives the hotel his credit card number. The hotel confirms that from the credit card company and then blocks the room for prospective guest. In case of the no show the hotel will make the charge to the guest credit card number and the credit card company will bill it to card holder.

- *<u>AIRLINES GUARANTEE:</u>*

In this case the airlines management takes the responsibility of the payment of the stay of their crew members. In case of no-show the charges are paid by airlines company. Though this situation rarely occurs.

- *<u>COMPANY GUARANTEE:</u>*

In this the company who makes booking for their executive guest and visitors takes the responsibility of payment.

- ### *TRAVEL AGENT GUARANTEE:*

Sometimes some travel agents or tour operators have arrangement with hotel chains to book the rooms for their clients. In this case they take the responsibility of the payment.

Reservation amendment/modification and cancellation policy:
AMENDEMENT IN RESERVATION:

In certain cases the guest may change the original booking program and inform the same to the hotel with a request to make amendments in the records. The change usually is in dates of booking. Sometimes it may be in number of pax, type and rates of rooms also. The reservation section will first confirm from their record whatever the requests can be accepted or not. In case the hotel decides to accept the request of the guest, necessary amendments in the records shall be made and communicated to all concerned department. The process of amendment includes two basic steps: First the cancellation of previous booking and second is to create a new booking.

CANCELLATIONS:

It is for certain that some percentage of cancellation will be there in hotels having a large number of reservations. Hotels must communicate the cancellation policy to the prospective guest, particularly when the advance deposit has been received from the guest to avoid legal problem

Generally hotels located downtown do not charge any retention charges from guests who intimate about their cancellation 24 hours in advance of their date of arrival directly the hotel or 48 hours in advance if they intimate to central reservation officer.

In Resort hotels the request of cancellation should be made by the prospective guest 15 days to 3 days before the date of arrival during high and low season respectively. So that retention charges should not be charged.

Once the cancellation request of the guest is accepted it is important that hotel communicate back to the guest and inform him of the cancellation. The guest may be refunded any deposit as per the policy of the hotel.

Further the hotel will update the record as follows:

<u>DIARY SYSTEM:</u> The reservation form along with other set of documents concerning the booking will be filed and marked cancelled and also the room which is blocked in charts will be released.

<u>WHITNEY SYSTEM:</u> The concerned rack is approached and the whitney carrier or slip is being removed and filed with other relevant documents and marked cancelled.

<u>COMPUTER SYSTEM:</u> In this case the reservation module which includes the types of room etc which have been booked are updated. It is important to note that once the cancellation record is updated the room is now available for future booking.

RETENTION CHARGES:

These are the charges which may be collected from a guest having guaranteed reservation and does not come on the scheduled date due to the reasons best known to him. The guest/agency has made any advance payment, the same may be forfeited as retention charge, if the guest does not inform about his cancellation within the prescribed time mentioned by hotel.

Cancellations effected beyond the time limits may entitle hotel to levy retention charges on room rates as under:

For hotels located in towns other than Resort places- One day Charge

For Resort hotels:

During high season-

Cancellation made under 10 days but more than 7 days notice – 1 day charge as retention charges

Between 7 days and 48 hours- 2 days charge as retention charge

Less than 48 hours- 3 days charge as retention charge

During low season-

1 day charge provided that where a hotel has covered itself by demanding to deposit in advance from the guest against confirmed reservation, the retention charges shall be restricted to the charges mentioned above. Excess deposit is refunded back.

Reservation Network/Channel (CRS):

Central Reservation System:

Central reservation system is a computer based reservation system which enables the guest to make a reservation in any of the participating lodging property at any destination. The central reservation office typically deals directly with the public by means of a toll free telephone number. The central reservation offices operate 24 hour a day and almost round the year.

These centres typically exchange the room availability information with the member properties and communicate the reservation transactions as they occur through the computer. The hotel and central reservation office have accurate, up-to-date information on room availability. Central reservation office is equipped with necessary communication equipment like computer, a telephone, FAX machine etc. Hotel may pay a flat fee for obtaining the services of a CRS and additional fee for each reservation received through central reservation office. In turn, each property provides accurate and current room availability data to central reservation office.

The central reservation system is of two types:

• Affiliated system

• Non-affiliated system

Affiliated System: In affiliated reservation system all the participating hotel units belongs to same chain or group. E.g. Welcome net (Welcome group), Holidex (Holiday Inn), Image (Hyatt), ITT (Sheraton).

Non-Affiliated System: Non-affiliated system is a subscription based system, designed to connect independent or non chain property. This enables non-chain properties to enjoy the same benefits of affiliated system.

<u>Reservation supply chain (online companies)- Expedia, Make My Trip, Travel Related Services:</u>

If you are planning for a vacation or going on a trip, then you can take help from the best hotel booking sites in India that offer a variety of services along with hotel services and more. On these websites, you can enjoy the best facilities that allow you to plan your whole trip.

In India, there are a number of hotel booking sites that allow you to plan and book all the services that you need for your trip or vacation. Be it cabs, flight or train bookings or sight-seeing, you can get to compare hotel prices worldwide and enjoy your trip.

We will have a look at some of the hotel booking websites.

1. MakeMyTrip

There is a good reason why MakeMyTrip is at the top of our list. It is not only a good website, but its services are considered to be one of the best. The site has a large customer base and provides some of the best services a travel website can offer.

It is undoubtedly the best among all of the top 10 hotel booking sites in India.

Why book with MakeMyTrip?

- MakeMyTrip has the best hotels in Indian and International locations.
- It also provides great deals on hotel booking online.
- MakeMyTrip has excellent facilities and services.
- Thousands of hotel options are available on this website.

2. OYO Rooms

Oyo Rooms is one of India's biggest hotel and accommodation chains in India. It provides users with many hotels and stays options all over the country. It has managed to grow incredibly fast in India within a very short period of time.

This website is one of India's most popular and perhaps the best hotel booking site for India.

Why book with OYO Rooms?

- You can compare hotel prices and select the priced hotel.
- On Oyo, you can also check ratings of hotels.
- There are multiple options available for hotel booking on this website.
- OYO wizard membership provides cheaper booking rates.
- It is one of the top 10 Best Hotel Booking Websites in India.

3. Airbnb

Airbnb is another hotel and stays booking website where you can find homes from all types of categories. It is very easy to book on Airbnb, and the most significant benefit is that it is very affordable to book and stay.

It is available at almost all major locations throughout the world, making it one of the best hotel booking sites in India and the world.

Why book with Airbnb?

- On Airbnb, local travel experiences with native experts.
- More than 6 million holiday homes and rentals are available on the site.
- Airbnb is available in more than 191 countries.
- You can make bookings for solo travel, family vacation or work trips.

4. Expedia

Expedia has been one of the most popular travel websites in India because of the plethora of options that are available on its platform. Expedia has some excellent features that make it a sought after destination partner.

Expedia offers various discounts, offers and deals where customers can get some of the best booking rates and save a lot of money with each transaction. It also has its mobile app, which is considered the best hotel booking app in India 2022.

Why book hotels with Expedia?

- Over a million hotels are available on Expedia.
- Expedia rewards program provides reward points and booking with mobile.
- Free cancellation on select hotels is available on Expedia.
- Expedia provides exclusive perks and discounts on its website.

5. Trivago

Trivago is perhaps the most popular travel and hotel booking website in the country. It is well-known for its brilliant options for comparing different hotel booking platforms. This helps get the best rates and deals for each booking.

Because of its immense popularity, Trivago is one of the top 10 hotel booking sites in India 2022.

Why book hotels with Trivago?

- Over a hundred of sites available on its platform.
- On Trivago, you can compare different sites and select the one with the best price.
- You can enjoy excellent travel discounts on Trivago.
- Trivago Rating index selects the best hotels for users.

6. Yatra

Yatra is one of India's leading hotel booking websites and is known for its affordability and also the luxurious hotels it provides on its platform. They offer lucrative discounts and deals for hotel bookings, travel packages and flight bookings which make them a popular choice among many people.

Yatra is undoubtedly one of the best online hotel booking sites in India and is preferred by many people in the country.

Why book hotels with Yatra?

- You can make some of the most affordable travel bookings.
- Has a network of more than 70,000 domestic hotels and 5,00000 International hotels
- You can look for hotels by area, city name, hotel name and more.
- User and expert ratings of hotels are also available on this website.
- You can select amenities like free wifi, breakfast, free cancellation beforehand.

7. Cleartrip

Cleartrip is a popular travel partner for booking hotels, flight, trains and more. You can make travel plans for Indian and international destinations at some of the best prices that you can get. Cleartrip has a lot of options that help you make the best choice for your hotel bookings.

It is used by millions of travellers which makes it one of the best hotel booking websites. It also has its own mobile app that makes it even more popular.

Why book hotels with Cleartrip?

- It has 360-degree images of the hotels, which help you in making better decisions.
- You can check reviews and ratings from other users.
- It also has a smart tag feature which helps in decision making.
- You can look for hotels based on landmarks, locations and more on Cleartrip.

8. Hotels.com

As is evident from its name, Hotels.com is a site that is dedicated to hotel and stays booking only. It is a very popular website in India and across the world. It helps you find hotels based on your budget and are an excellent choice for those looking for affordable travel plans.

Hotels.com is immensely popular throughout the world and is rightly considered one among the best hotel booking websites in India.

Why book hotels with Hotels.com?

- You can book holiday cottages, luxury resorts, hostels and hotels on this platform.
- Before making the reservation, you can compare different hotels.
- It has a 5% discount on select hotels on its website.
- You can also win rewards and points for your bookings on Hotels.com.

9. Booking.com

Booking.com is one of the most trusted hotel booking websites in the world and is considered as one of the pioneers of hotel booking. It is a vast collection of hotels, resorts and more which you can book swiftly on their website.

It provides good quality images of the hotels that you want to book, which helps users in making the right decisions. It is, without a doubt, one of the best hotel booking websites in India and the world.

Why book hotels with Bookings.com?

- Booking.com allows hotel comparison for better decision making.
- It provides excellent options for a wide budget range.
- It has more than 135 million verified user hotel reviews.
- Multiple filters help to pinpoint the right hotel choice are present on Booking.com.

10. TripAdvisor

TripAdvisor is one of the most sought after hotels booking sites and is considered one of the premier sites because of its vast database and huge collection of user reviews. TripAdvisor ratings for hotels are considered to be the best, and many other platforms also depend upon the TripAdvisor ratings.

It connects almost 200 different websites to give you the best choice for hotel bookings and thus finds a prominent place among the top 10 hotel booking sites in India.

Why book hotels with TripAdvisor?

- On TripAdvisor, you can compare over 200 different sites for hotel booking.
- You can also browse articles, images and blogs to get more ideas on the best travel plans.
- It has the world's largest collection of attractions, tours and more.
- TripAdvisor forums help you in getting more knowledge from other travellers.

<u>**Reservation terminology and documentation:**</u> Please refer to Part A, Unit 1.

CHAPTER SEVEN

Unit 7: Registration

(Topics Covered: Define registration and importance of registration, Concept of registration, Activities of registration stage, Process of registration, Modes of registration, Front desk directed, Guest directed. Registration terminology, Documentation.)

Registration and its importance:

The process of registration starts in the second phase of guest cycle in case of a guest with confirmed reservation. The process begins with the arrival of the guest at the front desk. In the present chapter we will study the activities that speed up the registration of the guest to avoid queuing at the front desk during the peak hours of guest arrivals. The activity that supports the speedy check-in of the guest is termed as Pre-registration activity.

The registration of a guest at the front desk involves legal implications on the both hotel as well as the guest. This is a valid contract between guest and the hotel. A registration activity takes place at front desk. The check-in procedure of the guest varies with their status. In this chapter we will study the steps involved in check-in of the guest with confirmed reservation, walk-in, VIPs, Group, Crews and Scanty baggage guest in detail.

Concept of registration:

Registration is the process of gathering information from the guest that is mandatory the law prevailing in the country. According to the Foreigner's Act 1946 and The Registration of Foreigners Rules, 1992 the innkeeper is responsible to keep the records of the guest who are staying in their premises. The innkeeper should keep the records as contained in form F of The Registration of Foreigners Rules, 1992. Registration activity is also a proof of a valid contract between the guest and the hotel in which hotel offers safe and secure boarding and lodging facility to the guest and the acceptance of the guest to pay for the services and facilities received.

The registration is carried at front desk. The first step in guest registration process begins with capturing the data of the guest like name, address, purpose of visit, duration of stay etc.

<u>Activities of registration stage:</u>

The activities that are carried out before arrival of guest to accelerate the guest registration are termed as pre-registration activity. The necessary information to fill the registration form can be gathered mainly from the two sources namely:

- Reservation Form
- Guest History Card

The information contained in these forms are utilized to complete the registration form and guest can experience a quick check-in when they arrive at the registration desk as they only have to verify the information already entered in the registration card by putting their signatures whereas the walking guest's check-in activity may take little more time in completing the formalities of registration. The pre-registration activity may also include activities like room and rate assignment and creation of the guest folios. Most of the front office managers prefer the room and rate assignments at the time of arrival of the guest to adjust any changes. The pre-registration activity is carried out manually in manual and semi-automated system whereas in case of fully automated front office system the same task is carried out by the system which transforms the guest's data from reservation form and guest history card on registration card.

The flow of the transactions in registration process can be studied in following phases;

§ Identification of guests
§ Formation of registration records
§ Room and rate assignments
§ Establishment of credits
§ Completion of check in procedure and issuance of room keys
§ Generation of documents during registration

Identification of guests: The identification of guest's transient status is important as the hotel process the registration of guest with confirm reservation and walk-in in a slight different way. The front desk agent refers to the today's arrival list for guest with confirm reservation and for walk in they refer to the room availability status. The guest with confirmed reservation may be FIT (Free individual traveller) or group/ crew. The identification of the guest status leads in speedy check in of the guest.

Formation of registration records: The guest's signature to verify the records in the registration form results in formation of permanent and complete registration record. On the basis of this record hotel may process to develop other hotel records like guest folio, visitor's tabular ledger, arrival notification slip, guest history card etc. The completion of registration record is a legal requirement and this should be stored for a minimum period of three years or as required by the law prevailing in the state. The same record can be accessed by a competent local authority as and when required.

Room and rate assignment: After completing the registration formality the next step is to allocate and assign an available room in specific category as requested by the guest during reservation. In case of a chance guest (walk in) the hotel may exercise the option of up-selling. The details regarding the type of room and rate helps receptionist in deciding which room to be assigned to the guest. While assigning a room guest's preferences like floor level, near to the elevator, view, colour scheme etc. are entertained if they can be satisfied.

Establishment of credits: The determination of guest's creditability and the mode by which they will be settling their account is very important for the hotel. A cash and cash equivalent mode (traveller's cheque, demand draft and credit/ charge card) of account settlement is preferred. The determination of creditability of guest can be established by:

§ Asking the guest to produce their credit card at the time of arrival and by swiping the same for the authorization from the credit card company.

§ The guest may be asked to produce Travel Agent voucher/ authorization letter from the company in case if the bills are settled by the company.

§ Advance deposit may also be asked at the time of check in.

Completion of check in procedure and issuance of room keys: After the guest has registered, room is assigned and credit is established, the next step is to issue the room keys to the guest. The bell boy is called to escort the guest and install the guest luggage in their assigned room. The front desk employee carries out following activity after every check in:

§ Update of room status.

§ Preparation of arrival notification slips and sending them to concern department.

§ Creation of guest folio

§ Filling of form C in case of foreigners and sending the same to the concern authority.

Generation of documents during registration:

During the registration following records are generated:

§ Registration card

§ Room rack slip

§ Arrival notification slip

§ VIP or Group/ Crew arrival notification

§ Entries in AD register (Arrival/ departure register)

§ Form C, in case of registration of a foreigner

§ Creation of guest folio

<u>Process of registration under:</u>

Guest with reservation

- Walk-in guests
- Group guests
- Transient guest
- Airline crew member
- Incentive guest
- VIP and CIP
- SPATT

Check-in procedure guest with confirm reservation:

The check in procedure for the guest with confirmed reservation involves following steps:

- Welcome the guest with smile and greet them according to the time of the day.
- Ask them if they have confirmed reservation.
- Check with the today's arrival list.
- Pre filled registration card is given to guest to verify the registration record.
- Check the registration card completed by the guest for completeness of the registration card including even billing instructions.
- Allot the room and authorize the bell desk personnel to install the guest luggage into the room. The bell captain will fill the information in the arrival errand card and Lobby control sheet.

Check-in procedure Walk- in guest

The check in procedure for the walk- in guest involves following steps:

- Welcome the guest with smile and greet them according to the time of the day.
- Ask them if they have confirmed reservation.
- If the guest is not having reservation, then check room availability status for the requested duration of stay by the guest.
- If rooms are available for the requested duration, then you can proceed for the check in activity of the walk- in guest. (It is essential to ascertain the creditability of a walk- in guest.)
- Assist the guest to fill the registration card and sign.
- Check the registration card completed by the guest for completeness of the registration card.
- In case of an unknown guest, ask for the advance or take the imprint of credit card.
- Allot the room and authorize the bell desk personnel to install the guest luggage into the room. The bell captain will fill the information in the arrival errand card and Lobby control sheet.
- Issue the room keys to the guest, and ask the bell boy to escort the guest and install guest luggage into room.
- Wish the guest an enjoyable stay at your property.

Check-in procedure for VIP:

The VIP guest gets a special treatment and attention from the hotel employee due to their status. The guest can be treated as VIP if they are heads of states, ministers, senior media personnel, sports personnel, film and rock stars, travel writers, top executives of corporate houses, CEOs of large business houses, senior defence personnel, famous public figures etc. The VIPs check- in process may start with their arrival at the airport. The role of hotel in welcoming the political VIPs at airport is minimal due to security reasons. In case of corporate heads of business houses, the hotel person may receive them at the airport and escort the guest to the hotel room. The registration process may be carried out during the transfer from airport to hotel or in the hotel room.

The check in procedure of VIP guest involves following steps:

- Limousine facility may be offered to pick up the guest from airport.

- At the arrival of the guest at the hotel they may be welcomed by putting a tilak, garlanding followed by Aarti. The General Manager/ Front office manager are also present to welcome the VIP as per their status.
- The registration formality is carried out by the authorized representative of VIP in advance.
- The VIP is escorted to their room by the General Manager/ Front office manager.
- The arrival notification and any special instruction of VIPs are sent to all concerned department.

Check-in procedure Groups/Crew (domestic & international):

The check in procedure for group/crew requires specialised pre registration activity as group contains large number of people to be registered at the same time. The front desk assistant should be in constant touch with the group leader/ airport representative. Following pre registration activity is required in check in procedure of group/ crew:

- A group list containing details of each guest in the group is required. The list should contain the details like name, address, purpose of visit, duration of stay, meal preference (vegetarian/ non vegetarian), passport details (for foreigners) and any special instruction regarding the location of room.
- Number of required rooms for the group is preferably allocated at the same floor.
- Rooming list is prepared which contains the name and room number allotted to each member of group/crew.
- Keys are arranged according to room number and placed in an envelope to be handed over to the group leader.
- Registration cards are pre filled from the information received from the group leader/ airport representative and arranged alphabetically.
- Appropriate numbers of bell boys are retained for installing the guest luggage in their room.
- Food and beverage service department is coordinated for arrangement of welcome drink.

Check- in procedure:

The following steps are involved in the check in of group and crew at the hotel.

- When the vehicle arrives at the portico the guest luggage is handled by the Bell boys. They put the guest luggage tag on each luggage of individual guest as per the rooming list and luggage is transferred to the respective room using luggage trolley.
- The group leader is escorted to the reception desk where he completes the formalities of registration. The room keys and the registration form of all the members handed over to him for getting the signatures of every group member and dispersal of room keys.
- Meanwhile the group members are offered welcome drink in a pre scheduled area.
- The group leader handovers the signed registration card at the front desk, and guests may proceed to their respective rooms after having their welcome drinks.
- Meal schedule, wake call and pick up time may also be enquired from the group leader.

Check-In Procedure Scanty Baggage Guest:

A guest who arrives at front desk requesting for accommodation carrying very little or no baggage is known as a scanty baggage guest. The Bell boy carrying the guest luggage should report at front desk regarding the same. Following steps are involved in check in procedure of scanty baggage guests:

- The Bell boy informs the front desk regarding the scanty baggage.
- For registering a scanty baggage guest the front desk assistant takes the authorization from Duty manager.
- The registration formalities are completed as per the walk in.
- A full advance for the duration of stay may be asked from the guest.
- Scanty baggage Stamp should be imprinted on the guest registration card.
- APC (all payment cash) slip is prepared and sent to all point of sales.
- Room keys are allotted.

Check-in procedure Foreigner:

The check in procedure for foreigners is same as of a domestic guest with an exception that we have to fill form _C' for registering a foreigner guest. Form _C' is filled in duplicate, the top copy is sent to foreigner regional registration office (FRRO) or to the local intelligence unit (LIU) with in 24 hours of arrival of a foreign national. In case of Pakistan and Bangladesh, the same information should also be sent to local police station.

Form C:

According to the Registration of Foreigners' Rules 1992'; rule 14 makes it obligatory on the part of innkeeper to send information about foreigners registered at their hotel. Any person who is not an Indian national (person having the passport of country other than India except Nepal and Bhutan) is known as foreigner. The hotel is liable to send information contained in form C to the nearest FRRO or LIU within twenty four hours of arrival of a foreign national, in case of Pakistani, Bangladeshi and Chinese nationals this information should reach with in 12 hours to FRRO or LIU and local police station. The C form is prepared in duplicate and it should be serial numbered, the top copy is sent to competent authority and the second copy is kept for permanent record for the duration as specified in law related to the same.

Self Check-In Terminals:

Self check in terminal is an outcome of advancement of technology and —do it yourself‖ competent guest. A self check in terminal is like an interactive ATM machine. These terminals may be located at the airport and at convenient place in the lobby. The use of such machines reduces the manpower requirement. The guest by using their credit card can check in without any assistance. The room is assigned and keys are also dispensed by the machine. Such self check- in terminals is more common in smart hotels. The efficiency of front desk is increased when such terminals are used. Apart from dispensing the room keys the arrival notification to other department is sent instantaneously. Use of self check- in terminal lacks the personalized human touch from the hotel.

Modes of Check Out:

- Front desk directed (Express Check Out and Computerized Check Out)
- Guest directed (Video check-out and Self-Check-out)

The guest checkout involves the following steps:

1. Guest requests checkout.
2. Desk clerk inquires about quality of products and services.
3. Guest returns key to desk clerk.
4. Desk clerk retrieves hard copy of electronic folio.
5. Desk clerk reviews folio for completeness.

6. Guest reviews charges and payments.

7. Guest determines method of payment.

8. Guest makes payment.

9. Desk clerk inquires about additional reservations.

10. Desk clerk files folio and related documents for the night audit.

11. Desk clerk communicates guest departure to housekeeping and other departments in

the hotel if necessary.

The objective of the checkout process is to process the guest's request for settlement

of his or her account as quickly and efficiently as possible. The lodging establishment also

wants to maintain a quality-control system for both the guest and the hotel: posting errors

can mean erroneous charges for the guest and lost money for the lodging establishment.

Express Check-Out:

Most hotels are now using the Express Checkout service that allows customers to check out of their rooms and return the keys, without actually having to wait for their final bill to be produced. It is a great convenience for hotel guests at all times, but especially so when they are pressed for time, which is often the case with many of us.

Offering an Express Checkout service to your guests means that they can return their keys and go without having to wait for their bill to be made up. The benefits are obvious and here are some of them:

- Express Checkout saves your guests time when there are long queues at the front desk, because there is no need to wait to checkout.
- If a guest is in a hurry to catch a train or plain, you are helping her to avoid a stressful delay.
- If there is no one available at the front desk, your guests can simply drop in their keys and leave.
- The guest leaves the hotel without having to go through the standard C/O procedure The guest signs the ECO form and authorizes the hotel to charge the outstanding balance to his credit card The guest is given the Express C/O form on the morning of his date of departure.
- The hotel sends the signed ECO form and the credit card imprint to the credit card company towards payment of the bill The cashier prepares

the guest's final bill and mails a copy to the guest.

But the benefits go both ways. Using Express Checkout at your hotel also means that your staff can make up your guests' bills at the most convenient time of the day, not when they have a bunch of people in front of them, all waiting to check in or out.

In Room Computerised Checkout / Video Checkout:

In-room folio review and checkout functions generally rely on in room computer terminals or guestroom telephone to access and display guest folio data on the guestroom television screen. An interface to a front office accounting system allows the guest to access folio data and approve a method of settlement for his account. Newer technology may provide computer- synthesized voice responses through the guestroom telephone. Each method provides guests with folio totals and details and directs a self-checkout procedure. Printed folio copies are typically available to guests to pick up at the front desk. Similar to other self-checkout technologies, in-room computer applications automatically updates room status and creates a guest history file.

Self Check – Out:

- Only fully automated hotels are equipped with self service terminals, which allow guests to C/I and C/O promptly.
- Self C/I and C/O kiosks identify guests by their room number, credit card number.
- Guests can access and review their folios and settle their accounts using the credit card.

Express checkout guests do not have to go to the front desk to drop of their keys. Just leave the keys in the guest room and leave, at most major hotels.

CHAPTER EIGHT

Unit 8: Safety and Security

(**Topics Covered:** Safety and security of guest (their valuables) and hotel staff, Key control, Types of keys, Key control measures, Electronic keys, Safe deposit vaults and in room electronic safes.)

The front office is a hotel's communication center; it is the vital link between the hotel management and the guest. When a guest calls for assistance because of fire, illness, theft, or any other emergency, it is usually the front office that must respond. The staff on duty at the front office cannot leave and resolve the emergency because they must continue to provide communication services and process financial transactions. The security department staff must react with speed and efficiency to serve the guest.

The security department is often regarded as a passive department, reacting only when called on. In reality, it is a very active department, setting policies, organizing programs, and delivering training programs to promote guest and employee safety. The director of security is a trained professional who must ensure that a busy hotel filled with guests, employees, and equipment stays safe. One of the department's goals is to prevent emergencies through planning. Another goal, however, is to train all hotel employees to respond to emergencies.

The act of delivering hospitality is thought to occur naturally. However, throughout this text, delivering hospitality has been discussed as a planned concept, complete with research on guests' needs, policy and program development, establishment and delivery of training programs, and follow-up information systems. Hospitality also includes providing a safe environment for guests, which requires a well-organized department to oversee and implement safety programs. The security department of a hotel is vital to delivering hospitality to guests.

This department is responsible for establishing the details of the following systems:

- Guest and employee safety
- Room key security
- Fire safety systems
- Bomb threat action
- Emergency evacuation plans
- Employee safety training plans
- Emergency communication plans

Key control:

The access to the room is controlled by placing lock at the door. Hotel has a strict control over the room keys. People who possess the key can access the room. Hotel may have hard key system or electronic key system. If hotel is using hard key system following security measures can be followed:

§ Ask the guest to deposit room keys at reception while moving out of the hotel premises.

§ Discourage guest to carry room key along with them while going out of the hotel premises. This is mostly done by putting heavy and large key tags which is inconvenient to carry.

§ In an event of loss of keys the lock should be replaced immediately.

The electronic key system is an investment in guest safety and security. As each new guest registers, a fresh plastic, metallic or hard-pressed paper key is produced. The room door lock combination can be changed as and when required by option available through master computer, hence if a guest carries away the electronic key with them will not pose any security threat.

Types of Room Keys: Hotel, for security reason may use three types of room keys:

§ Emergency / Grand Master Key

§ Master Key

§ Guestroom Key

Emergency Key / Grand Master Key: An emergency/grand master key opens all guest room door lock even if they are double locked (Double lock is an internal safety locking device, if locked from inside the room, it cannot be opened from outside by its own keys and master key). Emergency key should be highly protected and should only be used in an event of emergency. A strict key control is maintained for the same. It should not be taken out of the premises. Generally emergency key is under control of the head of the property.

Master Key: A master key opens all guest room lock which is not double locked. This key may be such that it can unlock all guest room lock or may open only specific floor's guest room locks. The master key is under control of executive housekeeper of the hotel. There may be several floor master keys used by room attendant for cleaning guest room. These keys are strictly controlled and issued only to the staff on duty. They have to sign before taking the key and at the time of submitting.

Guestroom Key: These are individual room keys for each room. A guestroom key opens the lock of the individual guestrooms. These keys are under control of front desk. These are issued to guest who has registered and collected back when they depart from the hotel.

Safe deposit vaults and in room electronic safes:

Though hotel is not responsible for the guest valuables, the rule to this effect is written in the guest registration card and also notified in the in guest room but a hotel offers a free safe deposit facility for his valuables.

Hotels have bank type of lockers installed at the front office cash. A locker is allotted to guest that can be opened by using two keys .The master key is with the front office cashier and other key is issued to the guest. A contract is also signed in between the guest and the hotel. Whenever a guest wants to open his locker it has to be entered into the locker operating register. Signatures are always verified with the specimen .Head cashier inserts his key then a guest inserts his own key, and then only a lock can be opened. Guest is left alone to operate his locker. If the key is lost by the guest, then the locker will be drilled open in presence of the guest and can be charged for the replacement of the locker.

These days some hotels have installed electronic safe deposit boxes in each guest room .this safety box can be operated by using an electronic number. Guest can use any number to open the lock. The number selected by the guest becomes the locker's code number .The guests are advised to keep their valuables in the electronic safety box. Though hotel is not responsible for any lost item .But hotels take this issue as prestige issue so an inquiry is done on the hotel security level.

Manually operated Safe Lockers : A key concern for guest is the safety of their belongings, especially valuables like cash, jewellery, and important documents. Hotels provide safe deposit lockers for the same. Some hotels may also provide in-room safe deposit lockers which are electronically locked and operated through a password.

Manually operated lockers, usually found in the back office of Front Office department, are opened by the simultaneous use of two keys. One key is issued to the guest and the other is with the front office. Whenever a guest wishes to operate the locker, the front office assistant and the guest use their respective keys to open the lock. The hotel may provide this facility for a nominal charge or no charge depending upon the house policy. Guests who wish to use this facility have to sign in the safe deposit locker register to get the keys of the safe deposit box.

PROCEDURE FOR USING MANUALLY OPERATED SAFE DEPOSIT LOCKER

Every hotel has its own operating procedure for the allotment of safe deposit lockers. The standard procedure has two stages

1. Issue of locker
2. Surrender of locker.

Issue of Locker: Following procedure is used for issue of lockers

a. An empty safe deposit locker is allocated to the guest with the locker number.

b. A safe deposit registration card is handed over to the guest and the guest is requested to fill the necessary information.

c. The locker is assigned and the locker key is handed over to the guest.

d. The guest keeps his valuables and documents in the locker, locks the box and carries the key.

e. The guest can use the safe deposit box as and when required. He is required to make an entry in the locker register for each use.

Surrender of Locker: Following procedure is used for surrender of lockers

a. The guest is requested to withdraw the articles placed in the locker.

b. The guest is requested to sign an acknowledgement that he has taken all his belongings that had been placed in the safe deposit box.

c. The guest surrenders the locker key to the Front Office assistant.

<u>In room electronic safes:</u>

This type of safe is commonly found in mainstream hotels and resorts and in many ways is the one that MAY have the least amount of thefts from it. That's because it requires a handheld computer device to open the safe. These safes require the attachment of a handheld PDA, with either an infra-red USB or cable. The units store up to 50 entries, incorrect PIN entry, and it's all-time and date stamped. These can be attached to a PC, where audit reports can be printed for police and insurance purposes. These units DO NOT have a hotel override, it reveals the guest PIN.

Unit 9: Guest Account Settlement

(Topics Covered: Modes of account settlement, Cash, Credit (travellers check, travel agent voucher, foreign currency, charge cards, airline vouchers, third party billing), Control measures for cash and credit based account settlement policy, Forex (licences, exchange rates and policy), Currency exchange during arriving in India, Currency exchange during departing from India. Reservation section terminology. Documentation.)

<u>Guest Account Settlement:</u>

Orientation of Account Settlement

By Guest: The guest settles own account by cash/credit card/cheque.

By Organization: The organization settles guest account by transferring money to the

hotel account.

<u>Methods of Account Settlement:</u>

There are following popular methods of account settlement:

Account Settlement in Local Currency: A guest can pay in terms of a local currency where the payment is not chargeable with conversion fees.

Account Settlement in Foreign Currency: If the guest prefers to pay in foreign currency, the service of payment by the bank is chargeable for around 3% to 6% of the total payable amount.

Account Settlement Using Traveller Check: Travelers' cheques, the pre-printed cheques in the denominations of major world currencies are a good option to paying by cash.

Debit Card: Use of magnetic cards for payment against account is most common today. Paying by debit cards is as good as paying by cash as the amount of money is instantly transferred from the guest's bank account into the hotel's bank account. In case of credit card settlement, the accounting staff mails the charge vouchers signed by guests to the credit card company; preferably within a specified time. The credit card company then settles the guest account by transferring money against it.

Credit Settlement by Organization: Many national, international, private, or public organizations send their employees or students for attending workshops, seminar, or meetings. Such organizations tie-up with the hotel for paying the bills of their employees on credit. The organizations reserve accommodations depending on the number of room nights (number of rooms × number of nights the representatives are expected to occupy). This is popularly known as account Settlement using Direct Billing.

In **direct billing account settlement**, the front office staff verifies guest folios and transfers the guest account to non-guest or city account. The hotel's back-office accounting verifies the guest folios and is responsible to collect the direct billing amount from a direct billing agency such as embassy, university, or organizations. The accounting section also notifies the guests that if the direct billing agency fails or refuses to pay the charges then the guests need to settle the account by paying them from their pocket.

Combined Account Settlement: A guest can settle account by paying partial amount in cash and remaining amount on credit. The front office staff needs to prepare the supporting document for such kind of payment and hands it over to the back-office accounts.

<u>**Control measures for cash and credit based account settlement policy:**</u>
<u>**CREDIT CONTROL AFTER DEPARTURE OF GUEST:**</u>

Hotels must ensure that the guests who are given credit facility from the hotel are able to pay their bill in full within the scheduled period of time and only then the hotel should fix a house limit. Usually the hotel's credit policy allows credit to:

- Guaranteed payment reservation guests
- Company guarantee payment guests
- Credit card guarantee guests
- Deposit/advance payment reservation guests

<u>**PROBLEMS IN CREDIT CONTROL MAY ARISE IF:**</u>

- Guest is not explained clearly as to which credit cards/foreign currencies are accepted by the hotel.

- The guest is not informed that if his bill exceeds the house limit he will have to pay the balance in cash
- Communication gap between accounts department and cashier or night auditor and cashier
- Negligence by the staff to look at the black list

CASH CONTROL:

- All cash must be kept under lock and key and under the supervision of the cashier.
- The cash bank/float given to the cashier is also controlled and a check is kept on the same
- The cashier should take proper precautions when dealing with foreign currency
- Whenever the guest pays in cash the cashier has to make a cash receipt and hand it over to the guest.
- The cash collected everyday should be sent to the bank for deposit.

Cash control is important from the point of view of hotel as credit sales are usually discouraged.

Forex Policy: (Exchange Rates)

The Floating Exchange Rate

A floating exchange rate, or fluctuating exchange rate, is a type of exchange rate regime wherein a currency's value is allowed to fluctuate according to the foreign exchange market. A currency that uses a floating exchange rate is known as a floating currency. The dollar is an example of a floating currency.

Many economists believe floating exchange rates are the best possible exchange rate regime because these regimes automatically adjust to economic circumstances. These regimes enable a country to dampen the impact of shocks and foreign business cycles, and to preempt the possibility of having a balance of payments crisis. However, they also engender unpredictability as the result of their dynamism.

The Fixed Exchange Rate

A fixed exchange rate system, or pegged exchange rate system, is a currency system in which governments try to maintain a currency value that is constant against a specific currency or good. In a fixed exchange-rate system, a country's government decides the worth of its currency in terms of either a fixed weight of an asset, another currency, or a basket of other currencies. The central bank of a country remains committed at all times to buy and sell its currency at a fixed price.

To ensure that a currency will maintain its "pegged" value, the country's central bank maintain reserves of foreign currencies and gold. They can sell these reserves in order to intervene in the foreign exchange market to make up excess demand or take up excess supply of the country's currency.

The most famous fixed rate system is the gold standard, where a unit of currency is pegged to a specific measure of gold. Regimes also peg to other currencies. These countries can either choose a single currency to peg to, or a "basket" consisting of the currencies of the country's major trading partners.

The Pegged Float Exchange Rate

Pegged floating currencies are pegged to some band or value, which is either fixed or periodically adjusted. These are a hybrid of fixed and floating regimes. There are three types of pegged float regimes:

Crawling bands: The market value of a national currency is permitted to fluctuate within a range specified by a band of fluctuation. This band is determined by international agreements or by unilateral decision by a central bank. The bands are adjusted periodically by the country's central bank. Generally the bands are adjusted in response to economic circumstances and indicators.

Crawling pegs: A crawling peg is an exchange rate regime, usually seen as a part of fixed exchange rate regimes, that allows gradual depreciation or appreciation in an exchange rate. The system is a method to fully utilize the peg under the fixed exchange regimes, as well as the flexibility under the floating exchange rate regime. The system is designed to peg at a certain value but, at the same time, to "glide" in response to external market uncertainties. In dealing with external pressure to appreciate or depreciate the exchange rate (such as interest rate differentials or changes in foreign exchange reserves), the system can meet frequent but moderate exchange rate changes to ensure that the economic dislocation is minimized.

Pegged with horizontal bands: This system is similar to crawling bands, but the currency is allowed to fluctuate within a larger band of greater than one percent of the currency's value.

<u>**Currency exchange during arriving in India**</u>

Bringing in Foreign Exchange

- You can bring into India foreign exchange without any limit. If, however, the value of foreign currency in <u>cash</u> exceeds US$ 5,000 and/or the <u>cash plus TCs</u> exceed US$ 10,000 it should be declared to the customs authorities at the airport in the currency declaration form (CDF), on arrival in India.

Exchange Earners' Foreign Currency (EEFC) Account

- You can retain upto specified limits, your earnings in foreign exchange, in an Exchange Earners' Foreign Currency (EEFC) Account with a bank in India.

- These accounts are NOT interest bearing and there is no ceiling on the balances that can be built up in these accounts.

- Balances held in such accounts can be used for any purposes for which exchange can be otherwise purchased from authorised dealers in India.

<u>**Currency exchange during departing from India**</u>

Exporting Indian rupees is strictly prohibited for non-Indian residents. Residents of India can travel abroad with up to Rs. 25,000. There's no limit to how much of a foreign currency you can take out of India, but if it's US$5,000 or more in banknotes and coins, or US$10,000 or more in coins, notes and traveller's cheques, it will have to be declared

CHAPTER TEN

Unit 10: Situation and Complaint Handling

(Topics Covered: Situation handling, Usual situation (skipper, scanty baggage, walking, walk-in, paging, room change, luggage handling during check-in and check-out, left luggage procedure, etc.), Unusual situations (death, fire, theft, bomb threat and terrorist attack). Complaint handling, Types of guest, Types of guest complaints, Complaint as a gift philosophy, the complaints handling procedure and redressal.)

Situation handling:

Skippers:

Skippers often comes with little luggage or no luggage. The bell boys have to be alert to notify the front office about guests with scanty baggage in-order to take necessary advance from them and at the time of check-out.

How to Prevent Skippers?

Make sure you always ask guests to fill in registration cards with all details upon check in.

Preauthorize guests credit cards included deposit of a set amount.

On PMS activate a NO post on reservation to stop any extra charges from other outlets to be charged to the guest room.

Scanty Baggage:

A guest who checks in to the hotel with very less or no luggage. Scanty baggage means no baggage or a piece of light baggage consisting of briefcase or airbag.

Guest with scanty baggage is normal skippers from the hotel. Skippers are those persons who check out of the hotel without settling their bills. The scanty baggage guests also normally go out with their light baggage and the hotel never knows that if this guest is going out with an intention to come back or not. To save guard the hotels interest, normally guest with scanty baggage are requested to pay in advance.

There is a set procedure adopted by hotels to keep control of guests, with scanty baggage.

- Lobby manager and the reception are notified immediately on guest's arrival about the scanty baggage.
- Arrival errand card is stamped with scanty baggage.
- Guest registration card's all copies are stamped with 'scanty baggage'.
- The scanty baggage register is filled up by the bell desk.
- Get the guest registration cards and the scanty baggage register signed by the lobby manager.

Walkin Guest:

A Guest who arrives at a hotel without a reservation is called as 'Walk in'.

The Classic nightmare for any traveller who travel for miles and miles who then walk-in to the hotels and find that the hotel is fully occupied. Hotels have no obligations to accommodate guests who arrive without reservation when no rooms are available for the night.

When the hotel cannot accommodated a walk-in guest, the front office agent can make the situation a little easy for the guest by suggesting and providing directions to alternative hotels nearby.

The front office staff can even call other similar hotels and help the guest to make reservation.

If there seems to be no alternative to turning away the guest, a manager not a front desk agent, should explain the matter in a private office.

Registering one guest in view of another who cannot be accommodated can be extremely awkward and embarrassing.

Following steps to be clarified before accepting a Walk-in Reservation:

1. If the guest Presents a confirmation letter, verify the date and the name of the hotel; the guest may have arrived on a different date ir at the wrong hotel.
2. Check with the guest if the reservation was made by another person, it is possible that the reservation agent might have entered the reservation under the booker / caller name!

3. Re verify the reservation by searching the hotel software by last name, first name, reservation number, partial name search, mobile number, Booker name, company, travel agent, etc. If the guest had booked from the travel agent ask the guest to call up the travel agent and get more details of the booking.

4. Ask the guest to reconfirm the arrival date and departure date again, the guest may be arriving on a different date or it is possible that this guest was a no-show for the previous night.

5. If all of the above checks and given negative result then after checking the availability of rooms in the hotel the front desk agent can create a new reservation. When the reservation is created for walk-in guest the source segment of the reservation should be tagged as 'Walk-In'.

6. It is also a good practice to collect a advance deposit for the complete room rental and approximate incidental charges from a Walk-in guest.

GUEST MESSAGE HANDLING:

When there is a telephone call or visitor for a resident guest and the guest is not present in the hotel, the front desk agent takes the message for the guest and delivers the same as soon as the guest comes back. The process of receiving and delivering messages to resident guest is known as message handling.

MESSAGE HANDLING PROCEDURE:

1. When there is a visitor or a telephone call for a guest, the front desk assistant should look at the information rack /computer to see whether the guest is a resident guest, future guest or checked-out guest.

2. In case of a resident guest, the agent should check whether the guest is present in the room or not. If the guest is not present in the room, the agent must check the key rack for the location form. If the same is found act according to the instructions of the guest.

3. If the guest has not left any location form, the front desk assistant should take down the message for the guest on a message slip.

4. The message slip is prepared in duplicate. One copy is placed in the key rack and the second copy is placed in a message slip envelope and slipped through the door of the guest room by the Bell Boy.

5. If there is a visitor or a call for the guest who has checked-out of the hotel, then the front office agent should give information as per the instructions left by the guest.

6. If there is a call for a future guest, then the agent should send the message slip to the back office, where it will be placed along with the reservation record. On the date of arrival of the guest the message slip would be attached to the GRC .so that it can be delivered to the guest at the time of check-in.

7. In some hotels the telephone in the guest room has a message indicator which is switched on to inform the guest that there is a message for him. In some hotels the guest can read the message on the TV in the room.

PAGING OF GUEST:

Paging a guest means to locate a guest within the hotel. During their stay guest may be expecting a visitor or an important phone call while he is not in the room. So, in this situation while leaving the guest fills up a form called location form and hand it over to the reception staff. The reception staff should inform the same to the telephone operator. Such that any call for the guest or any visitor for the guest comes we can contact him based on the information on the location form.

Paging is generally done in three methods: - By Page board system: - In front office assistant writes the name of the guest on both sides of the page board and ask the bell boy to locate the guest in the place mentioned on the location form and once the guest is located the message is conveyed to the guest.

By Pager/Beeper System: - In this system the generally the guest is provided with a pager / a beeper and when there is a call or a visitor arrives for the guest the information is sent by the pager at information section and thus guest can contact to the reception. This is generally used in resort hotels where the public area is large.

HANDLING GUEST ROOM CHANGE:

Guest rooms are the most important commodity of a hotel. They form a large component of the guests over all experience at a hotel. In case a room doesn't match the guest's expectations, the guest may want to change room. There are times when the hotel may wish to change the room of a resident guest.

A guest may want to change his room for the following reasons:

- If the room assigned is not as per his choice.
- If one or more equipment's in the room are not working satisfactorily.
- If the number of occupants in the room changes.

The hotel may wish to change the guest's room for the following reasons:

- If the requested category of room is not available.
- If the guest overstays and the hotel does not have a room of the same type to allot to the next guest.
- If the room requires maintenance work.

PROCEDURE FOR CHANGING THE GUEST ROOM:

Any change in guest room, the front office agent should seek authorization from the Lobby Manager. Front office informs the guest about the room change in advance so that the guest packs his luggage properly. The front office agent fills six copies of room change slip-for reception, bell captain, front desk cashier, telephone exchange, housekeeping and room service-and takes authorization. A bell boy is called and given the keys of the new room. He proceeds to the guest room to shift the guest's luggage. If the change of room is done in the presence of the guest, it is called live move, and if it is carried out in the absence of the guest it is known as dead move. The bellboy collects the room key of the old room and deposits it at the front desk.

LEFT LUGGAGE:

The term "Left luggage" is attributed to luggage left by a guest who checks out of the hotel but wishes to collect the luggage later. Guest who wants to visit other cities in a country on a short tour may find. It in convenient tour carries their entire package with them or may find it once economical to retain room in the hotel where they can keep their luggage. Hotel provided the left luggage facilities to guest who are likely to checking to the hotel after they return from the tour. This is not strictly necessary.

Their might be guests who check out but ended to depend much later in the day the occupied they time sight-seeing he would find inconvenient cart their luggage with them. Leave their luggage in the hotel premises under the guarantee by the management luggage would be safe. Some may be charge fees for the facilities. But most of the hotels don't charge the facility. Guest baggage kept in custody of the hotel after the guest has checked out which will be later collected by the guest. The left luggage room is in close proximity to the bell desk where it has racks along the wall where the luggage is deposited. The procedure for handling left luggage is done by the Bell Captain who enters the details in the Left Luggage Register.

Procedure for Left Luggage Handling:

Hotels normally follow the following procedure while accepting the luggage to be stored in the left luggage room:

- The agent makes sure that the guest wishing to keep his luggage in the left luggage room has cleared his bills.
- The luggage tag is filled and tied to each luggage.
- The details of the luggage are entered in the left luggage register.
- The counterfoil of the luggage tag is torn and handed over to the guest.
- The guest is required to present the same for the collection of his luggage.
- The luggage is kept in the left luggage room.

While delivering the luggage to the guest, the following procedure is followed:

- The front office agent requests the guest is to show the luggage tag counterfoil.
- The front office agent tallies the counterfoil with the tag attached to the baggage.
- The front office agent makes an entry in the left luggage register and requests the guest to sign for the delivery of the luggage.
- The front office agent hands over the luggage to the guest.

Handling Unusual Events:
Terrorist activities and Bomb threat:
A lodging property that caters the VIPs may face the possible threat of terrorist activity and bomb threat. The hotel should take these threats seriously. The hotel in such situation should liaise with the local police authority and follow the instruction from them. The bomb threat may come by telephone. The person receiving such call should follow the below mentioned points:
§ Do not interrupt the caller
§ Write the exact words of the caller
If possible find out :
§ Time due to explode
§ Where the device is placed
§ Description of device
§ Why he has done it

§ Whom they represents

§ Write everything as soon as call is disconnected (a bomb threat form may be used for the same if used in hotel) such as: Callers voice, Mannerism, Determination, Age and sex, Accent, Any background noise etc.

§ Do not alter the exact talk that has occurred between you and caller while re-telling to the authorities.

§ Inform the competent authority immediately.

§ Do not spread the rumors.

§ Do not attempt to diffuse device if you are able to locate the same.

Robbery:

Robbery is a possibility in hotel as there may be a large sum at the front desk cash and bills sections and also at the point of sales. In an event of armed robbery hotel employees should normally follows the below mentioned procedures:

§ Comply with the robbers demand

§ Do not make sudden movement to provoke the robbers to use weapons or fire arms.

§ Remain quiet unless directed to talk by robbers

§ Do not attempt to disarm the robber, as this may jeopardize the life of person doing the act and other people in the vicinity.

§ The cashier may switch the secret alarm that might be installed in the cash drawer while following the direction of robbers without being suspicious to be noticed by them.

§ Observe the person carefully noting the physical characteristics like height, built, eye colour, hair colour, mannerism, complexion, clothing, scar marks or any thing that can be helpful to identification of the robbers.

§ The employees may also note the direction of escape, type and registration number of vehicle used by the robbers.

§ The employees should refrain themselves for touching any objects that might be touched by the robbers and restrict the movement of the people in the area so that the possible evidences are saved till the policemen comes to the premises.

§ The hotel may have a format to record the details of the robber that is gathered from the people who have witnessed the event.

Death of an In-House Guest in the Hotel:

Whenever information comes regarding the death of an in-house guest the Front Office Manager should be reported directly who informs the

General Manager and the Security Manager. Later on, the police authority is even told and the hotel doctor is summoned to confirm the death of the guest. The residential address of the guests is also identified and the relatives are informed. Once the doctor has confirmed the death and the police have given the permission the dead body is removed by the help of a stretcher. In the meanwhile, if the deceased guest was under some other doctor consultation then that doctor is also enquired.

A death certificate is also prepared and a report is prepared to mention the time, room number and other details related to the deceased guest. The guest room is locked and sealed and after the permission and clearance of police the room is opened and spring cleaned and can be resold again after the approval of the local authority.

Accident Emergency Situation:

Accidents can take place in the hotels at any point of time due to faulty stairs, ramps, and balconies and even due to the parking places. The hotels should ensure that handrails, the nonslip surface should be used while framing the architecture plan for the hotels.

Lost and found:

This is a term used in hotel parlance to refer to any item which is left by the guest or temporarily misplaced by the guest but traced later by the hotel staff. Such articles to be handed over to the housekeeping department which maintained a special locker for this purpose. If the item belongs to the guest who has already checked out, then a letter has to be sent to the forwarding address left by the guest while checkout or which is there in the registration card. If no reply is received by the hotel within a certain time limit, that may be auctioned to the hotel employees or take a decision as per the hotel policies and rules.

Illness and Epidemics Emergency Situation:

There should always be a Doctor on call available for the hotel so that in case if any guest suffers from any kind of problem, he /she can be given the concern treatment as soon as possible.

Vandalism:

The front office staff must call the hotel security and order the main door to be locked. If the situation gets out of the hand then the security manager should call the police immediately.

Damage to property by the resident guest:

The front office cashier is instructed to raise a charge for the value of the damages to property, a responsible guest will never argue but if he does the subject to be referred to the general manager.

Handling Drunken Guest:

A drunken guest may disturb another guest. In order to avoid this, the drunken guest should be escorted to an isolated area like a back office. Hotel staff should calmly handle the situation by following the SOP for handling drunken guests.

GUEST COMPLAINTS:

Guest Complaints When guests are not satisfied with some services and express their discontent to hotel employees, most often to the front desk staff, their grievances are recorded as guest complaints.

The guests' complaints can be grouped into four major categories:

• Mechanical

• Attitudinal

• Service-related

• Unusual complaints.

Mechanical complaints are related to the malfunctioning or non-functioning of systems and equipment's installed in guest rooms, like television, mini-bar, weather control, channelled music, geyser, and so on.

Attitudinal Complaint: When a guest feels insulted by the rude or tactless hotel staff and lodges a complaint, it is referred to as attitudinal complaint. A guest may also make attitudinal complaints when the hotel staffs bother him with their problems.

Service-related complaints are about the problems in services provided by the hotel, like delay in the room service of lunch, or delay in the clearance of soiled crockery from the room after meals, etc.

Unusual complaints are those over which the hotel does not have any control. For example, a guest may complain about the lack of golf course in the hotel, or the lack of central heating facility, etc. The front office should handle guests' complaints tactfully, exercising patience, empathy, and decision-making skills.

As hospitality is a service-oriented industry, the hotel staff should always try to resolve the customer's problems immediately and thus appease him. If a front office agent is unable to handle a guest's complaint, she should call her superior before the situation gets out of control or becomes worse.

The following guidelines may be followed while handling guest complaints:

• Listen silently without interruption, with empathy.

- Show concern and take complaints seriously.
- Never argue. Remember the guest is always right.
- Never try to win an argument you may win the argument but lose the guest forever.
- If possible, isolate the guest so that other guests may not overhear.
- Offer choices and never make a false promise.
- Monitor the corrective measures.
- Follow up and inform the guest about the solution.
- If unable to resolve the guest problem, consult your superiors.
- Address guests by name all communication should be in the first person.
- Use "I am sorry" not "we.
- Don't be defensive. Be composed at all times. Don't take criticisms personally.
- Offer an apology even if the dis-service is not your fault.
- Show empathy by using such phrases as: "I can understand how you feel", "I appreciate what you're saying."
- Tell them what you can do...not what you can't do.
- Find out what it will take to turn their dissatisfaction into satisfaction If they agree to that solution, act quickly before they change their mind.
- Follow-up and inform the guest about the solution.
- If unable to resolve the guest problem, consult your superiors.

Part B: Principles of Accounts

Principles of Accounts

CHAPTER ELEVEN

Unit 1: Introduction to Accounting

(**Topics Covered**: Meaning and definition. Types and classification. Principles of accounts. System of accounting. Generally accepted principle of accounting-GAAP)

<u>Meaning of Accounting:</u>

- An accounting system shows detailed information regarding each of the account categories, and it governs recording, reporting, and preparation of financial statement
- Accounting is concerned with the recording of financial transactions and analyzing the effect of such transactions; which will assist in the development of business decisions.
- Hospitality Accounting is concerned with providing specialized internal data to operational managers of the core departments of Hotel & Hospitality Industry.
- Executives from Food Production Department can direct stores for specific orders based on current & foreseen data of Hotel Occupancy. Duty Roasters can be altered across all core departments to enhance operational efficiency with available data.

Definitions of Accounting:

The committee of the ***American Institute of Certified Public Accountants*** has defined Accounting as:

"Accounting is the art of recording, classifying and summarizing in a significant manner and in terms of money, transactions and events, which are, in part at least of financial character and interpreting the results thereof".

Further, According to ***American Accounting Association***, Accounting is defined as –

"The process of identifying, measuring and communicating economic information to permit informed judgments and decisions by users of the information".

Types and classification:

The changing business scenario over the centuries gave rise to specialized branches of accounting which could cater to the changing requirements. The branches of accounting are:

- Financial accounting;
- Cost accounting; and
- Management accounting.

Financial Accounting:

The accounting system concerned with the financial state of affairs and financial results of operations is known as Financial Accounting. It is the original form of accounting. It is mainly concerned with the preparation of financial statements for the use of outsiders like creditors, debenture holders, investors and financial institutions. The financial statements i.e., the profit and loss account and the balance sheet, show them the manner in which operations of the business have been conducted during a specified period.

Cost Accounting:

It is that branch of accounting which is concerned with the accumulation and assignment of historical costs to units of product and department. Cost Accounting has been primarily being use for the purpose of valuation of stock and measurement of profits. It also seeks to ascertain the cost of unit produced and sold or the services rendered by a business entity. Cost Accounting is mostly related to the future aspects of the business. The process of cost accounting is based on the data provided by the financial accounting.

Management Accounting:

It is an accounting for the management i.e., accounting which provides necessary information to the management for discharging its functions. According to the Anglo-American Council on productivity, "Management accounting is the presentation of accounting information is such a way as to assist management in the creation of policy and the day-to-day operation of an undertaking." It covers all arrangements and combinations or adjustments of the orthodox information to provide the Chief Executive with the information from which he can control the business e.g. Information about funds, costs, profits etc. Management accounting covers the area of accounting beyond the perspectives of cost accounting. These areas can be capital expenditure decisions, capital structure decisions, and dividend decisions.

<u>Principles of Accounts:</u>

<u>Assumptions:</u>

The basic assumptions of accounting are like the foundation pillars on which the structure of accounting is based. The four basic assumptions are as follows:

Accounting entity

According to this assumption, business is treated as a unit or entity apart from its owners, creditors and others. In other words, the proprietor of a business concern is always considered to be separate and distinct from the business which he controls. All the business transactions are recorded in the books of accounts from the view point of the business. Even the proprietor is treated as a creditor to the extent of his capital.

Money Measurement

In accounting, only those business transactions and events which are of financial nature are recorded. For example, when Sales Manager is not on good terms with Production Manager, the business is bound to suffer. This fact will not be recorded, because it cannot be measured in terms of money.

Accounting Period

The users of financial statements need periodical reports to know the operational result and the financial position of the business concern. Hence it becomes necessary to close the accounts at regular intervals. Usually a period of 365 days or 52 weeks or 1 year is considered as the accounting period.

Going Concern

As per this assumption, the business will exist for a long period and transactions are recorded from this point of view. There is neither the intention nor the necessity to wind up the business in the foreseeable future.

<u>Modifying Principles:</u>

To make the accounting information useful to various interested parties, the basic assumptions and concepts discussed earlier have been modified.

These modifying principles are as under.

Cost Benefit

This modifying principle states that the cost of applying a principle should not be more than the benefit derived from it. If the cost is more than the benefit then that principle should be modified.

Materiality

The materiality principle requires all relatively relevant information should be disclosed in the financial statements. Unimportant and immaterial information are either left out or merged with other items.

Consistency

The aim of consistency principle is to preserve the comparability of financial statements. The rules, practices, concepts and principles used in accounting should be continuously observed and applied year after year. Comparisons of financial results of the business among different accounting period can be significant and meaningful only when consistent practices were followed in ascertaining them. For example, depreciation of assets can be provided under different methods, whichever method is followed, it should be followed regularly.

Prudence Conservatism

Prudence principle takes into consideration all prospective losses but leaves all prospective profits. The essence of this principle is "anticipate no profit and provide for all possible losses". For example, while valuing stock in trade, market price or cost price whichever is less is considered.

Accounting Concepts:

The term accounting concept is used to mean the necessary accounting assumptions upon which the accounting is based on.

Business Entity Concept: -Accounting assumes that a business is separate and distinct from the person who owns it. All the transactions of the business are recorded in the books of accounts from the sole view of business & not with the point of view of owner.

Money Measurement Concept: -Accounting records only those all transactions and events that can be expressed in terms of money.

Going Concern concept–In this concept, The Accounting assumes that the business will continue to operate for an indefinitely long period in the future. This will lead to clear distinction between assets &expenses.

Cost Concept–According to this concept asset is recorded as its actual cost. This cost of assets is the basis of all subsequent accounting norms.

Dual Aspect Concept–In this concept, every transaction entered into by a firm will have two aspects. In the business, the resources earned are assets and the claims of different parties against these assets are called equities. Accordingly, based on this concept, Total assets must be equal to equal to the claims of different parties against these assets. Thus,

Assets = Equities

Assets = Capital + Liabilities

Capital = Assets - Liabilities

Realisation Concept–This concept is also known as Revenue concept.According to this concept, Revenue is deemed to be realized when the goods have been transferred or the service has been rendered to a customer.

Accounting Period Concept – In this concept,the business entity sets a time frame (generally one year) for determining the profit and loss of the business. Such time interval is known as Accounting period.

Matching Concept–According to this concept, all expenses that are incurred in an accounting period should be matched with revenue realized in that period.

Accrual Concept–In this concept, a recorded transaction will affect the assets &liabilities of the business entity. Further, this concept requires all events and transactions, both cash & credit transactions to be taken into account.

<u>System of Accounting:</u>

Systems of accounting refer to the two systems of recording the financial transactions in the books of accounts. These two systems are the single entry system and the double or dual entry system.

Single Entry

It is the incomplete system of recording business transactions. The business organization maintains only cash book and personal accounts of debtors and creditors. Henceforth, the complete recording of transactions cannot be made. Further, Trail Balance – a important constituent of Accounting cannot be prepared in this system.

Double Entry

It this system every business transaction is having a twofold effect of benefits giving and benefit receiving aspects. The recording is made on the basis of both these aspects. Double Entry is an accounting system that records the effects of transactions and other events in at least two accounts with equal debits and credits.

Generally accepted principle of accounting (GAAP):

Generally Accepted Accounting Principles (GAAP) are basic accounting principles and guidelines which provide the framework for more detailed and comprehensive accounting rules, standards and other industry-specific accounting practices. For example, the Financial Accounting Standards Board (FASB) uses these principles as a base to frame their own accounting standards. Thus GAAP encompasses:

Basic accounting principles/guidelines

Accounting Standards usually issued by the premier accounting body of the country.

Industry-specific accounting practices to cover unusual scenarios.

In India, financial statements are prepared on the basis of accounting standards issued by the Institute of Chartered Accountants of India (ICAI) and the law laid down in the respective applicable acts (for example, Schedule III to Companies Act, 2013 should be compulsorily followed by all companies). The ICAI also releases guidance notes from time to time on various topics to help in the accounting process and provide clarity. While the basic accounting principles may not directly form part of the accounting standards and the related laws, they are assumed and expected to be universally followed.

Generally Accepted Accounting Principles

The following are the general accounting principles as mentioned earlier:

Business Entity Assumption: It states that every business entity should be treated as an entity that is separate from its owners. Therefore, all financial transactions should also be distinguished in such a manner. This concept is especially important while recording financial transactions of a sole proprietor. When the entire business with its assets and liabilities belong to the proprietor, the financial transactions need to be distinguished between those related to the business and those related to the proprietor personally.

Monetary Unit Assumption: All the financial transactions of a business should be capable of being expressed in a monetary unit (Indian Rupees, for example) and if it is not possible to do so, then it should not be recorded in the books of accounts of the business.

Accounting Period: This principle entails that the accounting process of a business should be completed within a certain time period which is usually a financial year or a calendar year. Thus, every transaction which relates to a particular accounting period will form a part of the financial statements prepared for that period.

Historical Cost Concept: As a general rule, when certain economic resources or assets are acquired by an enterprise, they are recorded as per the cash or cash equivalent actually spent to acquire that resource or asset on the transaction date – even if the transaction happened the previous day or ten years ago. This would result in the value of the remaining asset constant irrespective of the accounting period. The market value of the asset is not taken into account unless specifically required by law or an accounting standard.

Going Concern Assumption: The business entity is assumed to be a going concern, i.e., it will continue to operate for an indefinite amount of time. This assumption is important because if the business entity were to liquidate in the near future, it would have to restate its assets and liabilities in the accordance with the actual amount that could be realised or payable as the case may be so as to reflect the true financial position of the entity.

Full Disclosure Principle: An accounting entry may not independently be able to provide all the relevant information relating to the transaction. Hence the full disclosure principle requires the entity to disclose all the financial information relevant to the investor/user to assist him in decision making. At the transactional level, this is done by recording an adequate narration with every transaction and at the financial statement level, this is implemented by providing notes to the accounts.

Matching Concept: This concept requires the revenue for a particular period to be matched with its corresponding expenditure so as to show the true profit for the period.

Accrual Basis of Accounting: This principle requires all revenue and expenditure to be recorded in the period it is actually incurred and not when cash or cash equivalent has been received/spent. The earning of the income and the incurring of the expenditure is important, irrespective of the corresponding cash flow.

Consistency: An entity may decide to follow a particular accounting procedure in relation to a series of transactions. Such accounting procedures need to be followed consistently over the following accounting periods so as to facilitate comparison of the results between two periods. For example, an entity might choose to adopt the straight-line method of depreciation of its tangible fixed assets. This method needs to be consistently followed even in the coming years.

Materiality: This accounting principle allows an entity to disregard another accounting principle if the result of the same does not affect the decision making of the user of the financial statements. Certain errors or omissions may also be ignored if their effect is immaterial to the financial statements. For example, when a fixed asset is purchased, the matching concept requires the entity to recognise the expenditure over the useful life of the asset. If an entity purchases a keyboard for Rs. 300 and the turnover of such an entity is in crores of rupees, it would be immaterial to the user of financial statements whether such an asset is recognised as an asset or expense. Thus, even if the computer keyboard is considered as an expense in the year of purchase, it would not be violating the basic accounting principles since the amount involved and the impact of the same is immaterial.

Conservatism: In the process of accounting, one might come across various situations where there are two equally acceptable ways of accounting for a particular transaction. One might even have to choose between recording a transaction or not recording the same. In such a situation, a conservative approach should be followed. This means that while accounting for a particular transaction, all anticipated expenses or losses will need to be accounted for but all potential income or gains should not be recorded until actually earned/received. This is why a provision for expenses like bad debts is made but there is no corresponding record provided for an increase in the realisable value of an asset.

Unit 2: Books of Original Entry (Journal)

(**Topics Covered:** Meaning and definition. Format of Journal, Rules of debit and credit. Opening entry, simple and compound entries.)

The books in which a transaction is recorded for the first time from a source document are called **Books of Original Entry** or **Prime Entry**.

<u>**Meaning and definition:**</u>

Journal is one of the books of original entry in which transactions are originally recorded in a chronological order according to the principles of Double Entry System.

It is also called a 'Day Book'.

The process of recording a transaction in the journal is called 'Journalising' and the entries made in this book-are called 'Journal Entries'.

<u>**Format of Journal:**</u>

The journal has five columns:

(1) Date

(2) Particulars with "Narration"

(3) Ledger Folio

(4) Amount (Debit)

(5) Amount (Credit)

Explanation: The columns of journal are as under:

1. **Date:** In each page of the journal at the top of the date column, the year is written and in the next line, month and date of the first entry are written.

2. **Particulars:** In this column, the details regarding account titles and description are recorded.

3. **Ledger Folio:** The page number of the ledger in which the accounts are appearing is indicated in this column.

4. **Amount (Debit):** The amount to be debited along with its unit of measurement at the top of this column on each page is written against the Account that is debited.

5. **Amount (Credit):** The amount to be credited along with its unit of measurement at the top of this column on each page is written against the Account that is credited.

Rules of debit and credit:

Every business transaction which can be measured in monetary terms finds a place in the accounting transactions of a firm. In order to record such transactions, a system of debit and credit has been devised, which records such events through two different accounts.

The net effect of these accounting entries is the same in terms of quantity. However, by debiting and crediting two different accounts, the correct and apt accounting treatment can be depicted. In a ledger account, usually the debit column is on the left and the credit column is on the right.

- A debit is an accounting entry that either increases an asset or expense account. Or decreases a liability or equity account. It is positioned on the left in an accounting entry.
- A credit is an accounting entry that increases either a liability or equity account. Or decreases an asset or expense account. It is positioned on the right in an accounting entry.

Whenever an accounting transaction happens, a minimum of two accounts is always impacted, with a debit entry being recorded against one account and a credit entry being recorded against another account. There is no upper limit to the number of accounts involved in a transaction but the minimum cannot be less than two accounts.

The totals of the debits and credits for any transaction must always equal each other so that an accounting transaction is always said to be in balance. Thus, the use of debits and credits in a two column transaction recording format is the most essential of all controls over accounting accuracy. This is how debit and credit find their use.

The following are the rules of debit and credit which guide the system of accounts, they are known as the Golden Rules of accountancy:

- First: Debit what comes in, Credit what goes out.
- Second: Debit all expenses and losses, Credit all incomes and gains.

- Third: Debit the receiver, Credit the giver.

<u>Opening entry, simple and compound entries:</u>
Opening entry is referred to as the first entry that is recorded or which is brought forward from a previous accounting period to the new accounting period. In an ongoing business, the closing balance of the previous accounting period serves as an opening balance for the current accounting period.

Every transaction affects two accounts – one is debited and another is account is credited. Thus in recording a transaction in a journal one account is debited and another account is credited. This type of entry is called **simple entry**.

The entry in which more than one account is debited or more than one account is credited, is known as a compound entry. Three or more accounts are connected with a **compound entry.**

Example of Simple Entry:
For example, on 10.04.21 we bought furniture from S. The entry is:

Date	Particulars	L.F	Amount	Amount
10.04.21	Fumiture A/C ....Dr. S A/C (Being furniture purchased on credit)		10,000	10,000

<u>Simple Enrty Example</u>

Example Compound Entry:
For example, on 16.05.21 we paid Rs. 1,000 on account of salaries and Rs. 600 on account of rent. For this the entry will be:

Date	Particulars	L.F	Amount	Amount
16.05.21	Salary A/C ....Dr. Rent A/C Cash A/C (Being salaries and rent)		1,000 600	10,000

<u>Compound Entry Example</u>

Here two accounts have been debited and the entry involves three accounts. Hence, it is a **compound entry**.

CHAPTER THIRTEEN

Unit 3: Ledger

(**Topics Covered:** Meaning and uses. Formats. Posting)

In order to ascertain the net effect of all the transactions relating to a particular account are collected at one place in the Ledger. A Ledger is a book which contains all the accounts whether personal, real or nominal, which are first entered in journal or special purpose subsidiary books.

Ledger is a book that contains the accounts. Any financial statement related to the financial position of the company emerges only from the accounts. Thus, this ledger is known as the Principal Book. Hence, it is necessary to relate all the information for any account available is from the ledger. This book of accounts is the most important book for any business and that is why it is known as the king of all books. Also, the ledger book is also known as the book of the Final Entry.

<u>**Format of a Ledger:**</u>

Dr.   Name of the ledger account   Cr.

Date	Particulars	J.F.	Amount ₹	Date	Particulars	J.F.	Amount ₹

Format of a Legder

i. Each ledger account is divided into two parts. The left hand side is known as the debit side and the right hand side is known as the credit side. The words "Dr" and "Cr" are used to denote Debit and Credit.

ii. The name of the account is mentioned in the top (middle) of the account.

iii. The date of the transaction is recorded in the date column.

iv. The word "To" is used before the accounts which appear on the debit side of an account in the particulars column. Similarly, the word "By" is used before the accounts which appear on the credit side of an account in the particulars column.

v. The name of the other account which is affected by the transaction is written either in the debit side or credit side in the particulars column.

vi. The page number of the Journal or Subsidiary Book from where that particular entry is transferred, is entered in the Journal Folio (J.F) column.

vii. The amount pertaining to this account is entered in the amount column

Ledger Posting:

The procedure of posting is given as follows:

i. ***Procedure of posting for an Account which has been debited in the journal entry.***

Step 1 → Locate in the ledger, the account to be debited and enter the date of the transaction in the date column on the debit side.

Step 2 → Record the name of the account credited in the Journal in the particulars column on the debit side as "To..... (name of the account credited)".

Step 3 → Record the page number of the Journal in the J.F column on the debit side and in the Journal, write the page number of the ledger on which a particular account appears in the L.F. column.

Step 4 → Enter the relevant amount in the amount column on the debit side.

ii. ***Procedure of posting for an Account which has been credited in the journal entry.***

Step 1 → Locate in the ledger the account to be credited and enter the date of the transaction in the date column on the credit side.

Step 2 → Record the name of the account debited in the Journal in the particulars column on the credit side as "By...... (name of the account debited)"

Step 3 → Record the page number of the Journal in the J.F column on the credit side and in the Journal, write the page number of the ledger on which a particular account appears in the L.F. column.

Step 4 → Enter the relevant amount in the amount column on the credit side.

Following image shows the format of General Ledger Account:

Date	Particulars	DR or CR	Account No.	Post ref	Debit $	Credit $
	1) Name of the Business:					
	2) Name of the document - General Ledger					
1/1/2014	Owner contributes $100					
	Bank	Dr			100	
	Capital	Cr				100
31/3/14	The Ship buys Pall Mall for $200					
	Bank	Decreasing - Cr				200
	Property	Increasing - Dr			200	
1/4/2014	The boot lands on Pall Mall and pays $10 rent to the ship (we are the ship)					
	Bank	increasing - Dr			10	
	Revenue - rent	increasing - Cr				10

General Ledger Account Format:

CHAPTER FOURTEEN

Unit 4: Subsidiary Books

(**Topics Covered:** Need and uses. Classification. Purchase book, Sales book, Purchase return book, Sales return book, Debit note, Credit note, Practical Problems)

Subsidiary Books:

Transactions are classified and grouped according to their nature. Transactions are of two types: **Cash** and **Credit**.

Cash transactions are grouped in one category – *Cash Book*

Credit transactions are sub-grouped in separate book is used for each category or group of transactions which are repetitive and sufficiently large in number. – *Purchases Book* & *Sales Book.*

Need and uses:

I. **Purchases Book** records only credit purchases of goods by the trader.

II. **Sales Book** is meant for entering only credit sales of goods by the trader.

III. **Purchases return Book** records the goods returned by the trader to suppliers.

IV. **Sales return Book** deals with goods returned (out of previous sales) by the customers.

V. **Bills receivable Book** records the receipts of bills (Bills Receivable).

VI. **Bills Payable Book** records the issue of bills (Bills Payable).

VII. **Cash Book** is used for recording only cash transactions i.e., receipts and payments of cash.

VIII. **Journal Proper** is the journal which records the entries which cannot be entered in any of the above listed subsidiary books.

Advantages of Subsidiary Books:

The advantages of maintaining subsidiary books are :

i. **Division of Labour** : The division of journal, resulting in division of work, ensures more clerks working independently in recording original entries in the subsidiary books.

ii. **Efficiency** : The division of labour also helps the reduction in work load, saving in time and stationery.

iii. **Prevents errors and Frauds** : The accounting work can be divided in such a manner that the work of one person is automatically checked by another person.

iv. **Easy reference** : It facilitates easy references to any particular item. Example :- Total credit sales for a month can be easily obtained from the Sales Book.

v. **Easy Postings** : Posting from the subsidiary books are made at convenient intervals depending upon the nature of the business.

<u>**Classification:**</u>

I. Purchase book

II. Sales book

III. Purchase return book

IV. Sales return book

V. Debit note

VI. Credit note

Purchase Book or Purchase Journal:

Purchase book is a book of original entry in which only credit purchases of goods are recorded. Cash purchases of goods are recorded in the cash book. Credit purchases of other assets are also not recorded in the purchase book; they are recorded in the journal proper.

Goods here mean the items or articles in which business enterprise is dealing with or we can say that goods are the items which are used by the business enterprise for regular sale. For example, purchase of a computer by a business enterprise which is dealing in cloth shall not be treated as its goods and items related to computers shall be regarded as its assets. Similarly, purchase of cloth by a business enterprise which is dealing in computers shall not be treated as its goods since items relating to only computers are its goods.

Instead of recording transactions in the journal, the transactions relating to credit purchases of goods are directly recorded in the purchases book. However, the total of the purchases book shall be recorded on the debit side of the 'Purchases Account'. The main intention for preparing the purchases book is to know the credit purchases at any particular period of time.

Sales Book or Sales Journal:

Sales book is a book of original entry in which only credit sales of goods are recorded. Cash sales of goods are recorded in the cash book. Credit sales of other assets are also not recorded in the sales book; they are recorded in the journal proper.

Goods here mean the items or articles in which business enterprise is dealing or we can say that goods are the items which are used by the business enterprise for regular sale. For example, sale of furniture by a business enterprise which is dealing in stationery shall not be treated as its goods and items related to stationery alone shall be regarded as its goods.

Instead of recording transactions in the journal, the transactions relating to credit sales of goods are directly recorded in the sales book. However, the total of the sales book shall be recorded on the credit side of the 'Sales Account' The main intention for preparing the sales book is to know the credit sales at any particular period of time.

Purchases Return Book or Purchases Return Journal:

Purchases return book is a book of original entry in which transactions related to the return of purchases of goods are recorded.

There may be several reasons for returning the goods to the supplier; some of them are as under:

(a) On finding some defects in the goods.

(b) When goods sent are not as per the samples or specifications.

(c) If the quantity of goods supplied is more than the requirements.

(d) When there is a breach of an agreement between the seller and the purchaser.

When the business enterprise returns the goods to the supplier, a debit note is sent to the party to whom this document is sent. The business enterprise may make a debit note against the supplier for an amount which is to be recovered from him when the business enterprise returns some goods which are defective in nature or not as per specifications.

In this document, all details about the date and amount of transaction, the name of the party whose account is debited along with the reason for debiting his account shall be mentioned. It should be noted that the trade discount availed at the time of purchase shall also be adjusted at the time of returning the goods.

Sales Return Book Or Sales Return Journal:

Sales return book is a book of original entry in which transactions related to the return of sales of goods are recorded. The sales return book does not record return of goods sold on cash basis. There may be several reasons for returning the goods by the customers.

Some of them are as under:

(a) On finding some defects in the goods.

(b) When there is delay in supply of goods to the customers.

(c) When goods sent are not as per the samples or specifications.

(d) If there is an oversupply of goods.

(e) When there is a breach of agreement between the seller and the purchaser.

When a business enterprise receives back the goods sold earlier, it makes a credit note in favour of the purchaser showing that his account has been credited in the books of business enterprise. In this document, all details about the date and amount of transaction, the name of the party whose account is credited along with reason for crediting his account shall be mentioned.It should be noted that the trade discount allowed at the time of credit sale shall also be adjusted at the time of receiving goods.

Debit note:

A debit note is also known as a debit memo. It is a document that is issued from a buyer to a seller indicating a request to return funds as a result of incorrect or damaged goods or services or cancellation of purchase. A **debit note** is issued before a credit note can be issued by the supplier and acts as a buyer's formal request to issue a **credit note.**

A debit note can be issued by a buyer to the seller requesting the return of the partial or whole amount of payment already made. It could be due to incorrect or damaged goods received or cancellation of the order, or other special circumstances. A debit note serves as evidence of a purchase return in the buyer's accounting books. On the other hand, a credit note is proof of a sales return.

It is issued when, as a customer, you receive goods or services that may not be of expected standard while you are in receipt of the final invoice from the seller. As a buyer of goods from a supplier, if you would like to return the purchased goods for any valid reason, you can issue a debit note. **Some common reasons for issuing debit notes:**

- Damaged or defective goods received.
- The purchaser has overbilled the invoice.
- Incorrect invoice amount

Let's look at a **debit note example.**

Company A is the purchaser, and Company B is the seller or supplier. The sequence of events below will lead to the issuance of a debit note.

1. Company A makes a purchase of goods worth Rs. 1000 from Company B
2. Company A receives the goods, along with the final invoice, but finds some goods to be damaged.
3. Company A communicates to company B about the damaged goods and its intention of returning the goods as is.
4. Company A raises a debit note against company B, containing information about the original purchase and the value of the damaged goods.
5. On receipt of the debit note, Company B, after some due diligence, issues an appropriate credit note.

Credit note:

Acredit note is also known as a credit memo. It is a document that is issued by the seller to indicate a full or partial return of funds. It may arise in the event of an incorrect or damaged supply of goods, cancellation of a purchase or an invoice error. It is usually raised in response to a debit note from a customer. This document can also be used by the customer or purchaser against a future order.

As long as the total invoice amount is not exceeded, you may issue multiple credit notes.

Some common reasons for the issuing credit notes:

- If you are the supplier and have supplied goods of unsatisfactory quality to the buyer and the buyer wants to return the same, you can issue a credit note for adjustments against the invoice already raised.
- Corrections in already issued invoices.
- Correction of discount rates.
- Cancelling any pending payments against invoices.

There are 2 types of credit notes, based on where it is applicable.

- Credit notes issued on outgoing payments.
- Credit notes issued on incoming payments.

Let's take an **example of a credit note.**

Company A is the purchaser, and Company B is the supplier. Company A places Rs.10000 worth of order from Company B. After sampling the delivered goods, company A informs company B about the low quality of goods detected in the sample. Company B verifies the sampled items to confirm the defects and issues a credit note against the original invoice for the amount mutually decided on.

In such cases, the original invoice can be cancelled against the credit note issued, and a corrected invoice can be raised. This credit note may be used by Company A for further purchases from company B in the future. A refund of the amount may also be agreed on.

CHAPTER FIFTEEN

Unit 5: Cash Book

(Topics Covered: Meaning. Advantages. Single, Double and Three columns. Handling cheque.)

Cash Book:

Cash transactions are numerous transaction in a business entity ; it becomes easier to maintain all these in a separate book of records . This book that upkeep"s only the cash transactions is the **Cash Book.** The cash book is both a journal and a ledger. Cash Book will always show debit balance, as cash payments can never exceed cash available.

Advantages of using Cash Book:

1. *Saves time and labour*: All cash transactions are straight away recorded in the cash book which is in the form of a ledger.

2. *To know cash and bank balance*: It benefits the proprietor to know the cash and bank balance at any point of time.

3. *Mistakes and frauds can be prevented*: Regular balancing of cash book reveals the balance of cash in hand. In case the cash book is maintained by business concern, it can avoid frauds. Discrepancies if any, can be identified and rectified.

4. *Effective cash management*: Cash book provides all information regarding total receipts and payments of the business concern at a particular period.

Single, Double and Three columns:

Simple Column Cash Book: For recording cash transaction only.

This is the simplest form of Cash Book and is used in businesses where payments are made and received mostly in cash and where usually no cash discount is received or given. However, if there are any discount or cheque transactions, it is recorded in a separate account in the ledger. The ruling of a one-column Cash Book is like an ordinary cash account.

Double Column Cash Book: For recording and cash discount transaction.

This type of cash book has two columns, viz., cash column and discount column. Usually, the cash discount is allowed or received when payment is made. So, it is necessary to record this fact at the same place where the cash transaction is recorded. This type is similar to Simple Cash Book, except that one additional column on each side is provided for recording cash discount. As discount is a nominal account, discount allowed being a loss is shown on the debit side and discount received being a gain is shown on the credit side.

Triple Column Cash Book: For recording cash, bank and discount transaction.

These days, it is difficult to carry on any business without having dealings with the bank. Normally, the bulk of its funds is kept by the business at a bank in a current account where frequent withdrawals and deposits are permitted. Bank transactions are numerous than cash transactions. Therefore it is appropriate as well as convenient that cash book should have on the additional column on each side to record money's deposited at the bank and the payment out of the bank.

Handling Cheque:

If you are accepting a cheque as payment from someone you do not know, confirm the following information:

- Full name.
- Home address.
- Phone number.
- PAN / Aadhar number.

Check with the bank the cheque will be drawn on to confirm that the person writing the check has an account with funds available to cover the check.

CHAPTER SIXTEEN

Unit 6: Bank Reconciliation Statement

(Topics Covered: Meaning. Reasons of difference in pass book and cash book balances. Preparation of bank reconciliation statement.)

A bank reconciliation statement is a summary of banking and business activity that reconciles an entity's bank account with its financial records. The statement outlines the deposits, withdrawals, and other activities affecting a bank account for a specific period.

The balance of the bank column in the double or triple column cash book represents the customers cash balance at bank. It should be the same as shown by his bank pass book on any particular day. In case of disagreement in the balance of the cash book and the pass book, the need for preparing Bank Reconciliation Statement arises.

Definition - Bank reconciliation Statement: „Bank reconciliation statement is a list in which the various items that cause a difference between bank balance as per cash book and pass book on any given date are indicated".

<u>Reasons of difference in pass book and cash book balances:</u>
<u>Causes of Disagreement</u>

It is between the balance shown by the cash book and the balance shown by the pass book

<u>1. Cheques paid into bank but not yet collected</u>

The cheque paid into bank for collection but not credited into the account of the customer, because the cheque is

i. not collected and credited till that date.

ii. collected but the bank staff has forgotten to make entry.

iii. collected but credited to wrong account.

iv. dishonoured.

v. collected for No. I account but credited to No. II account of the same customer.

<u>2. Cheques issued but not yet presented for payment</u>

The cheques issued but not debited customers account may be because the cheque is

i. not cashed till date.

ii. not presented till date.

iii. presented but dishonoured for some reasons or other.

iv. lost by the party to whom the cheque was issued.

v. cashed out of No. I account but wrongly debited to No. II account of the same customer.

Amount credited by the banker in the pass book without the immediate knowledge of the customer.

<u>3. Amounts debited by the banker in the pass book without the immediate knowledge of the customer</u>

<u>Preparation of Bank Reconciliation Statement (BRS):</u>

Check for Un-cleared Dues

Step 1: First of all, compare the opening balances of both the bank column of the cash book as well as the bank statement. The two can be different in terms of uncleared dues like un-presented or un-credited cheques from the previous month.

Compare Debit and Credit Sides

Step 2: Start by comparing the credit side of the bank statement to the debit side of the bank statement. Also, compare the credit side of the cash book to the debit side of the cash book. The two must be equal in both documents. Tick the columns if you can't find any error.

Check for Missed Entries

Step 3: Analyse entries in the bank column of the cash book as well as in checkbook. Look for records that have been missed to be posted in the bank column of the cash book. Make a separate list of all such items and list them in cash book.

Correct them

Step 4: Correct the errors present in the cash book, if any.

Revise the Entries

Step 5: Calculate the balance after revising the updated cash book's bank column.

Make BRS Accordingly

Step 6: Prepare Bank Reconciliation Statement accordingly. Make sure to add the updated version of records.

Add Un-presented Cheques and Deduct Un-credited Cheques

Step 7: Banks are not aware of Un-presented cheques because the beneficiary doesn't get the cheque. It is the case when the business firm forgets to deliver the signed cheque to the issued name.

This situation leads to the addition of the cheque amount in the bank statement.

On the other hand, cheques which beneficiary has not yet collected are called un-credited cheques. These must be deducted.

Make Final Changes

Step 8: Make all the final adjustments and check for bank errors in the bank statement and the firm's errors in the cash book. During heavy transaction days, firms or banks may make mistakes in noting entries.

The process removes those errors. Although it consists of fine work, reconciliation becomes a helping hand at hard times (large transaction days).

Left-Hand Side Equal to the Right-Hand Side

Step 9: The results from both the documents i.e. bank statement and cash book must match with each other.

CHAPTER SEVENTEEN

Unit 7: Trial Balance

(**Topics Covered:** Meaning, Methods, Advantages, Limitation)

Trial Balance:

Trial balance is a statement prepared with the balances or total of debits and credits of all the accounts in the ledger to test the arithmetical accuracy of the ledger accounts.

Step 1 - After recording and classifying the transactions in the various accounts along with balancing thereof.

Step 2 - Then the next step in the accounting process is to prepare a statement to check the arithmetical accuracy of the transactions recorded so for. This statement is called „Trial Balance".

A business entity prepares a trail balance on the closing date of an accounting year.

Definition - Trial Balance

"Trial balance is a statement, prepared with the debit and credit balances of ledger accounts to test the arithmetical accuracy of the books" – J.r. Batliboi.

Methods:

A trial balance can be prepared in the following methods.

i. **The Total Method**: According to this method, the total amount of the debit side of the ledger accounts and the total amount of the credit side of the ledger accounts are recorded.

ii. **The Balance Method**: In this method, only the balances of an account either debit or credit, as the case may be, are recorded against their respective accounts.

Advantages of Trial Balance:

- To check the debits equal the credits
- To find the uncover errors in journalizing

- To find the uncover errors in posting
- To locate the errors in ledger accounts
- To make financial statements
- To list the accounts at a single place
- To know the ending balance of each account at a glance
- To make the adjustments for unrecorded transactions
- To find the missing amount of an account in the special case
- To test the mathematical accuracy of recording process

In short, the trial balance is an essential tool to verify the accuracy of the recording process.

Limitations of Trail Balance:

The following are the important limitations of trail balances:

- The trail balance can be prepared only in those concerns where double entry system of book- keeping is adopted.
- This system is too costly.
- If the trail balance is wrong, the subsequent preparation of Trading, P&L Account and Balance Sheet will not reflect the true picture of the concern.

CHAPTER EIGHTEEN

Unit 8: Final Accounts

(**Topics Covered:** Meaning. Procedure for preparation of final accounts. Difference between trading accounts profit & loss accounts and balance sheet. Adjustment - Closing stock.)

<u>Final Accounts:</u>

As the name suggests final accounts are the accounts which are prepared at the last stage of an accounting cycle. Final accounts show both financial position of a business along with the profitability; they are used by external and internal parties for various purposes. Final accounts are a bookkeeping term that refers to the final trial balance at the end of an accounting period from which the financial statements are derived. This final trial balance includes all of the journal entries used to close the books, such as: Wage and payroll tax accruals etc.

Parts of Final Accounts:

The final accounts of business concern generally include two parts.

The first partis <u>**Trading and Profit and Loss Account**</u>. This is prepared to find out the net result of the business.

The second part is <u>**Balance Sheet**</u> which is prepared to know the financial position of the business.

<u>Trading Account:</u>

Trading account is prepared for an accounting period to find the gross margin of the business. The balance of this account shows gross profit or loss which is transferred to the profit and loss account.

Items Shown in Trading Account: (A) Debit Side

Opening stock: The stock at the beginning of an accounting period is called opening stock. This is the closing stock as per the last balance sheet.

Purchases: The total value of goods purchased after deducting purchase returns is debited to trading a/c.

Direct expenses: Direct expenses are incurred to make the goods saleable.

Items Shown in Trading Account :(B) Credit Side

Sales: - It includes both credit and cash sales.

Closing stock: - Closing stock is the value of goods remaining at the end of the accounting period.

Balancing of Trading Account

The difference between the two sides of the Trading Account, indicates either Gross Profit or Gross Loss. If the credit side total is more, the difference represents Gross Profit. Also, if the total of the debit side is more, the difference represents Gross Loss. Then, the Gross Profit or Gross Loss is transferred to Profit & Loss Account.

<u>Profit and Loss Account:</u>

In the words of Prof. Carter "Profit and loss account is an account into which all gains and losses are collected in order to ascertain the excess of gains over the losses or vice versa."

Preparation of Profit and Loss Account:

Step 1 - Profit and loss account starts with gross profit brought down from trading account on the credit side. (If gross loss, on the debit side).

Step 2: - All the indirect expenses are debited and all the revenue incomes are credited to the profit and loss account and then net profit or loss is calculated.

Step 3: - If incomes or credit is more, than the expenses or debit, the difference is net profit. On the other hand, if the expenses or debit side is more, the difference is net loss.

Items Appearing in The Debit Side (Profit and Loss Account):

Those expenses which are chargeable to the normal activities of the business are recorded in the debit side of profit and loss account. They are termed as indirect expenses.

i. Office and Administrative expenses

ii. Repairs and Maintenance expenses

iii. Financial expenses

iv. Selling and distribution expenses

Items Appearing in the Credit Side (Profit and Loss Account):

The following are some of the incomes and gains.

i. Interest received on investment & fixed deposits.

ii. Discount earned.

iii. Commission earned.

Balancing of Profit & Loss Account:

The difference between the two sides of profit and loss account indicates either net profit or net loss. If the total on the credit side is more the difference is called net profit. Also, if the total of debit side is more the difference represents net loss. The net profit or net loss is transferred to capital account.

<u>Preparation of Balance Sheet:</u>

Balance sheet is prepared by taking up all personal accounts and real accounts (assets and properties) together with the net result obtained from profit and loss account. On the left-hand side of the statement, the liabilities and capital are shown. On the right-hand side, all the assets are shown.

"Balance sheet is a „Classified summary" of the ledger balances remaining after closing all revenue items into the profit and loss account." - Cropper.

<u>Assets:</u>

Assets represents everything which a business owns and has money value. In other words, asset includes possessions and properties of the business.

<u>Classification of Assets:</u>

Fixed assets: Fixed assets are the assets which are acquired and held permanently and used in the business with the objective of making profits. Example: - Land and building, Plant and machinery, Furniture and Fixtures.

Current assets: The assets of the business in the form of cash, debtors bank balances, bill receivable and stock are called current assets as they can be realized within an operating cycle of one year to discharge liabilities.

Tangible assets: Tangible assets have definite physical shape or identity and existence. Example land, cash, stock etc.

Intangible assets: The assets which have no physical shape but have value are called intangible assets. Example: - Goodwill, patents, trademarks.

Fictitious assets: Fictitious assets are not real assets. Example: - Past accumulated losses or expenses which are capitalised for the time being, expenses for promotion of organisations.

<u>Liabilities:</u>

A liability is an amount which a business firm is „liable to pay" legally.

<u>Classification of Liabilities</u>

Liabilities are classified into bur categories as given below.

Owner's capital: Capital is the amount contributed by the owners of the business.

Long term Liabilities: They do not become due for payment in the ordinary „operating cycle" of business or within a short period of lime. Examples are long term loans and debentures.

Current liabilities: Liabilities which are repayable during the operating cycle of business, usually within a year, are called short term liabilities or current liabilities. Examples of current liabilities are trade creditors, bills payable, outstanding expenses, bank overdraft, taxes payable and dividends payable.

Contingent liabilities: Contingent liabilities will result into liabilities only if certain events happen. Examples are: Bills discounted and endorsed which may be dishonoured, unpaid calls on investments.

Balance Sheet Equation:

The liability to the owner - capital, is always made up of the difference between assets and liabilities.

Thus,

Assets = Liabilities + Capital or

Capital = Assets - Liabilities

Adjustments:

An adjusting entry is simply an adjustment to your books to make your financial statements more accurately reflect your income and expenses, usually — but not always — on an accrual basis. Adjusting entries are made at the end of the accounting period. This can be at the end of the month or the end of the year.

Types of Adjusting Entries:

The amount of adjusting entries a business makes depends on their number of financial transactions. However, we divide adjusting entries into three main types: accruals, deferrals, and non-cash expenses.

Accruals

A business may earn revenue from selling a good or service during one accounting period, but not invoice the client or receive payment until a future accounting period. These earned but unrecognized revenues are adjusting entries recognized in accounting as **accrued revenues**.

You record accrued revenues by:

- Debiting the accounts receivable account and,
- Crediting the service revenue account.

Another type of accrual in accounting is the **accrued expense**. Accrued expenses are expenses made but that the business hasn't paid for yet, such as salaries or interest expense.

They are recorded as an adjusting entry by:

* Debiting the expense account
* And crediting accounts payable.

If you want to learn more on how to pay back expenses owed to your suppliers in a timely manner, check out our business guide on invoice payments.

Deferrals

When your business makes an expense that will benefit more than one accounting period, such as paying insurance in advance for the year, this expense is recognized as **a prepaid expense**.

These prepayments are first recorded as assets, and as time passes by, they are expensed through adjusting entries.

The adjusting entry for prepaid expenses includes:

* A debit to the expense account (insurance expense, for example)
* A credit to prepaid expense account previously recorded.

The other deferral in accounting is **the deferred revenue**,which is an adjusting entry that converts liabilities to revenue.

More specifically, deferred revenue is revenue that a customer pays the business, for services that haven't been received yet, such as yearly memberships and subscriptions.

When cash is received it's recorded as a liability since it hasn't been earned yet by the business. Over time, this liability is turned into revenue until it's fully earned.

This change is done by recording the following adjusting entry:

* Debiting the unearned revenue account
* Crediting the service revenue account

Non-Cash Expenses

The most common method used to adjust non-cash expenses in business is **depreciation**.

By definition, depreciation is the allocation of the cost of a depreciable asset over the course of its useful life. Depreciable assets (also known as fixed assets) are physical objects a business owns that last over one accounting period, such as equipment, furniture, buildings, etc.

In simpler terms, depreciation is a way of devaluing objects that last longer than a year, so that they are expensed according to the time that they get used by the business (not when you pay for them).

For instance, if a company buys a building that's expected to last for 10 years for $20,000, that $20,000 will be expensed throughout the entirety of the 10 years, rather than when the building is purchased.

And since depreciation doesn't involve any actual cash exchange, it's purely an **estimate** of how much a physical asset gets used in one accounting period. The most commonly used formula to estimate depreciation is by the straight-line method in which:

Depreciation (per accounting period) = Cost of the asset / Estimated Useful Life

The adjusting entry to record the depreciation expense includes:

- A debit to the depreciation expense account
- A credit to the accumulated depreciation account

Other methods that non-cash expenses can be adjusted through include amortization, depletion, stock-based compensation, etc.

Closing Stock: Goods remaining unsold at the end of the accounting year. Cost of Conversion: Expenses incurred in the factory (for converting raw materials into finished goods.) I Cost of Goods Sold: Difference between the cost of goods available for sale and the cost of goods in stock.

CHAPTER NINETEEN

Unit 9: Capital and Revenue Expenditure

Expenditure:

Expenditure means spending on something. This can be a payment is cash or can also be the exchange of some valuable item in exchange for goods or services. It is the process of causing a liability by a commodity. Receipts and invoices keep the records of expenditures. An expense is a word very similar to expenditure but expense shows the deduction in the value of the asset while expenditure simply denotes the obtaining of assets. Two types of expenditures are present on the basis of time durations, That is

1. Capital expenditures
2. Revenue expenditures

Capital Expenditures

These are expenditures for high-value items that holds longer duration requirements. Capital expenditures are long-term expenditures. In other words, when the expenses are made for a particular asset but they do not get completely consumed in the specific time. Due to this the earning capacity increases, and in the meanwhile, the price of the assets decreases.

Consequently, the future costs are reduced because the costs of the assets are continuously revised according to the depreciation taking place. There is a requirement to redo the capital expenditures in the accounting year. These do not get exhausted in the accounting year and benefits the user in the future years. Besides that, capital expenditures enhance the position of the business and trade.

There different types of capital expenditure, for example

- Cash money spent on business purposes.
- Purchasing of Plants and machinery items
- IT items
- Electric power equipment
- Permanent additions to existing fixed assets

Revenue Expenditures

In contrast to the capital expenditure, revenue expenditures are not the high-value items, instead, they are the routine expenditures that takes place in the normal business. In other words, this kind of expenditure maintains fixed assets.

Unlike capital expenditure, earnings do not increase but stay maintained in revenue expenditure. The assets get consumed in an accounting year and no future benefits are available. Also, the prices of assets remain fixed. The assets are consumed in less than a year so there is a need to purchase them again. This is a recurring type of expenditure. There are two sub-categories of revenue expenditures:

1. **Direct Expenses:** These include the cost of manufacturing of raw material to turn it into a finished product. For instance, Productive wages and salaries to workers, shipping costs, legal expenses, electricity, and water bills, fuels costs, rent, commissions, packaging charges.
2. **Indirect Expenses:** These connect with only selling and distributing goods other than manufacturing. For example, salaries, depreciation, machinery, items of furniture and fixing, etc.

Revenue expenditures and capital expenditures are both completely different things as a one. Revenue expenditure is a periodic investment of money that does not benefit the business nor leads to any loss in any way. While on the other hand, capital expenditure is the long-term investment that only benefits the business.

It is very necessary to determine its capital nature or revenue nature. Because both have their own advantages and shortcoming that are not understandable separately.

CHAPTER TWENTY

Unit 10: Depreciation

(**Topics Covered:** Meaning & causes. Methods- fixed instalments. Diminishing balance)

In the process of preparing final accounts, allocation for depreciation on all fixed assets is done, in order to arrive at an appropriate amount of profit or loss for the accounting period.

Depreciation – Meaning: Depreciation is a method associated with tangible long-lived assets. It allows the recovery of the cost of a tangible asset over a period of time, commonly known as the asset's useful life.

Depreciation – Definition: Depreciation may be defined as the loss in value of assets or amount of expense arising out of physical deformation and other causes that has to deduct from profit.

According to Institute of Cost and Management Accounting, London (ICMA) terminology "The depreciation is the diminution in intrinsic value of the asset due to use and/or lapse of time."

Examples: -machines, plants, furniture, buildings, computers, trucks, vans, equipment, etc.

<u>Methods for Providing Depreciation:</u>

The depreciation amount to be charged for during an accounting year depends up on depreciable amount and the method of allocation. There are eight methods used for providing depreciation, which are: -

- Fixed Instalment Method
- Diminishing Balance Method

<u>Fixed Instalment Method:</u>

This method is based on the assumption of equal usage of the asset over its entire useful life. It is called straight line method or fixed instalment method because the amount of depreciation remains constant from year to year over the useful life of the asset. It is also known as fixed percentage on original cost method because same percentage of the original cost (in fact depreciable cost) is written off as depreciation from year to year.

The depreciation amount to be provided under this method is computed by using the following formula:

Depreciation = (Cost of Asset – Estimated Net Residential Value) / Estimated useful life of the Asset

Diminishing Balance Method:

Under this method, the rate of depreciation is calculated on the **written down value** of the asset & is charged on the book value of the asset. This method involves the application of a pre-determined proportion/percentage of the book value of the asset at the beginning of every accounting period, so as to calculate the amount of depreciation. The amount of depreciation reduces year after year.

Merits of Diminishing Balance Method

- In this method it is easy to calculate the depreciation on additions made during the year
- The income tax authorities in India, certify this method of depreciation.
- It ensures a fairly even charge to Profit and Loss Account on account of both depreciation and repairs

Demerits of Diminishing Balance Method

- The value of an asset cannot be brought down to zero
- This method also does not take into account the loss of interest on the money invested in the asset.
- The determination of a suitable rate of depreciation is also difficult under this method.

Part C: Hotel Accounts

Hotel Accounts

CHAPTER TWENTY-ONE

Unit 1: Uniform System of Accounts for Hotels

(**Topics Covered:** Introduction to Uniform System Of Accounts. Advantage & disadvantages)

Introduction to Uniform System of Accounts:

1. Regardless of the business size, Accounting in the perspective of Hotel Industry is all about recording and retrieving in & out cash-flow.
2. Hotel Accounting is considered as the boon for better decision making that brings in good fortune to hoteliers if handled efficiently.
3. Beyond that it involves summarizing, reporting and analyzing the hotel's financial position for a particular period, further helps in budgeting, forecasting and future cost planning.
4. In general, a Certified Public Accountant (CPA), accountant or a bookkeeper takes care of handling the accounting activities and generates the financial statements such as Balance Sheet, Profit & Loss (Income) and Cash Flow, etc.
5. And, these are the most crucial components that communicate the financial information of an individual hotel or group of hotels.
6. Staying accountable doesn't end here! Hotel Accounting also involves in keeping the bank account in sync, streamlining the payables & receivables, analyzing
7. department- wise expenses, generating general ledger, tracking inventory supplies and 1099 payment reports.
8. In terms of Operations front, the accounting plays a key role in Tracking Bills, Recurring Dues, Sales & Journals Approval, while keeping a tab on

Occupancy %, Rooms Sold, Average Daily Rate (ADR), RevPar, Room Revenue and Guest Satisfaction Surveys, Competition Analysis through STR, Variance Analysis, Labor Management, Operating Budgets and Financial Benchmarking.

9. On the other side, the Time & Payroll Management, Daily Activity Tracking, Performance Monitoring, Daily Sales, Profitability Forecast fall in the lineup of Accounting in Hotel Industry.

Meaning of USA:

When several hotels and restaurants follow the same accounting principles and practices, it is called the uniform system of accounting. It is not a separate system or method of recording the transactions of a business enterprise like double entry system or single entry system or cash system or mercantile system of accounting. It simply denotes a situation in which a number of hotel units use the same accounting principles and practices. This system is followed in hotels and restaurants to make meaningful comparison of cost, sales and profit figures of one unit with another.

Advantages of USA:

1. In the uniform system of accounting, the staff members of a hotel unit can easily be transferred to other unit because it will not take much time for the staff members to adjust themselves in the new hotel.
2. It facilitates inter-firm comparison and identification of the causes for higher costs, lower sales, lower profit etc., if any, to take suitable measures.
3. The proposed investors become able to compare the profitability and financial position of different hotels in a comparative form for investment purposes.
4. It becomes easier to decide the amount of rent or royalty of a property to be leased out.

Difficulties in implementing the USA:

1. There may be lack of proper co-operation, mutual trust and understanding amongst the member units.
2. There may not be free exchange of ideas, knowledge and technology amongst the member units.
3. There may not be free exchange of information regarding the method of valuation of closing stocks, depreciation etc.
4. There may be rivalry and sense of jealousy amongst the member units.
5. There may not be use of common heads to record sales of hotels like room sales, food sales, beverage sales, telephone income, laundry income, etc.
6. There may not be the use of common terminology and procedure regarding cost apportionment and cost control.
7. The bigger units may not be prepared to share their experience with the smaller units in order to improve the latter.

Removal of difficulties in implementing the USA:

1. There should be proper co-operation, mutual trust and understanding amongst the member units.
2. There should be free exchange of ideas, knowledge and technology amongst the member units.
3. There should be free exchange of information regarding the method of valuation of closing stocks, depreciation etc.
4. There should be no rivalry and sense of jealousy amongst the member units.
5. There should be the use of common heads to record the sales of hotels like room sales, food sales, beverage sales, telephone income, laundry income, etc.
6. There should be the use of common terminology and procedure regarding cost apportionment and cost control.
7. The bigger units should always be prepared to share their experience with the smaller units in order to improve the latter.

CHAPTER TWENTY-TWO

Unit 2: Income Statement under Uniform System of Accounts

(Topics Covered: Revenue and non-revenue producing departments of the hotel. Contents of the income statement)

The income statement is a financial statement that is used to help determine the past financial performance of the enterprise, predict future performance, and assess the capability of generating future cash flows. It is also known as the profit and loss statement (P&L), statement of operations, or statement of earnings.

The income statement consists of revenues (money received from the sale of products and services, before expenses are taken out, also known as the "top line") and expenses, along with the resulting net income or loss over a period of time due to earning activities. Net income (the "bottom line") is the result after all revenues and expenses have been accounted for. The income statement reflects a company's performance over a period of time. This is in contrast to the balance sheet, which represents a single moment in time.

<u>**Revenue and non-revenue producing departments of the hotel:**</u>

On the basis of Revenue there are main three types of departments in a hotel.

a) Operating and Revenue producing department.

b) Operating and Non - Revenue Producing Department.

c) Non- operating and Revenue Producing Department.

a) Operating and Revenue Producing Department:

Major revenue producing department ment: There are two departments which produce major revenue or more revenue than other departments - F & B department & Rooms.

Minor revenue producing department: These departments produce revenue in minor amount. Examples: Business centre, Telephone, Health club, Laundry,

B) Operating and Non - Revenue Producing Departments:

Under this there are those departments which operated by hotel but produce no revenue. There are some examples. Sales and marketing, H R D, Accounts, Store and receiving, Security, Maintenance.

C) Non - Operating and Revenue Producing Departments:

Under it there are those departments which are non- operated by hotel but produce revenue on the basis of rental contract. There are some examples – Shopping arcade, Other Rental Income, Travel Desk, Beauty Parlour, etc.

<u>Contents of the Income Statement:</u>

The income statement is a financial statement that is used to help determine the past financial performance of the enterprise, predict future performance, and assess the capability of generating future cash flows. It is also known as the profit and loss statement (P&L), statement of operations, or statement of earnings.

The income statement consists of revenues (money received from the sale of products and services, before expenses are taken out, also known as the "top line") and expenses, along with the resulting net income or loss over a period of time due to earning activities. Net income (the "bottom line") is the result after all revenues and expenses have been accounted for. The income statement reflects a company's performance over a period of time. This is in contrast to the balance sheet, which represents a single moment in time.

In the Hotel Industry, we see that at the end of each accounting period, the cycle is completed by the preparation of financial statements. The financial statements primarily constitute a statement of Income and & Balance Sheet. A Statement of income is prepared for the period with the year to date. Further, Financial statements (as stated above) can be two different statements or combined into one statement using two columns. With The use of computer technology in form of Hotel Information system (HIS) or Property Management System (PMS) have simplified the basic recording steps in Hotel accounting in form of Accounting Modules.

Hotel operations, besides the traditional Income statement & Balance sheet, have the following inclusive in Financial statement: -

- Individual department schedules
- Operating schedules – Rooms Division
- Operating schedules – Food & Beverage
- Operating schedules – Rental & other incomes
- Overhead schedules – Administrative & General
- Overhead schedules – Sales & Marketing
- Overhead schedules – Hotel Operations & Maintenance
- Relevant Statistics for Financial Interpretations

CHAPTER TWENTY-THREE

Unit 3: Departmental income Statements Under Uniform System of Hotel Accounts

(**Topics Covered:** Room departmental income schedule. Food and beverage department income schedule)

A hotel P&L statement includes the following elements:

1. Revenue or Top Line

This is typically itemised into individual revenue sources. These include room turnover, food and beverage revenue (restaurant, breakfast, bar, room service), and if applicable, events, activities, spa membership and gift shop income, among other possible revenue sources.

Once you have the figure of the total sales revenue, the cost of sale (commissions that are paid to different sales channels, for example to the OTAs) should be diminished to obtain your gross profit.

2. Costs

a) Operational expenses

These are the operational costs for delivering the services of each revenue source, for instance: restaurant, bar, banquets, front office, housekeeping, cleaning, engineering and others.

b) Undistributed expenses

Overheads such as administration, staff, and property-related costs.

c) Fixed expenses

These costs remain constant. They include property tax, property-related costs such as building and/or equipment rental, amortization, depreciation, insurance and the interest to pay on loans or debt, such as from loans, lease and insurance.

d) Interest, taxes, amortization and depreciation

3. Earnings or Bottom line

Difference of deducting the cost from the revenue. It is also known as net income, profit or earnings.

Here's a sample hostel profit and loss statement:

1. Revenue or Top line

To calculate the total revenue generated:

- - - Room Revenue
  - Food & Beverage

    - Breakfast Revenue
    - Bar Revenue
    - Restaurant Revenue
    - Room Service Revenue

  - Other Departmental revenue:

    - Events
    - Activities
    - Spa
    - Telephone
    - Gift Shop
    - Parking

2. Costs

a) Operational expenses:

Rooms

- Payroll
- Cleaning
- Laundry
- Other

F&B

- Food Cost
- Beverage Cost
- Payroll

- Cleaning
- Laundry
- Other

Other departments: spa, events and others

- Purchasing Costs
- Payroll
- Other

b) Undistributed costs:

- Administration, excluding what has been taken into account already for being related to services of the hotel.
- Marketing and distribution expenses, you can take into account: cost of commission to OTA, cost of metasearch, marketing expenses and other sales channels cost
- Staff not directly related to rooms, including F&B, spa and events staff
- Cleaning
- Other

c) Fixed expenses:

- Property tax
- Property rental
- Equipment rental
- Insurance

By applying the following formula we obtain our NOI (net operating income) or EBITDA (Earnings Before Interest Taxes Depreciation Amortization):

Revenue – Expenses before Interest, Taxes, Depreciation and Amortization

To conclude with the P&L statement, the final step is to calculate the following:

- Interest
- Taxes

- Depreciation
- Amortization

The above sample is of course a simplified version of a hotel P&L statement. Your accounting department may wish to break your own P&L statements down into more detail to aid greater understanding and provide deeper insight.

Conclusion: To understand your P&L as well as possible, what it boils down to, simply, is this: total sales minus total costs equals hotel profits. While it doesn't need to become complicated, the more detailed your P&L, the better for your understanding and insight regarding overall hotel operability and performance.

Any hotel management business that wishes to achieve healthy financial results, should invest a good amount of time to build a well structured profit and loss statement, and review it monthly with the members of the hotel executive and management team.

CHAPTER TWENTY-FOUR

Unit 4: Internal Control

(**Topics Covered:** Meaning & Objectives of internal control. Characteristics of internal control)

Definition:

The whole system of control, financial and otherwise, established by the management in order to carry on the business of the enterprises in an orderly and efficient manner, ensure adherence to management policies, safe-guard the assets and secure as far as possible the completeness and accuracy of the records.

Objectives of Internal Control:-

1. To check frauds and thefts.
2. To safeguard the assets of the business from thefts and misuse (cutlery and small equipment).
3. To improve the efficiency.
4. To follow the policies of the management.
5. To improve the quality.
6. To complete the records up to moment.

The following are the main types of internal control:

1. Organisation
2. Division of duties
3. Physical Control
4. Supervision
5. Financial Accuracy

Organisation

The management must make the organisation chart of all the departments. The authorities, responsibilities, reporting to, must be clearly identified, each job must be clearly described and specified. In case of delegation of power, it should be in writing with the approval of superiors. It must be clear to superiors that the authority/power can be delegated to subordinates but the responsibility cannot beelegated. The superiors are always responsible for the deed and misdeeds of subordinates. In larger hotels a lot of power is delegated to juniors because one person cannot perform all the duties. In smaller hotels the owner himself supervisors almost everything. The organisation chart of a hotel may differ from hotel to hotel, depending upon the size of the hotel, policy of the hotel, mechanical devices available, etc.

Division Of Duties

The duties among different employees must be divided to have an effective control but in smaller hotels, the broad division of duties may not be possible. For example, in a large hotel the bill clerk and cashier can be a separate person; this will have a control of one person over other and fewer chances of cash pilferage.

Physical Control

In hotels, the security is assigned to an outside agency so that security guards and hotels staff do not become friendly. All the departments, when not in operation must be locked and key, after sealing, must be kept with the security officer. The employees must use only staff gate for coming and leaving the hotel. This gate must be manned by a security officer round the clock. Each staff member must be checked physically to ensure that they are not taking away hotel's property, maybe by mistake, like matchboxes, hand towels, knife etc. The stores must be locked after normal working hours and no unauthorised person should be allowed to enter. The cash book, keys, cheque, books, etc. must be kept in safe custody of the responsible person.

Supervision

The supervisors must authorise/approve all the transactions of the hotel. All cutting/overwriting must be countersigned. The power of the supervisors must be specified in writing to avoid confusion.

Financial Accuracy

The totals, calculations, pricing of each bill must be checked for its accuracy. The overcharging and under-charging are very bad for the hotel. The bank account must be reconciled on weekly basis. The checks and K.O.T.'s must be numbered. At the end of every month ledgers must be balanced and trial balance prepared.

To ensure the effective control, the staff must be regularly trained. It is rightly said that training is a continuous process; every employee must be trained for a minimum of 100 hours in a year. The new employees must be imparted training before putting them on the actual job. The old staff knowledge must be updated and in case of shifting to new systems/methods the staff must be trained and motivated. The supervisors and management must ensure that the systems developed by the hotel must be followed by everyone and this will always ensure the perfect internal control.

Characteristics of Internal Control

1. Experienced, Qualified and Trustworthy Personnel

The personnel should be well qualified, experienced and trustworthy and this helps in providing better services
than competitors. This also ensures in having a better internal control on
pilferages.

2. Division of Duty

The duties are segregated to improve the efficiency, quality and for controlling the pilferage.

3. Leadership

Board of Directors, General Manager and other managers and supervisors must lead the person by communicating the policies of the hotel to one and all and encourage the person to have the best output and control.

4. Organisational Structure

The chain of hotels or hotel as the case may be must have a clear organisational structure and the personnel must know from whom to take orders and whom to report.

5. Sound Practice

These are policy measures generally set up and implemented by the board of directors and other senior executives in order to create an environment which facilitates internal control.

6. Authorise Personnel

The management must authorise clearly the personnel for taking the certain decision. For example a person should be authorised to extend the discount, cancel a bill, extend complimentary food/room, etc.

7. Records

The records must be maintained to ensure internal control. The records like guest registration cards, bills, K.O.T's, control sheets, etc. Are not only maintained, checked, verified but are also stored for future references.

8. Manual Procedures

Each job should be reduced to writing. Log books must be maintained in each department. The manual procedures should list the details of each position including how and when to perform each task.

9. Control

Control includes security services and measures for protecting assets, stores, guest's valuables, etc. The security services, as far as possible, must be hired from professionals.

10. Budget

The Budgets like short-term, long-term, specific budgets, etc. Must be made for sale, cost, production etc. The budgets must be achievable but not achievable so easily. The goals of the hotel must be clearly mentioned and the goals must be made not only for sale, cost etc. but must also be made for controlling pilferages.

11. Reports

For each job reports, must be made and circulated among the executives of the hotel for information and control.

12. Independent Checks

The personnel responsible for performing the jobs should not be asked for the internal checks but internal checks must be performed by different personnel either from the permanent personnel employed in the hotel or sometimes maybe hired from outside.

CHAPTER TWENTY-FIVE

Unit 5: Ledger &Computerised Accounting

(Topics Covered: Types of ledger used in hotel. Point of sale. Property management system. Introduction to computerised accounting system)

Ledger

In order to ascertain the net effect of all the transactions relating to a particular account are collected at one place in the Ledger. A Ledger is a book which contains all the accounts whether personal, real or nominal, which are first entered in journal or special purpose subsidiary books.

A. Types of ledger used in hotel:

There are two types of ledgers in front office accounting system:

Guest Ledger – It refers to the set of accounts related to the registered hotel guests. It is also known as Transient ledger, Front Office ledger or Rooms ledger.

City Ledger – Also called the non-guest ledger, it is the collection of non-guest accounts.

B. Point of sale:

Point of sale is the interaction when and where a transaction occurs between a business and a customer. This is where the brand calculates how much is owed from the customers and the customer chooses a payment method.

What is a Point of Sale (POS) System?

A point of sale is the moment when a customer makes a purchase, changing the profits and inventory for the vendor and influencing the customer's relationship with the brand; a POS system is the operation through which that transaction is completed.

Simply put, a POS system is a central hub where businesses can easily operate and monitor sales and store data collected from each transaction to improve and manage business better for future transactions. This includes tracking inventory, collecting data for financial reports, and keeping track of customer information.

Hospitality point of sale systems are computerized systems incorporating registers, computers and peripheral equipment, usually on a computer network to be used in restaurants, hair salons or hotels. Like other point of sale systems, these systems keep track of sales, labor and payroll, and can generate records used in accounting and bookkeeping. They may be accessed remotely by restaurant corporate offices, trouble shooters and other authorized parties.

Point of sale systems have revolutionized the restaurant industry, particularly in the fast food sector. In the most recent technologies, registers are computers, sometimes with touch screens. The registers connect to a server, often referred to as a "store controller" or a "central control unit". Printers and monitors are also found on the network. Additionally, remote servers can connect to store networks and monitor sales and other store data.

Typical restaurant POS software is able to create and print guest checks, print orders to kitchens and bars for preparation, process credit cards and other payment cards, and run reports. In addition, some systems implement wireless pagers and electronic signature-capture devices.

In the fast food industry, displays may be at the front counter, or configured for drive-through or walk-through cashiering and order taking. Front counter registers allow taking and serving orders at the same terminal, while drive-through registers allow orders to be taken at one or more drive-through windows, to be cashiered and served at another. In addition to registers, drive-through and kitchen displays are used to view orders. Once orders appear they may be deleted or recalled by the touch interface or by bump bars. Drive-through systems are often enhanced by the use of drive-through wireless (or headset) intercoms. The efficiency of such systems has decreased service times and increased efficiency of orders.

Another innovation in technology for the restaurant industry is wireless POS. Many restaurants with high volume use wireless handheld POS to collect orders which are sent to a server. The server sends required information to the kitchen in real time. Wireless systems consist of drive-through microphones and speakers (often one speaker will serve both purposes), which are wired to a "base station" or "center module." This, in turn, will broadcast to headsets. Headsets may be an all-in-one headset or one connected to a belt pack.

In hotels, POS software allows for transfer of meal charges from dining room to guest room with a button or two. It may also need to be integrated with property management software.

Newer, more sophisticated systems are getting away from the central database "file server" type system and going to what is called a "cluster database". This eliminates any crashing or system downtime that can be associated with the back office file server. This technology allows 100% of the information to not only be stored, but also pulled from the local terminal, thus eliminating the need to rely on a separate server for the system to operate.

C. Property management system:

A **property management system (PMS)** is software that facilitates a hotel's reservation management and administrative tasks. The most important functions include front-desk operations, reservations, channel management, housekeeping, rate and occupancy management, and payment processing. Although PMS software mostly controls reservation and financial transactions, it may allow you to manage housekeeping and perform human resources management as well. In general, PMS facilitates the main processes in a hotel related to internal and external operations.

The Hotel PMS streamlines operations for front office staff and guest services in a hotel business to check-in and check-out guests, see room availability, make adjustments to existing reservations, and even can have back office functionality (schedule housekeeping or maintenance). With a central system, hoteliers can better manage and monitor the key metrics needed to run their business (e.g. average daily rate, occupancy, and RevPAR).

Here are some of the things a hotel PMS can do:

- Guest check-in and check-out
- Room availability
- Reservations management (both OTA and direct bookings)
- Rate management
- Billing, and scheduling
- Housekeeping/maintenance
- Channel management (e.g. Booking channels like Expedia, GDS, etc.)

- Check-in kiosk
- Payment processing

D. Introduction to computerised accounting system:

In computerized hotel accounting, all postings are done at the point of sale (POS) by means of electronic input of data from the revenue outlet. The audit in hotels is done after arbitrary time line known as *"end of the day "*. Most of the hotels set the end of the day after 11:59 p.m. or according to the policy or standard procedures set by management of the hotel.

Types of Account

The Hotel accounts are broadly classified as Guest Accounts and non-guest accounts (mostly referred as *Guest Folio & Non-guest Folio*)

Assigning billing numbers for different accounts:

The use of unique billing number alerts the guest accounting module to the type of account to be processed.

Example: - a 6-digit account number may signal a non-guest account. Similarly, a 4- digit number may signal an in-house guest account.

Folios:

Folios in most of the accounting modules are: -

Individual (Guest) Folios: assigned to in-house guest. The input involves the Room Number. The Room Number acts as the designated account number.

Master Folios: - These apply for more than one guest or Room. These are created for billing service required by groups, corporate clients, Event managers & MICE Companies Etc.

Employee Folios: - These folios offer charge privileges to hotel employees. The transactions are processed in a manner similar to non-guest accounts

Control Folios: - These folios are used to track transactions that are posted to other folios (Individual guest folio, Master folio, non-guest folio, or employee folio).

Control folio acts as a cross checking of all balances in all the electronic folios.

Example: -

Step 1: -When an in-house guest makes orders of a Screw Driver cocktail in the Bar, the amount is posted (debited) to the appropriate individual folio (Room Number being the reference point).

Step 2: - The same amount is simultaneously posted (credited) as a deferred payment to the control folio of the Bar outlet.

Tracking: - it also tracks allowances, discounts, or corrective vouchers prepared for the day [A correction voucher is a voucher that is used to rectify mistakes posted in a guest account on the same day. an Allowance voucher refers to the amount posted to a folio that cannot be rectified.]

§ It simplifies auditing function (because it serves as a powerful internal control document – in line with the principles of Double entry system)

Non-guest Folios: -

These folios are created for individuals who have in-house charge privileges but are not registered as guests in the hotel.

Example: - Health Club members, corporate clients, local celebrity Etc.

Non-guest account numbers are assigned at the time of creation pf accounts

CHAPTER TWENTY-SIX

Unit: 6 Night Auditing

(Topics Covered: Need of night auditing. Night auditors duties & responsibility. Reports prepared by night auditor)

Auditing is nothing but conducting **Financial inspection** of the organization. For a hotel business, the finance management starts at the front office. Accurate posting of transactions on the guest folios start at the front office, which is further carried to the back-office accounting department. The guest accounts are counterchecked on a daily basis during auditing.

Experts recommend the hotel management team to go through the night audit reports daily to get an insight of the hotel occupancy and finances.

What is Night Audit?

It is the process of auditing where the night auditor reviews all financial activities of the hotel that has taken place in one day.

The auditing process for the day is generally conducted at the end of the day during the following night, hence the name 'Night Audit'. It can be performed by the conventional method of using papers, receipts, vouchers, coupons, and files. But performing audit using modern PMS systems is easy, fast, and efficient.

Basic Activities During Night Audit:

The night auditor performs the following steps during night audit activity:

- *Posting accommodation and tax charges*
- *Accumulating guest service charges and payments*
- *Settling financial activities of various departments*
- *Settling the account receivables*
- *Running the trial balance for the day*
- *Preparing the night audit report*

The Need for Night Audit:

The objective of night audit is to evaluate the hotel's financial activities. Night audit not only reviews guest accounts by checking credits and debits but also tracks the credit limits of the guests and tallies projected and actual sales from various departments. Night audit reviews daily cash flow into and out of the hotel's account.

Night audit has a large significance in hotel business operations. The management body refers night audit report to plan future goals and control the expenses. The managers can react immediately on the acquired information.

Responsibilities of a Night Auditor:

Apart from the basic audit activities listed above, the night auditor carries out the following responsibilities:

- *Taking over from the last shift.*
- *Checking-in or checking-out the guests after 11:00 PM at night.*
- *Registering the guests.*
- *Allocating accommodations to the newly checked-in guests.*
- *Settling transactions in the newly created guest accounts.*
- *Verifying guest folios.*
- *Verifying room status report.*
- *Balancing all paperwork with the accounts in the PMS.*
- *Remaining liable for security of the premises.*
- *Handling guest accommodation keys.*
- *Taking backup of the PMS generated reports.*
- *Preparing lists of expected guest arrivals for the next day.*
- *Closing financial activities for a day.*
- *Starting financial activities for the next day.*
- *Receiving and recording bank deposits.*

Types of Night Audit Reports:

Today, the PMS helps night auditors to a great extent in auditing and generating accurate reports.

Here are some typical reports generated during night audit:

- **Night Audit Accommodation Report**: It gives a snapshot of the days when accommodations are occupied, the days when the accommodations are available, check-ins, check-outs, no-shows, and cancellations. This report can show further details for any of the items listed above.

- **Night Audit Counter Report**: It gives details on cash and credit card receipts and withdrawals.

· **Night Audit Revenue Report**: It delivers information on accommodation revenue, cancellation and no show revenue, and other POS revenue. Revenue generated through various agencies and bodies such as travel agents, corporate organizations, internet booking. etc., is also listed in this report.

· **Night Audit Tax Report**: Contains all the tax information on reservation revenue and other POS revenues such as VAT, luxury tax, and service tax.

· **Cashier's report**: It is the detailed list of cashier activity of cash influx and out flux, credit cards, and PMS totals. Cashier's report is very important part of the financial control system of a hotel. The front office manager reviews the night audit and looks for any divergences between the actual amount received and the PMS total.

· **Manager's Report**: It is a statistical list of previous day's occupancy. It includes details about available accommodations, occupied accommodations, sold and vacated accommodations, rack-rate, number of guests in the hotel, number of noshows, and so on.

· **General Manager's Report**: Each department in the hotel is required to send daily sales report to the front office. Using their information, a departmental total report is generated for the general manager's assessment. The General Manager determines the profit-generating departments and evaluates the success of sales and marketing.

· **High Balance Report**: This is a detailed report about the guests who have exceeded the credit limit set by the hotel management.

· **Ledger Balance Summary Report**: It displays the opening and closing balances for the Advance Deposit Ledger, Guest Ledger, and City Ledger.

· **Room Rate Audit Report**: It lists all rates that are applied to each guest and the difference from the rack rate with the predetermined rack code.

Balancing Night Reports:

Here are some formulae used to balance night audit:

Formula for Balancing Bank Deposit

The formula for balancing bank deposit is:

Total Bank Deposits

- Total Cash Sales

- Credit card received A/R

– Cash received A/R

= 0

Formula for Balancing Guest Ledger

The formula for balancing guest ledger is:
Total Revenue
- Paid-outs and non-collect sales
= Daily revenue
- Total cash income
- Today's outstanding A/R income
= 0

Formula for Balancing City Ledger
The formula for balancing city ledger is:
Yesterday's outstanding A/R
+ Today's outstanding A/R income
= Total outstanding A/R
- Credit card received and applied to A/R
– Cash received and applied to A/R
= balance of A/R

CHAPTER TWENTY-SEVEN

Unit 7: Room Rates

(Topics Covered: Fixing room rates. Basis of charging room rates. Calculation of single rate & double rate. Calculation of average room rate)

Room rate could be typically defined as the price or cost that is charged by the hotel or lodging industry for overnight lodging. Usually, the front office department and the sales and marketing department are responsible for ensuring effective room rate according to several market-sensitive aspects. The market sensitive factors basically include:

- Expected sale rooms.
- Expenses to beat market competition.
- Hotel operations.
- Tax investment opportunities.
- Price sensitivity.
- Marketing and sales endeavor.

Fixing room rates:

Determining a standard **room rate** is one of the challenging and tough jobs for hotel as designated room rate must be capable of generating revenue and compensate other costs of the hotel, such as administrative costs, overhead, and utility costs.

A hotel generally assigns a standard rate for each room category which is termed as the rack rate (a retail rate of guest room). Despite of its high charge; rack rate does not always ensure profit for the hotel. Rack rate for room could be varied due to the other room rate schedules along with room types, pattern, and designation.

Basis of charging room rates:

Room rates are basically established as part of the reservation process. Thus, the front office personnel must be skilled in assigning a special room rate during the registration process. Minimization and maximization of room rate depends respectively on the cost structure of the hotel and other competitive prices. The front office manager must consult with the hotel owners, general manager, and other department heads in case of maximization or minimization of competitor's room rate.

Calculation of Single rate & Double rate:

Even, in some special cases the front office manager or personnel is permissible to minimize the room rate then its standard rate. Front office department usually uses certain methods for establishing the room rate. Such as:

Rule-of-Thumb Method: Under this method room rate rates will be charged $1 for every $1,000 of construction and furnishing costs. Suppose, a new hotel has established where $ 30,000 construction cost has incurred, then under this method room rate will be $30. However, this method is now less applicable comparing to other methods.

Hubbart's Formula Method: Under this method, room rates are established based on certain factors. For example: operating expenses, revenue generated from other departments of hotel, expected return on investment etc. This method is very effective in determining average room rate. Hubbart's formula method depends on the front office to provide revenue to pay off operating expenses, overhead, and return on investment.

To determine the room rate, Hubbart's formula method basically applies the following steps:

- Figure out the expected profit, multiply the expected rate of return on investment with the total invest of the owner.
- Determine the pre tax profit, divide expected profit by 1 and deduct from the tax rate of the hotel.
- Figure out the fixed charges (ex- interest expense, depreciation, insurance, taxes of property, mortgage etc.) and management fees by subtracting from the pre tax profit.
- Determine operating expenses that are undistributed (ex- data processing, guesstimate administrative and general, human resource, marketing, accounting, utility etc) by subtracting from the fixed charges.
- Figure out income or loss which is derived from other revenue generated outlets, such as business center, food and beverage centers, telephone center and so on. And add this amount to the undistributed operated expense.

- Add the amounts arrived at step 2, 3, 4 and other operated losses and then deduct it from the amount arrived at step 5, to determine the income from required room department.
- Calculate the room department revenues by adding the required room department income, direct expenses of payroll and other expenses from room department and other direct expenses.
- Divide the amount arrived at step 7 by the estimated number of rooms to be sold, to determine the average room rate.

Market Tolerance: Market tolerance method is considered as the most time-consuming methods in establishing a hotel's average daily room rate. But, this method is established by estimating the competitive set (monitor the competitive price of same product) rather than scientifically approached. Management approaches this competitive set by considering the following areas:

- Compare the room rate with other competitive rate.
- Ensure more return on investment comparing to other hotels.
- Determine the occupancy percentage of both own and other comparable industries.
- Consider the emerged trend analysis of comparable industries.
- Compare maximization and minimization of room rate of other hotel industries in the market.

However, these methods for establishing room rate are not standard procedure or mandatory for each hotel. Room rate must be applied in way that it can ensure expected rate of investment by the hotel or the hotel owner. Room rate of each category should be considered and approached according to the current demand of the market.

<u>**Calculation of average room rate:**</u>

Average Room Rate: The average room rate (ARR) is an average selling price of all the paid rooms occupied.

The formula is as follows: **Rooms Revenue / Paid Rooms Occupied**

CHAPTER TWENTY-EIGHT

Unit 8: Yield Management

(**Topics Covered:** Meaning & importance in selling rooms)

Meaning of Yield Management:

Yield management is the technique which is used to increase the room revenue. In hotel industry yield management is also sometimes called revenue management. Hotel's daily performance like most of other industries is evaluated on the basis of either occupancy percentage or average daily revenue. The tariff may be reduced or discount percentage may be increased to increase the occupancy but it may not increase the revenue in the same proportion. Some hotels prefer to keep the tariff low in order to increase the occupancy percentage and on the contrary some hotels prefer to increase the tariff in spite of low occupancy percentage. The most appropriate room tariff will be which gets the maximum possible revenue and maximum possible occupancy percentage and this is called yield management.

Importance of Yield Management

1. Improved forecasting
2. Improved seasonal pricing
3. Identification of new market segments
4. Identification of market segment demands
5. Enhanced coordination between the front office and sales divisions
6. Determination of discounting activity

7. Improved development of short-term and long-term business plans
8. Establishment of a value based rate structure.
9. Savings in labour costs and other operating expenses
10. Planned responses to guest inquiries or requests regarding reservations.

Selling Rooms & Yield Management:

Yield management in the hotel industry is a dynamic pricing strategy for maximizing revenue from a fixed, time-limited inventory, such as hotel rooms.

It's based on understanding and predicting consumer behaviour to influence future hotel guests and generate maximum revenue per available room (RevPAR).

In simpler terms, yield management in hotels refers to selling the right room to the right customer at the right time and at the right price or rate.

It means that you can sell the same room to different guests at different rates, depending on the demand, your hotel's occupancy rate, the time of year, and many other factors.

But just because it boosts your profitability doesn't mean it's not beneficial to consumers as well.

If there are dips in demand, you can use yield management practices to offer rooms at discounted rates and attract more guests. That can lead to even more future bookings, as your customers would be thrilled to have paid less than usual to stay at your hotel.

The same goes for high demand. You can use yield management techniques during busy seasons to increase your room rates because it's highly likely your occupancy rates will be higher. Hence, you can boost revenue while helping customers make their desired bookings even during high demand.

The **key elements of hotel yield management** include:

- Group bookings
- Transient or FIT (Free Independent Traveller) rooms
- Food and beverage outlets
- Local activities and events

Group room sales can bring a lot of revenue to a hotel. To get the most out of them, your front office should collect data on group booking trends, lead time, and pace to forecast demand.

Transient or FIT rooms bring a higher revenue than group room bookings, as travellers typically book them closer to the arrival date. However, when demand is low, it can be wise to offer discounts.

Food and beverage outlets in a hotel can also impact room revenue. For instance, a group looking to book both rooms and catering services can bring in more revenue than one needing catering only with no room bookings.

Activities and events in or near your hotel (e.g., festivals, concerts, sporting events, etc.) can boost hotel revenue yield as well. Your front office should stay up-to-date with any and all events in the area to optimize the room rates according to the demand.

CHAPTER TWENTY-NINE

Unit 9: Ratio Analysis

(Topics Covered: Meaning of ratio. Profitability ratio. Turnover ratio)

<u>**Meaning of ratio:**</u>

A relationship between two quantities, normally expressed as the quotient of one divided by the other.

<u>**Ratio Analysis:**</u>

Definition: Ratio analysis is the process of examining and comparing financial information by calculating meaningful financial statement figure percentages instead of comparing line items from each financial statement.

Managers and investors use a number of different tools and comparisons to tell whether a company is doing well and whether it is worth investing in. The most common ways people analysis a company's performance are horizontal analysis, vertical analysis, and ratio analysis. Horizontal and vertical analyzes compare a company's performance over time and to a base or set of standard performance numbers.

What Does Ratio Analysis Mean?

Ratio analysis is much different. Ratio analysis compares relationships between financial statement accounts. This means that one income statement or balance sheet account is being compared to another. These relationships between financial statement accounts will not only give a manager or investor an idea of the how healthy the business is on a whole, it will also give them keen insights into business operations.

Example

Take inventory turns for example. Inventory turnover is the ratio between cost of goods sold and average inventory. Inventory turnover tells managers and investors not only how much inventory the company maintained, it also tells them how efficient the company was with its inventory. A high inventory turnover ratio means that the company is lean and is able to move its inventory quickly. This could indicate proper management and thoughtful inventory purchasing.

<u>Profitability ratio:</u>

Profitability ratios are a class of financial metrics that are used to assess a business's ability to generate earnings relative to its revenue, operating costs, balance sheet assets, or shareholders' equity over time, using data from a specific point in time.

Profitability ratios can be compared with efficiency ratios, which consider how well a company uses its assets internally to generate income (as opposed to after-cost profits).

<u>Turnover ratio:</u>

In accounting, turnover ratios are the financial ratios in which an annual income statement amount is divided by an average asset amount for the same year. Generally, the larger the turnover the better. The turnover ratios indicate the efficiency or effectiveness of a company's management.

How do you calculate turnover ratio? Inventory turnover indicates the rate at which a company sells and replaces its stock of goods during a particular period. The inventory turnover ratio formula is the cost of goods sold divided by the average inventory for the same period.

CHAPTER THIRTY

Unit 10: Departmental Accounting

(**Topics covered:** Introduction to departmental accounting. Allocation & apportionment of expenses. Basis of allocation. Method - Gross profit method, Net profit method)

<u>Introduction to Departmental Accounting:</u>

Departmental Accounting:

Department accounting or departmental accounting is a system of financial accounting which is used in the organizations whose all works are done through their different departments or departmental stores. Departmental accounts are prepared separately for each department and trial balance will also be prepared. Departmental P&L Account is prepared to ascertain the profit or loss of each department separately and at the end of the year it is transferred to General profit and loss account of the whole organization.

<u>Allocation & apportionment of expenses</u>

Cost Allocation:

Cost allocation is the process of identifying, aggregating and assigning costs to cost objects. A cost object is any activity or item for which you want to separately measure costs. Examples of cost objects are a product, a research project, a customer, a sales region, and a department.

Cost allocation is used for financial reporting purposes, to spread costs among departments or inventory items. Cost allocation is also used in the calculation of profitability at the department or subsidiary level, which in turn may be used as the basis for bonuses or the funding of additional activities. Cost allocations can also be used in the derivation of transfer prices between subsidiaries.

Apportionment:

Apportionment of costs is the process of sharing a group's expenditure among the individual funding streams/programmes being implemented. This process is generally used to cover central cost items such as salaries, general overhead and ongoing running costs.

Cost apportionment occurs when a specific cost cannot be directly identified with one specific cost centre. Any cost that does not belong to one department and is shared by a number of departments will be divided among these departments using apportionment.

Taking an example of the F&B manager's salary, such as expense would have to be apportioned (between Bar, Banquet, Restaurant etc.) depending on fair criteria. This could be something like the percentage of the manager's time taken up in each specific department. Other overheads that require apportionment include property rent, water and utility bills, general administration salaries, etc. Expenses such as rent, water and utilities can be fairly shared among departments by using a basis such as square feet per department space.

<u>Basis of Allocation:</u>

Normally, all direct expenses are charged to the respective departments, in case of indirect or general expenses, proper allocation among the departments must be made in order to ascertain the profit and loss made by each department. Each department is charged with proper business expenses.

Some expenses cannot be apportioned and no basis of apportionment is practicable. For instance, interest on Loan, Income Tax, Salary to General Manager, Share Transfer expenses, Bank charges, Audit fees etc. Here these expenses can safely be transferred to General Profit and Loss Account.

Similarly, income of general nature such as Interest on Calls-in-arrears, Interest on Investment, fees on share transfer etc. credited to General Profit and Loss Account. The Departmental Trading Account shows the Gross Profit or Loss and Departmental Profit and Loss Account shows the Net

Profit or Loss earned or suffered by each department.

Method:

I. Gross profit method

II. Net profit method

I. Gross profit method:

The gross profit method is a way of calculating the amount of ending inventory in a reporting period. It is used for monthly financial statements when a physical inventory is not possible, for interim periods between physical inventory counts, and when inventory has been destroyed by fire, theft, or other disaster and you need to estimate your losses for the purpose of insurance.

However, a gross profit method should not be used to determine year-end inventory, nor is it an acceptable method for tax purposes, or annual financial statements.

Gross profit method formula

To calculate the gross profit method, you need to follow these steps:

Add together the cost of beginning inventory and the cost of goods purchased during a period to get the cost of goods available for sale

Take the expected gross profit percentage of the total sales figure during a period to get the cost of goods sold

Then calculate the estimated cost of goods available for sale minus the estimated cost of goods sold to get the ending inventory

It can be helpful to compare the cost of goods sold as a percentage of sales with the recent trend line for the same percentage to see if the outcome matches.

II. Net profit method:

Net profit refers to the amount of money left over after various expenses have been subtracted from the total revenue. These expenses can include interest, operating expenses, taxes and more. Net profit is also known as the net income, bottom line and net earnings and is expressed in dollars. It is known as the bottom line since it can be found on the last line of a company's income statement.

A low or negative net profit is indicative of various issues such as less sales, poor management of expenses, poor marketing, ineffective pricing, poor customer service experience from employees and more. A high or positive net profit can be attributed to several favourable variables.

Net profit is important for several reasons. Ultimately, it helps determine a company's financial stability. Depending on your role in the business world, it can present various advantages. For example, investors use net profit to determine whether a company is worth the risk of investment. Creditors use it to determine whether they should offer a business loan. As a business owner, net profit helps you to assess where you stand financially in comparison to other similarly related businesses.

How to calculate net profit

For net profit to be useful, you'll need to know how to calculate it. Here are the various formulas you can use to calculate net profit:

net profit = total revenue - total expenses

You can also use the following formula:

net profit = gross profit - expenses

Part D: Business Communication

Business Communication

CHAPTER THIRTY-ONE

Unit 1: Introduction to Business Communication

(**Topics Covered:** Definition. Objectives. Principles of effective communication. Importance of good communication)

1.1.The main purposes of business communication are:

- To inform
- To request or persuade
- To build goodwill
- To encourage action
- To instruct
- To affirm shared goals

1.2. Definitions of Communication:

Communication is the sum of all the things one person does when he wants to create understanding in the mind of another. It involves a systematic and continuous process of telling, listening and understanding. (Louis A Allen)

Communication can be defined as the process through which two or more persons come to exchange ideas and understanding among themselves. The word Communication describes the process of conveying messages (facts, ideas, attitudes and opinions) from one person to another, so that they are understood. (M.W. Cumming)

Communication is the process whereby speech, signs or actions transmit information from one person to another. This definition is concise and definitive but doesn't include all the aspects of communication. There are other definitions, which state that communication involves transmitting information from one party to another. This broader definition doesn't require that the receiving party obtain a full understanding of the message. Of course, communication is better when both parties understand... but it can still exist even without that component

Communication is a process of transmitting and receiving verbal and non verbal messages that produce a response. The communication is considered effective when it achieves the desired reaction or response from the receiver, simply stated, communication is a two way process of exchanging ideas or information between human beings.

Communication can be defined as the process through which two or more persons come to exchange ideas and understanding among them. Communication is the understanding, not of the visible but of the invisible and hidden. These hidden and symbolic elements embedded in the culture give meaning to the visible communication process. Equally, if not of more importance is the fact that communication is a personal process that involves the exchange of behaviours.

No matter the type or mechanism of communication, every instance of communication must have a message that is being transferred from sender to receiver. In order for communication to be successful, the sender and receiver must have some signs, words or signals in common with each other so the sent message can be understood. The ideal definition of communication is a 2-way interaction between two parties to transmit information and mutual understanding between themselves. The interchange of information from one party to another is best communicated when a discussion is available so the receiver can ask questions and receive answers to clarify the message.

<u>There are at least three general types of communication goals:</u>

- Self Presentation Goals (who we are and how we want to be perceived),
- Relational Goals (how we develop, maintain, and terminate relationships),
- Instrumental Goals (how we manipulate others, gain compliance, manage interpersonal conflict, use and recognize interpersonal influence strategies (anchoring and contrast effects, reciprocity, commitment, liking, social proof, authority, and scarcity etc.)

<u>1.3. Objectives of Communication:</u>

Communication is the lifeblood of an organization. It is the vehicle that ensures proper performance of organizational functions and achievement of organizational goals. As a separate field of study, business communication has the following objectives:

a. **To exchange information**: The main objective of business communication is to exchange information with the internal and external parties. Internal communication occurs within the organization through orders, instructions, suggestions, opinions etc.

a. **To develop plans**: Plan is the blueprint of future courses of actions. The plan must be formulated for attaining organizational goals. In order to develop a plan, management requires information. In this regard, the objective of communication is to supply required information to the concerned managers.

c. **To implement the plan**: Once a plan is prepared, it is to be implemented. Implementation of a plan requires timely communication with the concerned parties. Thus, communication aims at transmitting a plan throughout the organization for its successful implementation.

d. **To facilitate policy formulation**: Policies are guidelines for performing organizational activities. Policies are also termed as standing decisions to recurring problems. Every organization needs to develop a set of policies to guide its operation. Preparing policies also require information from various sources. Therefore, the objective of communication is to collect necessary information for policy formulation.

e. **To achieve organizational goal**: Collective efforts of both managers and workers are essential for achieving organizational goals. Communication coordinates and synchronizes the efforts of employees at various levels to achieve the stated goals of the organization.

f. **To organize resources**: Various kinds of resources are available in organization such as human resources, material resources, financial resources and so on. In organizing these resources in an effective and efficient way is a key challenge to the managers. Communication is the vehicle to overcome this challenge.

g. **To coordinate**: Coordination is a basic management function. It involves linking the various functional departments of large organizations. Without proper and timely coordination, achievement of organizational goals is impossible. Therefore, the objective of communication is to coordinate the functions of various departments for the easy attainment of organizational goals.

h. **To direct the subordinates**: The job of a manager is to get the things done by others. In order to get the things done, management needs to lead, direct and control the employees. The performance of these managerial functions depends on effective communication with subordinates.

i. **To motivate employees**: A pre-requisite of employee motivation is the satisfaction of their financial and non-financial needs. Financial needs are fulfilled thorough monetary returns. However, in order to satisfy non-financial needs, management must communicate with employees on a regular basis both formally and informally.

j. **To create consciousness**: Employees of an organization must be conscious regarding their duties and responsibilities. Communication supplies necessary information and makes them conscious about their duties and responsibilities.

k. **To increase efficiency**: In order to increase employee efficiency, they should be provided with necessary information and guidelines. Communication supplies such information and guidelines for them.

ax. **To bring dynamism**: Organizations should be dynamic to cope with the internal and external changes. Bringing dynamism requires finding new and better ways of doing things. For this purpose, communication helps to seek new ideas and suggestions from the internal and external parties.

all. **To improve labour-management is relationships**: Harmonious relationship between workers and management is a prerequisite for organizational success. In this regard, the objective of communication is to ensure the free and fair flow of information and to create good understanding between them.

n. **To increase job satisfactions**: Communication enhances job satisfaction level of employees. It creates a friendly environment where employees can express themselves. As a result, they become more satisfied with their job.

- **To convey employee reaction**: Communication conveys employees' reactions, opinions, suggestions and complaints to their superiors about the plans, policies, programs and strategies of the company.

p. **To orient employee**: Communication orients the new employees with the company's policies, rules, regulations, procedures etc.

<u>1.4.. Principles of effective communication:</u>

In order to remove barriers to communication an open door communication policy should be prepared and followed by managers at all levels. The superiors in the organisation must create an atmosphere of confidence and trust in the organisation so that the credibility gap may be narrowed down.

<u>Major efforts in this direction are:</u>

(i) Two-way communication: The organisation's communication policy should provide for a two-way traffic in communication-upwards and downwards. It brings two minds closer and improves understanding between the two parties, the sender and the receiver. A should feedback system should be introduced in the organisation so that distortion in the filtering of damages should be avoided. There should be no communication gap.

(ii) Strengthening Communication Network: The communication network should be strengthened to make communication effective. For this purpose, the procedure of communication should be simplified; layers in downward communication should be reduced to the minimum possible. Decentralisation and delegation of authority should be encouraged to make information communication more efficient, through frequent meetings, conferences and timely dissemination of information to the subordinates.

(iii) Promoting Participative Approach: The management should promote the participate approach in management. The subordinates should be invited to participative in the decision-making process. It should seek cooperation from the subordinate and reduce communication barriers.

(iv) Appropriate Language: In communication certain symbols are used. Such symbols may be in the form of words, pictures and actions. If words are used, the language should be simple and easily comprehensible be avoided. The sender must use the language with which the receiver is familiar. The message should be supported by pictures or action, wherever necessary, to emphasise certain points. The sender must also practise in action what he says to others or expects from others.

(v) Credibility in Communication: One criterion of effective communication is credibility. The subordinates obey the orders of their superior because they have demonstrated through their actions that they are trustworthy. They must practices whatever they say. The superior must also maintain his trustworthiness. If the superior is trusted by the subordinates, communication will be effective.

(vi) Good Listening: A communication must be a good listener too. A good manager gives his subordinates a chance to speak and express their feelings well before him. The manager also gets some useful information for further communication and can also have a better understanding of the subordinates needs, demands etc.

(vii) Selecting on Effective Communication Channel: To be effective, the communication should be sent to the receiver though an effective channel. By effective channel we mean that the message reaches its destination in time, to the right person, and without and distortion, filtering or omission.

1.5. Importance of Good Communication:

Good communication has many advantages for a business:

- Motivates employees – helps them feel part of the business (see below)
- Easier to control and coordinate business activity – prevents different parts of the business going in opposite directions
- Makes successful decision making easier for managers– decisions are based on more complete and accurate information
- Better communication with customers will increase sales
- Improve relationships with suppliers and possibly lead to more reliable delivery
- Improves chances of obtaining finance – e.g. keeping the bank up-to-date about how the business is doing

Communication is to an organisation what the nervous system is to the human body. Effective Communication will lead to the smooth working of any organisation.

<u>The following points illustrate the importance of Communication in Business:</u>

- Smooth Working of a Business Firm
- Basis of Managerial Function
- Maximum Production and Minimum Cost
- Prompt Decision and its Implementation
- Building Human Relations
- Job Satisfaction and Good Morale
- Avoids Illusion
- Contacts with external Parties.

CHAPTER THIRTY-TWO

Unit 2: Types of Communication

(Topics Covered: Formal, Informal, Verbal, Written, Horizontal, Vertical)

2.1. Types of Communication:

Communication in an organization carries innumerable kinds of messages which may be difficult to map out; but it may be possible to classify communications in regard to how to transmit, or who communicates to whom, or what kinds of relationships communication develops. Thus communication may be grouped on the following basis:

2.1.1. On the basis of Direction of Communication:

(i) Downward Communication

(ii) Upward Communication and

(iii) Horizontal or Lateral Communication

2.1.2. On the basis of Way of Expression:

(i) Oral Communication and

(ii) Written Communication

2.1.3. On the basis of Organizational Structure:

(i) Formal Communication and

(ii) Informal Communication

On the basis of Direction of Communication:

(i) Downward Communication:

Downward communication occurs when information and messages flow down through an organization's formal chain of command or hierarchical structure. In other words, messages and orders start at the upper levels of the organizational hierarchy and move down toward the bottom levels. Responses to downward communications move up along the same path.

(ii) Upward Communication:

Communication is a very important part of working in the business environment. Managers must be able to communicate with employees and employees must be able to communicate with managers in order to have a profitable business. Upward communication is the flow of information from front line employees to managers, supervisors, and directors.

(iii) Horizontal or Lateral Communication

Horizontal communication is the transmission of information between people, divisions, departments or units within the same level of organizational hierarchy. You can distinguish it from vertical communication, which is the transmission of information between different levels of the organizational hierarchy. Horizontal communication is often referred to as 'lateral communication.'

On the basis of Way of Expression:

(i) Oral Communication:

It occurs through the spoken word. In oral communication, the two parties to communication, the sender and the receiver, exchange their views through speech, either in face-to-face communication between individual and individual, or between an individual and the group, or any mechanical or electrical device, such as a telephone, public address systems etc. meetings, conference, lectures, etc. are some other media of communication.

(ii) Written Communication:

The Written Communication refers to the process of conveying a message through the written symbols. In other words, any message exchanged between two or more persons that make use of written words is called as written communication. The written communication is the most common and effective mode of business communication. In any organization, the electronic mails, memos, reports, documents, letters, journals, job descriptions, employee manuals, etc. are some of the commonly used forms of written communication.

On the basis of Organizational Structure:

(i) Formal Communication:

The Formal Communication is the exchange of official information that flows along the different levels of the organizational hierarchy and conforms to the prescribed professional rules, policy, standards, processes and regulations of the organization. The formal communication follows a proper predefined channel of communication and is deliberately controlled. It is governed by the chain of command and complies with all the organizational conventional rules.

(ii) Informal Communication:

'Informal Communication' is the communication among the people of an organisation not on the basis of formal relationship in the organisational structure but on the basis of informal relations and understanding. It may overlap routes, levels or positions. Informal communication creates a situation where the different workers communicate with each other, work side by side, hour after hour and day after day irrespective of their formal positions and relationships. It is referred to as the 'grapevine' which indicates informal means of circulating information or gossip. It is direct, spontaneous and flexible. It is personal, unofficial, and mostly verbal.

2.2. Verbal and Non-Verbal communication:

Verbal communication, or communication through words, provides the opportunity for personal contact and two-way flow of information. A large part of our communication, whether at work or outside, is verbal in nature. Verbal communication in turn, may be divided into two areas – oral and written communication. Oral communication may be defined as a process whereby a speaker interacts verbally with one or more listeners, in order to influence the latter's behaviour in some way or the other. Oral communication in a business context can take the form of meetings, presentations, one-to-one meetings, performance reviews and so on.

Written communication is a process whereby a writer interacts verbally with a receiver, in order to influence the latter's behaviour. Written communication at the workplace can take several forms such as letters, memos, circulars, notices, reports and email. We will examine some of these in more detail in later chapters. Non-verbal communication, on the other hand may be defined as communication without words. It refers to any way of conveying meanings without the use of verbal language. The game of dumb charades is a perfect example. Non-verbal communication is generally unintentional, unlike verbal communication. All of us tend to communicate silently and unknowingly send signals and messages by what we do, apart from what we say. Gestures, facial expressions, posture and the way we dress, are all part of non-verbal communication. Non-verbal communication can have a greater impact than verbal communication, since —how you say something‖ is sometimes more important than —what you say. Although non-verbal communication can affect both our personal and business relationships, it is particularly important in the workplace.

2.2.1. Verbal Communication:

We communicate most of our ideas to others through verbal messages, i.e., through spoken or written messages. However, verbal messages have some drawbacks – the message may not be properly worded, or the message may be misunderstood, or interpreted differently from its intended meaning.

- **Avoid Words with Multiple Meanings:** Words sometimes tend to have different meanings in different cultures. Therefore, when communicating verbally, it is important to use words that are precise, unambiguous and have a single accepted meaning.

- **Ensure Clarity through Highly Specific Statements:** Instead of describing an object or idea in general terms or in abstract language, use highly specific language to avoid a variety of interpretations.

- **Avoid overuse of Jargon:** Jargon refers to technical terms or specialized vocabulary. Every profession has its own jargon which only experts in that field can understand. For example, IT experts use terms like —computer architecture‖ which the layperson may not understand. The use of jargon depends on the audience with whom you are communicating. A certain amount of jargon may be permissible when writing a technical report for example, but should be avoided when communicating with a general audience, since the terms may not be understood. Above all, never use jargon just to impress your audience.

- **Avoid Biased Language and Offensive Words:** Language has the power to arouse negative feelings, if it is not used with care. This can happen when the words used seem to be objective, but actually contain an intentional or unintentional bias.

2.2.2. Non-Verbal Communication:

Non-verbal communication can be defined as communication done without speaking or writing. Let us now take a look at some of its characteristics, which distinguish it from verbal communication.

- **Non-verbal Communication Cannot Be Avoided** – While one can avoid verbal communication by refusing to speak or write, it is not possible to do the same with non-verbal communication. That is because non-verbal communication is not always intentional, unlike verbal messages, as pointed out earlier. Sometimes, silence itself may convey a lot of meaning. Example – A speaker making a presentation may find that the audience is not very interactive. Instead he notices people yawning during his presentation. At the end of the session, when he asks for some feedback, there is total silence. The message conveyed in the above example is that the audience is bored with the session. The silence indicates that they have not listened to the session and that the feedback is negative.

- **Non-verbal Communication is Powerful** – Non-verbal communication helps us to form first impressions and make judgments of others. First impressions generally tend to be lasting impressions. Let us say you go for a job interview fifteen minutes late and dressed in informal attire. When asked some questions, you avoid eye contact. This immediately reflects on your attitude and the impression formed of you is that of a person who takes things casually, is insecure and lacks knowledge.

- **Non-verbal Communication is Ambiguous** – While precise words can be used in verbal communication to ensure that that the message is clearly understood, non-verbal communication is not always clear and easy to understand. For example, sitting back in a relaxed posture may be a signal of boredom or fatigue. Similarly, avoiding eye contact with your audience could mean that either you are nervous or guilty of something. Therefore, it is not possible to accurately understand the messages conveyed by non-verbal behaviour.

- **Non-verbal Communication Cannot Express All Messages** – Non-verbal behaviour can only express a person's feelings, attitudes, level of interest, liking or dislike for something. Certain messages about ideas or concepts can only be expressed through the spoken or written word. Consider the following, example-A sales manager wanting to report that sales for the current year has exceeded targets, can only do so through a written report or oral presentation. If he is making an oral presentation, his non-verbal behaviour can only indicate how pleased he is about the increase in sales.

- **Non-verbal Communication Varies Across Cultures** – While certain types of non-verbal behaviour are universal, others may be different in different cultures. Examples – There are different rules regarding the appropriateness of the handshake in oriental and western cultures. Generally, in oriental cultures like India, any form of physical contact is not common and is interpreted as being intimate, while it is an accepted thing in western countries. Similarly, a nod of the head means yes in some cultures and no in other cultures. In this age of business communication across cultures, it is important for you to understand these differences, especially when doing business overseas.

CHAPTER THIRTY-THREE

Unit 3: Essentials of good business letter and types of letters – Official, D.O

3.1 A business letter is usually used when writing from one company to another, or for correspondence between such organizations and their customers, clients and other external parties. The overall style of letter depends on the relationship between the parties concerned. Reasons to write a business letter include: to request direct information or action from another party, to order supplies from a supplier, to identify a mistake that was committed, to reply directly to a request, to apologize for a wrong, or to convey goodwill. A business letter is useful because it produces a permanent written record, is confidential, and formal.

The basics of good writing letters are easy to learn. The following guide provides the phrases that are usually found in any standard business letter. This basic of business letters are important because certain formulas are recognized and handled accordingly. Think of a basic business letter in three steps:

1. **Introduction** - *The reason for writing*

The introduction helps the reader understand in which context the letter should be considered. Possibilities include job interview inquires, business opportunity requests, complaints, and more. Each type of business letter has its own standard phrases.

2. **Details** - *What you would like to accomplish*

The detail section of a business letter is extremely important. This is where you achieve your goals in writing a business letter.

3. **Conclusion / Next Steps** - *What you would like to happen in the future*

Provide a call for future action. This can be a chance to talk in person, a follow-up letter or more. It's important and expected to make it clear what you would like for the next step from the person reading your business letter. The phrases presented in this guide provide a frame and introduction to the content of business letters. At the end of this guide, you will find links to sites that give tips on the difficult part of writing successful business letters - arguing your business objective. By using these standard phrases, you can give a professional tone to your English business letters.

3.2. Business Letter Formats:

E-mail may be the quick and convenient way to relay daily business messages, but the printed business letter is still the preferred way to convey important information. A carefully crafted letter presented on attractive letterhead can be a powerful communication tool. To make sure you are writing the most professional and effective letter possible, use the business letter format and template below and follow these basic business letter-writing.

Ø **Select a professional letterhead design:** Your business letter is a representation of your company, so you want it to look distinctive and immediately communicate "high quality." For a convenient and economical alternative to using traditional pre-printed letterhead, try using our contemporary letterhead and envelope design templates. Simply create a letter within a predesigned colour letterhead template and then print.

Ø **Use a standard business letter format and template:** The most widely used format for business letters is "block style," where the text of the entire letter is justified left. The text is single spaced, except for double spaces between paragraphs. Typically margins are about 1 inch (25.4 mm) on all sides of the document, which the default is setting for most word-processing programs. Business letter format illustrates the specific parts of a business letter:

Ø **Business Letter Template Fields:**

- **Date:** Use month, day, year format, e.g., December 3, 2013 or 3 December 2013
- **Sender's Address:** It is a good idea to include sender's email and url, if available. Don't include this information if it's already incorporated into the letterhead design. This will allow customers to find your small business more quickly.
- **Inside Address:** Use full name. Mr./ Ms. is optional

- **Salutation:** Be sure to use a colon at the end of the name, not a comma as in personal letters
- **Body Text:** State why you are writing. Establish any connection/mutual relationship up front. Outline the solution, providing proof in the way of examples and expert opinions. Group related information into paragraphs
- **Closing "Call to Action":** State what the reader needs to do and what you will do to follow up
- **Signature Block:** Sign your letter in blue or black ink
- **Enclosures:** Use if you have an enclosure
- **Carbon Copy:** Use if you are sending a copy to additional person(s)

Ø **Use a professional tone:** Save casual, chatty language for email - your printed business letter should be friendly but more professional. As Scott Ober suggests in his book Contemporary Business Communication, "The business writer should strive for an overall tone that is confident, courteous, and sincere; that uses emphasis and subordination appropriately; that contains non-discriminatory language; that stresses the "you" attitude; and that is written at an appropriate level of difficulty". That said, be sure to sound like yourself - you don't want your letter to read as if a machine wrote it.

Ø **Write clearly:** State your point early in your letter. To avoid any miscommunications, use straightforward, concise language. Skip the industry jargon and instead choose lively, active words to hold your reader's attention.

Ø **Organize your information logically:** Group related information into separate paragraphs. In a long, information-packed letter, consider organizing information into sections with subheads. You may want to highlight key words to make them "pop" - this technique is possible with most word-processing programs.

Ø **Use bold or Colour Font to Emphasize Words in Text:** It's easy to put a few words in bold or colour to draw attention to them.

Ø **Be persuasive:**

- Establish a positive relationship with your reader right away. If you have a connection to the reader - you've met before or have a mutual colleague, for example - mention it in your introductory paragraph. Whether you think your reader will agree with the point of your letter or not, it is important to find common ground and build your case from there.

- Understand your reader well enough to anticipate how he or she will react when reading your letter. Address his or her needs or wishes, or a specific problem, and then outline your solution. Provide proof in the way of examples and/or expert opinions to back up your point. Make sure to maintain a friendly tone.

· Conclude your letter with a "call to action." State clearly what your reader needs to do or believe to achieve the desired solution and then state what you, the writer, intend to do next to follow up.

Ø **Proofread your letter:** All your careful crafting and printing can't cover up spelling or punctuation errors, which leave a lasting negative impression.

3.3. Types of Business Letters:

Letter writing is a prized skill in the world of work. The higher you advance in your career, the more you will need to write letters. Letters are more formal and official than other types of business communication. They offer personal, verifiable authorization. Unlike e-mail, letters often must be routed through channels before they are sent out. Letters are the expected medium through which important documents such as contracts and proposals are sent to readers. There are four basic types of business letters: inquiry letters, special request letters, sales letters, and customer relations letters. Business letters can be further classified as positive, neutral, or negative. Inquiry and special request letters are neutral, sales letters are positive, and customer relations letters can be positive or negative.

Inquiry Letters: An inquiry letter asks for information about a product, service, or procedure. Businesses frequently exchange inquiry letters, and customers frequently send them to businesses. Three basic rules for an effective inquiry letter are to state exactly what information you want, indicate clearly why you must have this information, and specify exactly when you must have it.

Special Request Letters: Special request letters make a special demand, not a routine inquiry. The way you present your request is crucial, since your reader is not obliged to give you anything. When asking for information in a special request letter, state that you are, why you are writing, precisely what information you need, and exactly when you need the information (allow sufficient time). If you are asking for information to include in a report or other document, offer to forward a copy of the finished document as a courtesy. State that you will keep the information confidential, if that is appropriate. Finally, thank the recipient for helping you.

Sales Letters: A sales letter is written to persuade the reader to buy a product, try a service, support a cause, or participate in an activity. No matter what profession you are in, writing sales letters is a valuable skill.

<u>To write an effective sales letter, follow these guidelines:</u>

(1) Identify and limit your audience.

(2) Use reader psychology. Appeal to readers' emotions, pocketbook, comfort, and so on by focusing on the right issues.

(3) Don't boast or be a bore. Don't gush about your company or make elaborate explanations about a product.

(4) Use words that appeal to readers' senses.

(5) Be ethical. The "four A's" of sales letters are attention, appeal, application, and action. First, get the reader's attention.

Next, highlight your product's appeal. Then, show the reader the product's application. Finally, end with a specific request for action.

In the first part of your sales letter, get the reader's attention by asking a question, using a "how to" statement, complimenting the reader, offering a free gift, introducing a comparison, or announcing a change. In the second part, highlight your product's allure by appealing to the reader's intellect, emotions, or both.

Don't lose the momentum you have gained with your introduction by boring the reader with petty details, flat descriptions, elaborate inventories, or trivial boasts. In the third part of your sales letter, supply evidence of the value of what you are selling. Focus on the prospective customer, not on your company. Mention the cost of your product or service, if necessary, by relating it to the benefits to the customer. In the final section, tell readers exactly what you want them to do, and by what time. "Respond and be rewarded" is the basic message of the last section of a sales letter.

<u>Customer Relations Letters</u>: These deals with establishing and maintaining good working relationships. They deliver good news or bad news, acceptances or refusals. If you are writing an acceptance letter, use the direct approach-tell readers the good news up front. If you are writing a refusal letter, do not open the letter with your bad news; be indirect.

- **Follow-up Letters:** A follow-up letter is sent to thank a customer for buying a product or service and to encourage the customer to buy more in the future. As such it is a combination thank-you note and sales letter. Begin with a brief expression of gratitude. Next, discuss the benefits already known to the customer, and stress the company's dedication to its customers. Then extend this discussion into a new or continuing sales area, and end with a specific request for future business.

- **Complaint Letters:** These require delicacy. The right tone will increase your chances of getting what you want. Adopt the "you" attitude. Begin with a detailed description of the product or service you are complaining about. Include the model and serial numbers, size, quantity, and colour. Next, state exactly what is wrong with the product or service. Briefly describe the inconvenience you have experienced. Indicate precisely what you want done (you want your money back, you want a new model, you want an apology, and so on). Finally, ask for prompt handling of your claim.

- **Adjustment Letters:** Adjustment letters respond to complaint letters. For an adjustment letter that tells the customer "Yes," start with your good news. Admit immediately that the complaint was justified. State precisely what you are going to do to correct the problem. Offer an explanation for the inconvenience the customer suffered. End on a friendly, positive note. For adjustment letters that deny a claim, avoid blaming or scolding the customer. Thank the customer for writing. Stress that you understand the complaint. Provide a factual explanation to show customers they're being treated fairly. Give your decision without hedging or apologizing. (Indecision will infuriate customers who believe they have presented a convincing case.) Leave the door open for better and continued business in the future.

- **Refusal of Credit Letters:** Begin on a positive note. Express gratitude for the applicant for wanting to do business with you. Cite appropriate reasons for refusing to grant the customer credit: lack of business experience or prior credit, current unfavourable or unstable financial conditions, and so on. End on a positive note. Encourage the reader to reapply later when his or her circumstances have changed.

CHAPTER THIRTY-FOUR

Unit 4: Letter Writing

(Topics Covered: Circular, Memo, Notice, U.O. Note, Applications, Bio-data (C.V.), Covering letter, Invitations, Greetings, Apologies)

4.1. Circular:

A circular is generally understood as a written communication addressed to a circle of persons and customers. A circular may cover a notice or advertisements, etc., reproduced for distribution. The process of sending circulars is referred to as circularizing.

Circulars are a highly effective way to communicate with employees or customers. Many companies use circulars to enforce dress codes and policies or invite employees to meetings or luncheons. Circulars can also be used as an advertising tool.

There are a number of benefits to using circulars, but a circular must include certain features to be most effective. Additionally, distribution is important for circulars in business communication.

4.2. Memos:

Memo is a short form for memorandum.

It is derived from a Latin word *memorare* which is later changed to *memorandus* which literally means to provide information.

It is used for internal and intra-departmental communication. It provides information by a person or a committee to other people. It is normally used for making communication with one or two persons. Memo is less formal than a letter. The style, tone and format vary from that of the letter.

Also when a memo is sent to peers and juniors, it is more informal in style. When a memo is sent to seniors the tone varies and the style tends to be slightly more formal.

With the advent of intranet system in organizations, internal communication is made via networking. The advantage is it is instantaneous. Memos are useful for brief notes which need to be put n record. The conversational tone makes it more communicative and interactive, which is a welcome relief from the rigid and formal style of writing.

Correspondence between sections/departments in government offices continues to be through formal notes which invariably end with —Submitted for orders, or —Compliance should be ensured.

Though memos are official, the tone and style depends upon the relationship between the sender and the receiver. Conspicuously the pronouns I and You will be used. The obligatory components of a letter – salutation and complimentary close will not be used in a memo. Most of the companies have their own printed formats for memos. Even on a network, there will be standard formats. It will be easier to jot down a few lines on such printed forms and to send across. When compared with letters the format of a memo can have minor variations.

Normally the obligatory component will be the subject. Captions such as —urgent or —immediate could be added to indicate the nature of the memo. Memos could be used for passing on instructions, information or for making proposals. In government offices, they are used for conveying orders or calling for explanation.

Government offices still use colonial style of writing. They are always in third person and passive voice. —It is submitted‖ It has come to the notice of the undersigned —It has been decided —He should therefore explain as to why disciplinary action should not be taken against him etc are the usual expressions.

4.3. Notice:

Notice writing is a formal means of communication. The purpose of notice writing is to bring to notice a certain piece of information to a group of people. They are generally pinned in any common area where the concerned people can read it.

It is one of the common methods of communication. It gives important information about something that is about to take place or has taken place. It is usually meant for a wider audience and is put up in a public place for easy accessibility.

Notice is a formal, written or a printed announcement for the group of people. It is written in a very precise language avoiding any extra details.

Basically, notices are a tool of disseminating information regarding any occasion or issues. They reach a large number of people in less time that is why they are precise and brief in nature.

Format of a Notice

- Name of the Organisation - It refers to the name of the institution of which the person writing a notice is a part of. It is written on the top of the page, it helps the readers identify who issued the notice.
- Title - 'Notice'- This title says" notice', It lets the readers know that they are going to read the notice.
- Date - The date is written on the left corner of the notice after leaving a tile. As the notices are the formal communication, date of issuing a notice is very important. The date should be written in a proper format, which is clear and easily understandable.
- Heading - Heading explains what is the notice about in brief. Heading should reflect the content of the meeting. It is just like a 'subject' of an email, which gives a synopsis or purpose of the communication
- Body - Body of the notice includes the main content for which the notice was issued. The body should contain all the necessary information required in the notice like time of an event, venue of the event and a date and it should be written in a passive voice without the use of first-person.

4.4. U.O. Note: (Un-Official Note):

This form of communication is used within the office. This is mostly used in Secretariat between the secretariat departments. It is also used in Heads of Departments.

One way is to send the file to the concerned section for their remarks. The other way is we obtain the information by sending a U.O. Note.

How it should be written?

1. The U.O. Note No. is given on the top with date. This is the file number as indicated in the note file and the date of approval of the communication indicated.

2. The address entry of the person to whom it is intended is indicated at the left hand side bottom after the body of the U.O. Note as in the case of a Memo & D.O. letter.

3. Unlike in the letter, no salutations are used.

4. After the words the "subject" is indicated. (Generally the subject will be the same that is noted in the Personal register and the note file)

5. Immediately after the subject, Reference is indicated. Here all the references that are required for following the case should be given.

6. Body of the U.O. Note in convenient paragraphs comes next.

7. Bears no subscription except the designation of the signatory.

8. Signed by Designation of the officer approving it.

9. Indication of Enclosures at the left end of the body. Purpose to obtain the advice, views, concurrence or comments on a proposal or to seek clarification of rules, instructions this form of communication is addressed to other sections.

Though the name is Un-official note, it is used to obtain information within the organization and it is not something un-official.

4.5. Applications or Cover Letters:

Definition: A letter of application, also known as a cover letter, is a document sent with your resume to provide additional information on your skills and experience.

A letter of application typically provides detailed information on why are you are qualified for the job you are applying for. Effective application letters explain the reasons for your interest in the specific organization and identify your most relevant skills or experiences.

Your application letter should let the employer know what position you are applying for, why the employer should select you for an interview, and how you will follow-up.

When writing an application letter you should include:

- First Paragraph: Why you are writing - mention the job you are applying for and where you found the listing.
- Middle Paragraph(s): What you have to offer the employer - mention why your skills and experience are a good fit for the job.
- Last Paragraph: Say thank you to the hiring manager for considering you and note how you will follow up.

4.6. Resume:

- It signifies a summary of one's employment, education, and other skills
- It is used in applying for a new position.
- A resume seldom exceeds one side of an A4 sheet, and at the most two sides.
- It does not list out all the education and qualifications, but only highlight specific skills customized to target the job profile in question.

• A resume is usually broken into bullets and written in the first person to appear objective and formal.

A good resume starts with a brief Summary of Qualifications, followed by Areas of Strength or Industry Expertise in keywords, followed by Professional Experience in reverse chronological order. Focus is on the most recent experiences, and prior experiences summarized. The content aims at providing the reader a balance of responsibilities and accomplishments for each position. After Work experience come Professional Affiliations, Computer Skills, and Education.

Types of Resume:

Chronological Resume:

• Lists your work history in reverse chronological order (most recent first).

• A resume format preferred by many employers

• The preferred format for undergraduate to use

• Works best for those who have progressed in titles and have a good work history

Functional resume:

• Centres around skill areas that relate to the position for which you're applying.

• Works well for those with limited education, significant employment gaps, lack of work experience or experience in a different field.

• This format can be used both by recent graduates and career changers.

• If someone likes to use a functional format, must seek assistance from a career adviser for feedback.

Combination resume:

• Combines both detailed work history and skills

• Usually includes a 'skill summary' or 'highlights' near the top.

• Skills section must be kept short, somewhere in four to six bullets

Mega resume:

• Lists skills, work experience, honours and awards, activities, internship, education, hobbies and interests

• Includes anything that an employer would want to know

• Easily customizable, i.e, each resume for each employer; and include only relevant information.

4.7. Invitations:

Written invitations signal to guests that the occasion is special, not just a routine gathering. And replying in kind is a great way to express your gratitude for your host's forethought and hospitality.

Formal **invitations** are standard for events that call for formal or cocktail dress, such as weddings. Addresses, dates, and times are typically spelled out. A formal invitation card should use third person (e.g., they, their) rather than first (e.g., I, we, my, our) and include the full names of the event's hosts. Letters may use first person, typically *we*, but should still maintain a formal tone. For social invitations, you may follow modified block format and omit the recipient's address.

Informal **invitations** are appropriate for more casual events, such as a picnic or a baby shower. They are usually written in a conversational tone. Informal invitation cards may be written in first person.

When you send an invitation, state the purpose, location, date, and time of the event, and include the host's contact information (address and phone number; email optional) in order for guests to RSVP.

Note: RSVP: Répondez s'il vous plaît; please reply (used at the end of invitations to request a response).

4.8. Greetings:

Greetings are the way we communicate; we convey good wishes and congratulate others. When someone achieves well in their lives, or they have come across something very new. Presently, greeting anyone is very easy and quick through messaging, but the best is the traditional way we follow is writing letters. However, It gives a feeling of affinity to whom you are writing and to the one who is receiving.

The greeting letters are welcomed in every field, either official or personal. The only difference is how you write and the tone you use if its formal or informal. The format of style could be the same, but the words you use matter.

Personal Greetings

When to use a person's first name: If you are writing to someone in a professional capacity that you have known personally for many years, it is appropriate to use only their first name.

Professional Greetings

When to use a professional greeting: If you don't know the person well, it is best to use Mr., Ms., or Dr. as an appropriate business letter salutation. If you have any doubts about which greeting you should use, err on the side of caution and use the more formal style of address.

Use a Formal Salutation

Keep it formal: Try to avoid the temptation to begin your professional letter with informal salutations like "Hello," "Greetings," "Hi There," or "Good Morning" if you don't know the name of your contact person.

While those informal greetings are fine for casual emails to friends or even for more formal emails you might send to groups of people, in a professional letter you'll need to use a personal salutation with either a first and/or last name ("Dear Mr. Doe") or a job title ("Dear Hiring Manager").

4.9. Apologies:

An Apologize Letter/Sorry Letter, as the name states, is used to apologize to someone for one's mistake. It can also be used to mend broken or troubled relationships between individuals. In the corporate world, an apology letter becomes a permanent record of an event and the consequent response to it, hence, it is important to draft the letter accurately and professionally.

Furthermore, there are a few etiquettes to be followed when drafting an apology letter. One of the most important etiquettes is to not get defensive. It is only natural to get defensive and justify your actions, but that does not constitute an apology. Another important aspect of a good apology is to accept responsibility for your actions. Do not try and justify as it will just make the apology seem forced and not genuine. If required, do explain and make the person understand what exactly happened, but do not try to deflect the blame. Lastly, read through the Apologize letter, letter of apology format once again before sending it.

Guidelines for an Effective Apology Letter:

- An apology letter is a formal document, hence, ensure that the tone and language is formal
- Apologize for the event and take responsibility.
- Describe the details of the event if required. However, do not try and justify
- Present a plan or a course of action for the mistake
- Ensure or convince the person that the mistake will not repeat itself in the future
- Proofreading for spelling and grammatical errors before sending it in.

CHAPTER THIRTY-FIVE

Unit 5: Communication with Guest and Body language

(**Topics Covered:** Effective Speaking – Polite and effective enquiries & responses, Addressing a group, Listening and note taking skills, Body language- Importance & application.)

5.1. Effective Speaking:

Some speakers are better than the other in getting across their messages, while the others are not that convincing in their oral communication. But according to experts we all can acquire the qualities of a good public speaker with learning and practice.

But before that we have to know what essential qualities churn out an outstanding public speaker.

- **Clear**
- **Relevant**
- **Insightful**
- **Succinct (To the point)**
- **Practiced**
- **Energetic**
- **Respectful**

Clear – If you're even slightly vague in your own mind about your core message, or you don't deliver your message in a logical order, with clear transitions from one point to the next – your audience will be confused. It does take time to work all this through, but it's really important. Content is usually the reason why you and your audience are in the same room and thinking it through well enough beforehand makes all the difference to your reception as a speaker.

Relevant – You need to know your audience, in as much detail as possible. Audiences are sophisticated, and don't appreciate generalities. Tailor what you're going to say by doing as much research you need to beforehand.

You cannot motivate, inspire, inform, or expect your listeners to 'buy in' to your ideas:

A. Unless you talk their language.

B. If you don't speak at their level of understanding on the subject.

C. If you use jargon and words unfamiliar to them.

Insightful – dictionary.reference.com defines the word 'insightful' as — the ability to perceive clearly or deeply; penetration. And Scott Berkun in his great book Confessions of a Public Speaker (O'Reilly 2010) goes so far as to say this: —The problem with most bad presentations I see is not the speaking, the slides, the visuals, or any of the things people obsess about. Instead, it's the lack of thinking.

Succinct – When you're listening to a speaker, no matter how interesting, isn't it true that when they say the magic words —to sum up‖ or —finally‖, you wake up? It just seems to be human nature, and one of the best ways to respect your audience is to be as brief as possible!

Practice – This is absolutely crucial. And it must be done out loud, at least part of the time. Yes, this is tedious, and most people don't do it, which is why it's a characteristic of good speakers.

Energy - Your audience follows your cue: every group who doesn't know you will be cool to start with, we're all metaphorically taking a step back and assessing, in the early moments of hearing a new speaker. But if you show some energy, some life-force, the audience will follow you. You need to set the tone. You can also gain energy from your audience (a topic for another day!).

Respect – Every member of your audience wants to feel respected by you as the speaker. And this applies even more as a speaker if an audience member is rude or difficult. No matter how much you want to retaliate, remember that an audience will feel —as one‖ to some extent, and if you get tetchy with one person, they will potentially all be offended. So even if someone hits your hottest button, continue to be pleasant. That way, you'll gain the respect of the group, and potentially avoid crashing in flames, too!

<u>**5.2. Listening and note taking skills:**</u>

Good note taking involves effective listening that includes concentrating on, selecting, summarizing, and finally, evaluating what is being said by the lecturer. The key to effective listening is to be an ACTIVE listener.

<u>Suggestions to improve your listening skills:</u>

1. Be prepared. Survey relevant test materials and notes. The more you know, the more interested you will be. Participate in an exchange of ideas rather than a bombardment of unfamiliar ideas and unrelated facts.

2. Acquaint yourself with a lecturer's general lecture method and mannerisms. Pay attention to style, tone inflection of voice, pauses, accentuation of words, and nonverbal cues. Use these as signals for identifying important points.

3. Try not to be affected or distracted by lecturer's mannerisms.

<u>Note taking:</u>

Effective note taking involves extracting and recording the important ideas covered in lecture in a way that will help you to recall them. Good notes provide a valuable means for review and learning, and can increase the probability of doing well on an exam.

<u>Suggestions to Improve your Note taking:</u>

1. Think before writing. Relate what is being said to what you already know or have reviewed. Use your own interests/needs as well as information common to the course to guide your thoughts.

2. Preparing for class is an aid in helping you to become aware of the major concepts and in deciding what to record.

3. Be selective. Listen to everything, but do not try to write it all down. Search for the main ideas and sort out the important sub points and details. Notes should be brief, legible and consistent.

4. Take accurate notes. Use our own words, but don't waste time thinking of synonyms. Lecturer's terms may be simplified later. Use brackets to separate your own ideas from those of the lecturer.

5. Abbreviate words whenever possible, but be consistent.

6. Don't worry about missing a point. Leave spaces and fill what you missed later. Also, leave spaces for expanding and clarifying notes.

7. Record all important facts: dates, names, places, formulas. Copy diagrams and illustrations which will clarify your notes.

8. Draw a single line through mistakes, rather than erase or black out completely. This saves time and energy, and you may find later that the mistakes may have been important to record after all.

9. Integrate lecture notes with text material. This is helpful for clarification and retention of material. If text material is repeated in the lecture, you can make a notation for later referral to the text. Be sure to note supplementary examples or elaborations.

10. Review notes after class. Reread and edit your notes as soon as possible while the information is still fresh in your mind, adding and clarifying in order to increase your understanding. Write a summary (a paragraph or two) or formulate a summary question at the end of your notes to consolidate ideas and to reflect the relationship of facts and ideas with each other and as a whole.

5.3. Body language:

Body language is a form of non-verbal communication. Body language is about using behaviour to communicate. Both people and animals use this form of communication. Part of this behaviour is done subconsciously. It is therefore different from communicating using sign language, for example. Communication using sign language is intentional, body language is not. The forms of behaviour used in body language include body posture, gestures, facial expressions, and eye movements.

Body language may provide clues as to the attitude or state of mind of a person. For example, it may indicate aggression, attentiveness, boredom, a relaxed state, pleasure, amusement and intoxication. Language is significant to communication and relationships. It is relevant to management and leadership in business and also in places where it can be observed by many people. It can also be relevant to some outside of the workplace. It is commonly helpful in dating, mating, in family settings, and parenting.

Although body language is non-verbal or non-spoken, it can reveal much about your feelings and meaning to others and how others reveal their feelings toward you. Body language signals happen on both a conscious and unconscious level.

We all subconsciously give away hints as to our true feelings, through our movements and gestures. Some important body gestures are as follows:

1. **Gesture:** Brisk, erect walk. **Meaning:** Confidence

2. **Gesture:** Standing with hands on hips. **Meaning:** Readiness, aggression

3. **Gesture:** Sitting with legs crossed, foot kicking slightly. **Meaning:** Boredom

4. **Gesture:** Sitting, legs apart. **Meaning:** Open, relaxed

5. **Gesture:** Arms crossed on chest. **Meaning:** Defensiveness

6. **Gesture:** Walking with hands in pockets, shoulders hunched **Meaning:** Dejection

7. **Gesture:** Hand to cheek. **Meaning:** Evaluation or thinking

8. **Gesture:** Touching, slightly rubbing nose. **Meaning:** Rejection, doubt or lying

9. **Gesture:** Rubbing the eye. **Meaning:** Doubt or disbelief

10. **Gesture:** Hands clasped behind back. **Meaning:** Anger, frustration, apprehension

11. **Gesture:** Locked Ankles. **Meaning:** Apprehension

12. **Gesture:** Head resting in hand, eyes downcast. **Meaning:** Boredom

13. **Gesture: Rubbing Hands. Meaning:** Anticipation

14. **Gesture:** Sitting with hands clasped behind head, legs crossed. **Meaning:** Confidence, superiority.

15. **Gesture:** Open palms. **Meaning:** Sincerity, openness, innocence

16. **Gesture:** Pinching bridge of nose, eyes closed. **Meaning:** Negative evaluation

17. **Gesture:** Tapping or drumming fingers. **Meaning:** Impatience

18. **Gesture:** Stapling fingers. **Meaning:** Authoritative

19. **Gesture:** Patting/fondling hair. **Meaning:** Lack of self confidence, insecurity

20. **Gesture:** Quickly tilted head. **Meaning:** Interest

21. **Gesture:** Stroking Chin. **Meaning:** Trying to make a decision

22. **Gesture:** Looking down, face turned away. **Meaning:** Disbelief

23. **Gesture:** Biting nails. **Meaning:** Insecurity, nervousness

24. **Gesture:** Pulling or tugging at ear. **Meaning:** Indecision

25. **Gesture:** Prolonged tilted head. **Meaning:** Boredom

Unit 6: Speech Improvement

(Topics Covered: Pronunciation, stress, accent. Importance of speech in hotels. Common phonetic difficulties. Connective drills exercises. Introduction to frequently used foreign sounds.)

6.1. Pronunciation, Stress, Accent:

(i) Clear Pronunciation: the first important prerequisite of effective oral communication is that words should be pronounced clearly and correctly. Oral messages are often misunderstood because the speaker doesn't talk distinctly. Inability to use the jaws freely, to speak with a limber tongue and limber lips, and to speak slowly often makes for poor oral transmission. If a person tries to talk as fast as he thinks, his words will run to gather and get rammed into one another, so that when he intends asking 'what did you have?' He will succeed only in saying 'wajuhave?'

(ii) Appropriate Word Choice: Words have different meanings for different people. So it is important to be careful in the choice of words. The speaker, while speaking something, knows what he means, so he presumes that his listener also does so, which may be a wrong presumption. In oral communication it is more important to use the terms familiar to the listener rather than the terms that are familiar to the speaker.

(iii) Natural Voice: Some speakers deliberately cultivate an affected style under the impression that it would make them look more sophisticated. Nothing is farther from truth, and nothing impresses so much as the natural way of speech. One of the manuals for office employees in an American firm says, "The most effective

speech is that which is correct and at the same time natural and unaffected. Try to tone down an unusual accent and discard all affectations of speech. Try to cultivate a pleasing voice and speak clearly and distinctly."

6.1. Importance of speech in hotels:

Good communication has many advantages for a business: strong communication:

- Motivates employees – helps them feel part of the business (see below).
- Easier to control and coordinate business activity – prevents different parts of the business going in opposite directions.
- Makes successful decision making easier for managers– decisions are based on more complete and accurate information.
- Better communication with customers will increase sales.
- Improve relationships with suppliers and possibly lead to more reliable delivery.

Importance of speech in hospitality Industry: The hospitality industry is a very fast-paced environment that deals with people on a daily basis. Hospitality staffs are not sitting behind a computer sending emails; they are interacting with customers every minute. Customers expect to receive exceptional service when staying at a hotel, visiting a restaurant, or flying on a plane. Without communication, this is not possible.

Communication with Customers:

The first critical part of communication in the hospitality industry is the communication with customers. The hospitality industry is also known as the service industry. In order to provide service to customers, there has to be communication. Customers have to communicate with service staff in order to make reservations for hotels, airlines, and restaurants. The service professionals in the hospitality industry need to be able to speak to customers and provide information.

For example, when checking into a hotel, if there is not clear communication with the customer, then the customer will not know where their room is located or how to get there. This needs to be communicated to them when they check in.

Also, if a customer has an issue, it is vital that the service staff communicate effectively in order to resolve the issue. For example, let's say that you are at a restaurant and your order is incorrect. The server needs to communicate to you that they are going to fix the situation and apologize for the error. If the server is not able to communicate properly in this situation, it could cause bigger issues.

Communication with Co-workers:

In addition to communicating with the customer, the staff and management need to be able to communicate with each other as well. In our example about the restaurant, the situation could have been a communication error that caused the wrong order to be served. It could have been avoided if proper communication was used between the server and the kitchen staff.

Also, managers will find that if proper communication is used between staff and management, they will have a better working atmosphere. If the information is not communicated to the staff, they may become frustrated with their jobs. For example, let's say that a restaurant keeps running out of items on the menu. If the servers are not told about these items, it can become frustrating for them when they are serving tables. This is why it is important for everyone to communicate in order to make it more efficient for both the staff and the customers.

There are two key elements of good communication across the board:

1. Training

The first tip is to make sure the staff is provided with proper training. For example, restaurants need to make sure the staff is trained on the menu so they can communicate with the customers about it. If a customer has a question about a menu item, the staff will not be able to explain it if they have not been trained properly. Hotels need to train their staff on the aspects of the hotel, including the location of rooms, restaurants, pools, and anything else they might need to explain to a customer.

2. Clear and Concise

In the hospitality industry, it is also important to keep communication clear and concise, whether dealing with the customers or the staff. If a restaurant server talks for twenty minutes about the specials, the chances are that the customer will be overwhelmed and forget what was said. If management holds long meetings with detailed information, the staff might not retain all of it. These situations are why it is important to keep communication clear and concise.

6.3. Common phonetic difficulties:

Spelling words in English is challenging work. As a matter of fact, many native speakers of English have problems with spelling correctly. One of the main reasons for this is that many, many English words are NOT spelled as they are spoken. This difference between pronunciation and spelling causes a lot of confusion. The combination "ough" provides an excellent example:

- Tough - *pronounced - tuf (the 'u' sounding as in 'cup')*
- Through - *pronounced - throo*
- Dough - *pronounced - doe (long 'o')*
- Bought - *pronounced - bawt*

Most Important Rules for Avoiding Common Spelling Mistakes
It's enough to make anyone crazy! Here are some of the most common problems when spelling words in English.

Three Syllables Pronounced as Two Syllables

- Aspirin - *pronounced - asprin*
- Different - *pronounced - diffrent*
- Every - *pronounced - evry*

Four Syllables Pronounced as Three Syllables

- Comfortable - *pronounced - comfrtable*
- Temperature - *pronounced - temprature*
- Vegetable - *pronounced - vegtable*

Words That Sound the Same (Homophones)

- two, to, too - *pronounced - too*
- knew, new - *pronounced - niew*
- through, threw - *pronounced - throo*
- not, knot, naught - *pronounced - not*

Same Sounds - Different Spellings

'Eh' as in 'Let'

- let
- bread
- said

'Ai' as in 'I'

- I
- sigh
- buy
- either

The following letters are silent when pronounced.

- **D** - sandwich, Wednesday
- **G** - sign, foreign
- **GH** - daughter, light, right
- **H** - why, honest, hour
- **K** - know, knight, knob
- **L** - should, walk, half
- **P** - cupboard, psychology
- **S** - island
- **T** - whistle, listen, fasten
- **U** - guess, guitar
- **W** - who, write, wrong

Unusual Letter Combinations

- **GH** = 'F': cough, laugh, enough, rough
- **CH** = 'K': chemistry, headache, Christmas, stomach
- **EA** = 'EH': breakfast, head, bread, instead
- **EA** = 'EI': steak, break
- **EA** = 'EE': weak, streak
- **OU** = 'UH': country, double, enough

6.4. Connective drills exercises:
1. Stressing individual words incorrectly:

If you usually speak with native English speakers, this will be the number one reason why they misunderstand you. It's very hard for native English speakers to 'translate' a word spoken as 'caLENdar' to the way they would pronounce it, 'CALendar'.

Non-native English speakers don't have as much of a problem with this, and will probably still understand what you're trying to say.

<u>Quick fix:</u> Listen carefully to the way people around you pronounce their words. If you hear a pronunciation that is different from yours, check the dictionary (even if it's a common word) to be sure that you're stressing it correctly. Some commonly mis-stressed words that we hear (with proper stress in capitals) include: PURchase, COLleague, phoTOGraphy and ecoNOMic.

2. Stressing the wrong words in a sentence:

Remember that you can completely change the meaning of a sentence by stressing different words in that sentence. For example, you could say this sentence in a number of different ways:

"I didn't say we should drive this way."

If you stress **I**, you emphasize that taking that route wasn't your idea. On the other hand, if you stress **drive**, you emphasize the mode of transport.

If you don't pay close attention to the words that you stress, you could end up sending a completely different message than the one you intended.

<u>Quick fix:</u>
Think about placing added emphasis on the word that is most important to your meaning. You can add emphasis by lengthening the word, saying it slightly louder and/or changing the pitch of your voice slightly.

3. Pronouncing certain consonant sounds incorrectly:

If people are misunderstanding you, it could very well be due to you confusing what is called 'voiced' and 'unvoiced' sounds. You might substitute 'p' for 'b' or 't' for 'd', for example. These sounds are so easily confused because their only difference is whether or not you use your voice to produce them. If you aren't careful, you could be making mistakes like saying 'tuck' for 'duck' or 'pay' for 'bay'.

<u>Quick fix:</u>
Pay attention to how you use your voice when you speak. You should be able to feel the vibration of your vocal cords when you make voiced sounds (b, d, g, v, z, r, l, m, n, ng, dge, zh, and voiced th). You can also try to make lists of pairs of words that use the sounds you find challenging and practice

repeating those. Record yourself so you can hear whether you're making any progress.

4. Mixing up short and long vowel sounds:

Vowel sounds, like consonant sounds, can also be confused easily. The main problem with vowels happens when you mix up long and short vowel sounds. For example, the long 'ee' sound in 'seat' with the short 'i' sound in 'sit.' If you confuse these sounds, you end up saying completely different words. This can get confusing in conversation and forces people to draw much more from the context of your speech than the speech itself.

Quick fix:

Make practice word lists like the ones you made for the consonant sounds and practice the sounds that are difficult for you.

5. Forgetting to finish your words:

Do you have a tendency to let your word endings drop? We often hear people drop the 'ed' ending off of words in the past tense, for example. This is a dangerous mistake because not only is your pronunciation wrong, but it also sounds like you're making a grammatical mistake. People could judge you based on this type of error.

Quick fix:

Do everything you can to articulate your word endings. One exercise that might help is to move the word ending onto the front of the following word. This will only work if the following word begins with a vowel sound. For example, try saying 'talk tuh lot' instead of 'talked a lot'.

6.5. Introduction to frequently used foreign sounds:

- **Ad nauseam:** From Latin meaning to a sickening degree. "Tom talked ad nauseam about the time he scored the winning run."
- **Bon voyage:** From French meaning has a nice trip. "We all shouted 'bon voyage' as Rosa left for her vacation."
- **Bona fide:** From Latin meaning genuine. "Emma's teacher was a bona fide expert in European history."
- **Carte blanche:** From French meaning unlimited authority. "As the owner of the store, Mr. Williamson had carte blanche regarding what merchandise to sell."
- **Caveat emptor:** From the Latin meaning let the buyer beware. "I learned what caveat emptor meant the hard way when I bought a bike that never seemed to work right."

- **En masse**: From French meaning in a large group. "The fans left the football stadium en masse once the score became 42 to 0."
- **Fait accompli**: From French meaning established fact. "Luis was disappointed, but his losing the election for class president was a fait accompli."
- **Faux pas**: From French meaning a social blunder. "Elizabeth realized too late that not attending Susan's party was a faux pas."
- **Ipso facto**: From Latin meaning by the fact itself. "A teacher, ipso facto, is in charge of his or her class."
- **Modus operandi**: From Latin meaning method of operating. "My modus operandi when studying is to set very specific goals."
- **Persona non grata**: From Latin meaning an unacceptable person. "Sally was a persona non grata in our club because she wouldn't follow the rules."
- **Prima donna**: From Latin meaning a temperamental and conceited person. "Laura wasn't popular with the other girls because they considered her to be a prima donna."
- **Pro bono**: From Latin meaning done or donated without charge. "The lawyer's pro bono work with the homeless gave him a sense of personal satisfaction."
- **Quid pro quo**: From Latin meaning something for something, usually an equal exchange. "Helping Ian with his math was quid pro quo for the time Ian helped me mow the lawn."
- **Status quo**: From Latin meaning the existing condition. "Because he didn't like change, Bert always tried to maintain the status quo."

CHAPTER THIRTY-SEVEN

Unit 7: Electronic modes of Communication

(**Topics Covered:** Use of telephone, Taking telephonic orders, Telephone etiquette's, Fax, E-mail and protocol, Responsible social media.)

Electronic communication can be defined as, the communication which uses electronic media to transmit the information or message using computers, e-mail, telephone, video calling, FAX machine, etc. This type of communication can be developed by sharing data like images, graphics, sound, pictures, maps, software, and many things. Because of this e-communication, there is a lot of changes have occurred in work areas, society, etc. Thus, people can simply access global communication with no physical movement.

7.1 Use of telephone:

Despite the rapid changes in technology over the years, the importance of telephone communication in business still remains. The advantage of actually speaking to your customers and co-workers in many cases is often more effective, personal, appropriate, and time-saving than written communications such as email and texting.

7.1.2 Reasons why talking with someone on the telephone is still important for your business:

- Talking with Your Customers on the Telephone is Much More Personal
- Tone is Very Important for Effective Communication and Your Tone Can Come through More Clearly on a Telephone
- You Can Get an Immediate Response When You Talk on the Phone
- Leaving a Voice Mail is Usually Easier and Your Message is not limited to a Number of Characters
- Sensitive Issues are Better Handled by a Telephone Call

7.2 Taking telephonic orders:

(Example of Room Service Telephonic Order Taking basic procedure)

- The telephone must be answered within the three (3) first rings.
- Greet Callers Warmly
- Identify your department and introduce yourself by name.
- Announce: "Good morning / Good afternoon / Good evening In Room Dining, (according to the time of the day), this is (name of the order taker), may I assist you Mr./Mrs./Miss" followed by the name of the guest according to the data digitally displayed by the phone system (if available).
- Use good telephone etiquette.
- Do a room enquiry on the POS (Point of Sale) machine and check the billing instructions entered for this guest by the front office team.
- If the guest is on Cash Only list, then politely explain that the guest will have to pay for order when it is delivered.
- If the guest is not on cash list then take the order without discussing the method of payment.
- Pay attention to orders, and know the menu thoroughly.
- Ask questions to find out the guest's choice or preferences for service, such as how he or she would like an item cooked or prepared (eg: medium rare, "on the rocks etc)
- Ask the guest for his or her choice of salad dressings and for any special requests such as fat-free preparation. Etc.
- Write down all information's clearly. Highlight special requests.
- Ask how many guests will be eating and note down the number on the guest check. As this will help the waiter to set the tray/ cart with the appropriate numbers of cutleries and crockery.

7.3 Telephone Etiquette:

The telephone is one of the most important and commonly used tools in business. Multitudes of businesses, companies, and departments use telephones in their work every day; however, most of us don't think of the telephone as a tool, and as a result, accidentally misuse it. The telephone is a link between us and the world outside our business or department. Unfortunately, sometimes we don't pay attention or make a conscious effort to monitor what kind of message we are sending to our callers and the outside world.

Some basic rules of telephone etiquette are. . .

- Speak directly into the mouthpiece of the phone or a headset while talking
- DO NOT eat or chew gum while talking on the telephone
- DO NOT cover the phone with your hand or put it against your chest to avoid the caller hearing you. Chances are, they will still be able to comprehend what you are saying.
- If you are interrupted or must talk to somebody else in your workplace while you are on the phone, simply ask the caller if they can hold and press the HOLD button.
- DO NOT place the handset in the cradle until you've pressed the HOLD button.
- DO NOT lay the receiver on the desk, without placing the caller on hold (the caller will hear everything being discussed in your office).
- Always be courteous.

7.4 Fax:

Fax is nothing but an acronym for facsimile. It is useful for sending letters faster. It also gives authenticity to the communications as it will bear the signature of the sender and is sent on his letter head. However it is necessary to take a photocopy of the message printed on such papers because the print on them fades out in course of time.

7.5 E-mail and protocol:

There are rules for them to manage the messages so the professionalism and politeness are kept.

- Subject: Subject line is very important. Email with no subject can be seen as spam or junk.. Subject is also useful if you want the recipients to read your email first by writing words like [URGENT] as their inbox might be filled with many emails. Please remember that you cannot write subject header with "Hello" or "Hi". Subject line must be relevant with your messages
- Header: Do not forget to change the header to correspond with the subject. By giving a new header, the recipients can find a certain document you sent in their inbox folder without having to check your emails one by one.

- Respect and personal: You have to show respect for example by giving a certain greeting. "Dear Mr. Pandey" is fine. Make sure you write the name of the recipient so it will be more personal.

- Tone: Unlike the face-to-face communication where communication is delivered verbally, exchanging emails need a specific tone so the reader can read the text carefully. Tone is crucial as it helps the reader to correctly understand the text.

- Spelling and grammar: The message you write represents who you are. So make sure you have checked all the spellings and grammar before sending the email.

- Short message: Do not write a long email. Three or four paragraphs are enough with two or three sentences per paragraph.

- Signature: Signature is totally important. Never forget to put your name below the message. You may also need to add contact information like street address, fax and phone. The signature helps you to show your professionalism.

- Quick response: Expecting a quick response is okay, but do not insist to have your email responded like 5 minutes after the sending.

7.6 Responsible social media:

You are 100 percent responsible for everything that appears on your social media accounts, from your status updates and comments to pictures, videos, and links you share. Here are some pointers for staying on top of your personal and professional responsibilities in today's social age.

- You won't agree with everything or everyone you encounter on social media networks, but treat each person with dignity and respect. The Golden Rule of treating others how you want to be treated is a good practice.

- Do not turn to social media as a way to harass, demean, or bully someone else. Sitting in front of a computer screen does not give you license to embarrass, intimidate, or spread hurtful rumours about others.

- Regardless of your privacy settings, keep in mind that anything can possibly be seen by anyone at any time, even by that person that you didn't want to see it. Think before you post!

- Whether you're concerned with maintaining good friendships or future job prospects, be responsible in what you post and how it could affect your reputation. Many employers now check up on job candidates' social media accounts for evidence of bad behaviour.

7.6.1 Social Media Etiquette:

Social media etiquette refers to both the spoken and unspoken set of social conventional rules of personal and business behaviour online. It dictates how people conduct themselves on social media so they remain respectful and respectable.

Bad social media etiquette on your personal account will probably leave you with posts that make your future self cringe. But for businesses, it could affect their brand reputation and can deter customers from returning.

7.6.2 Why is social media etiquette important for business?

With an increasingly vigilant internet population, a single mistake on social media can make or break a business.

Outlining proper social media etiquette in your social media policy will help you:

- **Protect against legal and security issues:** If your industry has stringent privacy and compliance laws, your system will keep you on the right side of the regulations.
- **Protect against privacy risks:** Social media etiquette outlines what's acceptable to share and what isn't. This helps prevent privacy violations for your business and for others.
- **Empower staff:** When your employees know how to share content safely online, they can represent and advocate for your organization, without harming your reputation.
- **Defend your brand:** Social media etiquette ensures that everyone who interacts with your brand on social media will see a respectable, professional business.

Part E: Application of Computers

Application of Computers

CHAPTER THIRTY-EIGHT

Unit 1: Characteristics of Computers

(**Topics Covered:** Speed, Accuracy, Diligence, Versality, Power of remembering)

"We may define computer as a device that transforms data"

Characteristics of computers:

Speed:

As you know computer can work very fast. It takes only few seconds for calculations that we take hours to complete. Suppose you are asked to calculate the average monthly income of one thousand persons in your neighbourhood. For this you have to add income from all sources for all persons on a day to day basis and find out the average for each one of them. How long will it take for you to do this? One day, two days or one week? Do you know your small computer can finish this work in few seconds? The weather forecasting that you see every day on TV is the results of compilation and analysis of huge amount of data on temperature, humidity, pressure, etc. of various places on computers. It takes few minutes for the computer to process this huge amount of data and give the result. You will be surprised to know that computer can perform millions (1,000,000) of instructions and even more per second. Therefore, we determine the speed of computer in terms of microsecond (10-6 part of a second) or nano-second (10-9 part of a second). From this you can imagine how fast your computer performs work.

Accuracy:

Suppose someone calculates faster but commits a lot of errors in computing. Such result is useless. There is another aspect. Suppose you want to divide 15 by 7. You may work out up to 2 decimal places and say the dividend is 2.14. I may calculate up to 4 decimal places and say that the result is 2.1428. Someone else may go up to 9 decimal places and say the result is 2.142857143. Hence, in addition to speed, the computer should have accuracy or correctness in computing. The degree of accuracy of computer is very high and every calculation is performed with the same accuracy. The accuracy level is determined on the basis of design of computer. The errors in computer are due to human and inaccurate data.

Diligence:

A computer is free from tiredness, lack of concentration, fatigue, etc. It can work for hours without creating any error. If millions of calculations are to be performed, a computer will perform every calculation with the same accuracy. Due to this capability it overpowers human being in routine type of work.

Versatility:

It means the capacity to perform completely different type of work. You may use your computer to prepare payroll slips. Next moment you may use it for inventory management or to prepare electric bills.

Power of Remembering:

Computer has the power of storing any amount of information or data. Any information can be stored and recalled as long as you require it, for any numbers of years. It depends entirely upon you how much data you want to store in a computer and when to lose or retrieve these data.

CHAPTER THIRTY-NINE

Unit 2: Computer and its Components

(Topics Covered: Input unit, Storage unit, Central Processing Unit, Output unit)

<u>Computer and its components:</u>

<u>Input Devices:</u>

You use input devices to provide information to a computer, such as typing a letter or giving Instructions to a computer to perform a task. Some examples of input devices are described in the following list.

- **Mouse:** A device that you use to interact with items displayed on the computer screen. A standard mouse has a left and a right button.
- **Trackball:** This is an alternative to the traditional mouse and is favoured by graphic designers. It gives a much finer control over the movement of items on the screen.
- **Other screen pointing** devices are pointing stick, touch pad, joystick, light pen, digitizing table.
- Keyboard: A set of keys that resembles a typewriter keyboard. You use the keyboard to type text, such as letters or numbers into the computer.
- Scanner: A device that is similar to a photocopy machine. You can use this device to transfer an exact copy of a photograph or document into a computer. A scanner reads the page and translates it into a digital format, which a computer can read. For example, you can scan photographs of your family using a scanner.
- **Barcode Readers:** When used in a business barcodes provide a lot of information. Made up of columns of thick and thin lines, at the bottom of which a string of numbers is printed.

Storage Units:

The system unit is the name given to the main computer box that houses the various hardware. How do we get the different computer parts to work together so that your computer can work? By the process devices as below...

Mother Board: Inside the system unit is a circuit board with tiny electronic circuits and other components which is called a mother board. It is sometimes called a system board. The motherboard connects input (keyboard, mouse and scanner), output (monitor, speakers, and printer), processing (CPU, RAM and ROM) and storage (hard drive, CD and flash drives) components together and tells the CPU how to run (Lubbe and Benson, 2010:18). Other components on the motherboard include the video card, the sound card, and the circuits that allow the computer to communicate with devices like the printer.

Expansion Cards: Yes you can play music and video files on your computer. But how is it possible? Inside the computer system box you also find an expansion card circuit board that can be attached to the motherboard to add features such as video display and audio capability to your computer. Expansion cards are also called expansion boards that enable your computer to use the multimedia devices. An performance of your computer or enhances its features.

All computers need to store and retrieve data for processing. The CPU is constantly using memory from the time that it is switched on until the time you shut it down. There are two types of storage devices...

Primary Storage: is also called main memory or immediate access store (IMAS). This is necessary since the processing unit can only act on data and instructions that are held in primary storage. Primary storage consist..

- Random Access Memory (RAM)
- Read Only Memory (ROM)

Secondary Storage Devices:

PCs use a simple method of designating disk drives to store data. Letters of the alphabet. Data and information stored on a permanent basis for later use. Secondary storage is cheaper to purchase and access. Hard disks, Zip drives, Optical disks (CD's and DVD's) are all examples of secondary storage.

Central Processing Unit (CPU):

FUNCTIONAL UNITS: In order to carry out the operations mentioned in the previous section the computer allocates the task between its various functional units. The computer system is divided into three separate units for its operation. They are 1) arithmetic logical unit, 2) control unit, and 3) central processing unit.

Arithmetic Logical Unit (ALU) After you enter data through the input device it is stored in the primary storage unit. The actual processing of the data and instruction are performed by Arithmetic Logical Unit. The major operations performed by the ALU are addition, subtraction, multiplication, division, logic and comparison. Data is transferred to ALU from storage unit when required. After processing the output is returned back to storage unit for further processing or getting stored.

Control Unit (CU) The next component of computer is the Control Unit, which acts like the supervisor seeing that things are done in proper fashion. The control unit determines the sequence in which computer programs and instructions are executed. Things like processing of programs stored in the main memory, interpretation of the instructions and issuing of signals for other units of the computer to execute them. It also acts as a switch board operator when several users access the computer simultaneously. Thereby it coordinates the activities of computer's peripheral equipment as they perform the input and output. Therefore it is the manager of all operations mentioned in the previous section.

Central Processing Unit (CPU) 9 The ALU and the CU of a computer system are jointly known as the central processing unit. You may call CPU as the brain of any computer system. It is just like brain that takes all major decisions, makes all sorts of calculations and directs different parts of the computer functions by activating and controlling the operations.

<u>Output Devices:</u>

Output devices in the computer system are the equipment whereby the result of a computer operation can be viewed, heard or printed. You use output devices to get feedback from a computer after it performs a task.

- **Monitor:** A device that is similar to a television. It is used to display information, such as text and graphics, on the computer.
- **Printer:** A device that you use to transfer text and images from a computer to a paper or to another medium, such as a transparency film. You can use a printer to create a paper copy of whatever you see on your monitor.

- **Multimedia Output Device:** The most common multimedia output is sound, including music. The audio output device on a computer is a speaker. Headphones can also be used to receive audio output.

CHAPTER FORTY

Unit 4: Computer Software

(Topics Covered: System software. Application software)

Computer software:

Computer software can be divided into two distinct categories. These are system software and application software.

System software is a type of software that is designed to communicate with the hardware or even application software. It acts as an interface between the hardware and the computer programs whereby it coordinates the tasks between these two components of a computer system.

There are different types of system software. They include the operating system, language processors, and device drivers. A typical system software ensures that the hardware handles its tasks successfully. For instance, an operating system does memory management and file handling for hardware. Drivers control the performance of the monitor and other devices such as printers.

<u>Examples:</u>

- Windows. The Windows Operating System is perhaps one of the most well-known system software.
- Mac OS. The Mac Operating System, along with Windows, is one of the most popular operating systems.
- Chrome OS.
- Ubuntu.
- Android.
- iOS.
- Blackberry.
- PlayStation System Software.

Application software is the type of software that is designed to accomplish specific tasks within the operating system. Some of these tasks include handling documents, handling calculations, image editing, video editing among others.

Example of application software includes word processors, spreadsheets, database software, image editors among others.

Examples:

- Microsoft Word.
- Google Chrome.
- Firefox.
- Skype.
- Windows Media Player.
- VLC Media Player.
- Microsoft Access.
- Photoshop.

CHAPTER FORTY-ONE

Unit 5: Operating System

(Topics Covered: Windows, Linux)

An operating system is a software programme required to manage and operate a computing device like smartphones, tablets, computers, supercomputers, web servers, cars, network towers, smartwatches, etc. It is the operating system that eliminates the need to know coding language to interact with computing devices. It is a layer of graphical user interface (GUI), which acts as a platform between the user and the computer hardware. Moreover, the operating system manages the software side of a computer and controls programs execution.

<u>Windows:</u>

The oldest of all Microsoft's operating systems is MS-DOS (Microsoft Disk Operating System).

MS-DOS is a text-based operating system. Users have to type commands rather than use the more friendly graphical user interfaces (GUI's) available today. Despite its very basic appearance, MS-DOS is a very powerful operating system. There are many advanced applications and games available for MS-DOS. A version of MS-DOS underpins Windows. Many advanced administration tasks in Windows can only be performed using MS-DOS.

<u>History</u>

<u>Windows versions through the years</u>

<u>1985: Windows 1.0</u>

The history of Microsoft Windows dates back to 1985, when Microsoft released Microsoft Windows Version 1.01. Microsoft's aim was to provide a friendly user-interface known as a GUI (graphical user interface) which allowed for easier navigation of the system features. Windows 1.01 never really caught on. The release was a shaky start for the tech giant. Users found the software unstable. (The amazing thing about Windows 1.01 is that it fitted on a single floppy disk). However, the point-and-click interface made it easier for new users to operate a computer. Windows 1.0 offered many of the common components found in today's graphical user interface, such as scroll bars and "OK" buttons.

1987: Windows 2.0 and 2.11

Windows 2.0 was faster, more stable and had more GUI features. The GUI was very slightly improved but still looked too similar to Windows 1.01.The system introduced the control panel and ran the first versions of Excel and Word. Windows 2.0 supported extended memory, and Microsoft updated it for compatibility with Intel's 80386 processor. It was during this time that Microsoft became the largest software vendor in the world, just as computers were becoming more commonplace. The fact that Windows systems were user-friendly and relatively affordable was a contributing factor to the growing PC market.

1990: Windows 3.0

Windows 3.0 supported 16 colours and included the casual games familiar to most Windows users: Solitaire, Minesweeper and Hearts. Games that required more processing power still ran directly on MS-DOS. Exiting to DOS gave games direct hardware access made more system resources available. Microsoft made an enormous impression with Windows 3.0 and 3.1. Graphics and functionality were drastically improved. The Windows 3 family provided multimedia capabilities as well as vastly improved graphics and application support. Building on the success of Windows 3.x, Microsoft released Microsoft Windows 3.11 for Workgroups. This gave Windows the ability to function on a network.

1993: Windows New Technology (NT)

Windows NT's release marked the completion of a side project to build a new, advanced OS. NT was 32-bit and had a hardware abstraction layer. DOS was available through the command prompt, but it did not run the Windows OS. Microsoft designed NT as a workstation OS for businesses rather than home users. The system introduced the Start button.

1995: Windows 95

In 1995 Windows went through a major revamp and Microsoft Windows 95 was released. This provided greatly improved multimedia and a much more polished user interface. The now familiar desktop and Start Menu appeared. Internet and networking support was built in. Although Windows 95 was a home user operating system, it proved to be very popular in schools and businesses. Windows 95 facilitated hardware installation with its Plug and Play feature. Microsoft also unveiled 32-bit colour depth, enhanced multimedia capabilities and TCP/IP network support.

1998: Windows 98

Microsoft Windows 98 was very similar to Windows 95, it offered a much tidier display and enhanced multimedia support. Microsoft improved speed and Plug and Play hardware support in Windows 98. The company also debuted USB support and the Quick Launch bar in this release. DOS gaming began to wane as Windows gaming technology improved. The popularity of the OS made it an attractive target for malware. Microsoft integrated web technology into the Windows user interface and built its own web browser into the desktop.

2000: Windows Millennium Edition (ME)

Windows ME (Millennium Edition) was the last use of the Windows 95 codebase. Its most notable new feature was System Restore. Many customers found this release to be unstable. Some critics said ME stood for "mistake edition." Microsoft released the professional desktop OS Windows 2000 (initially called NT 5.0) in the same year for the business market. Improvements to the overall operating system allowed for easier configuration and installation. Microsoft based this OS on the more stable Windows NT code. Some home users installed Windows 2000 for its greater reliability. Microsoft updated Plug and Play support, which spurred home users to switch to this OS. One big advantage of Windows 2000 was that operating system settings could be modified easily without the need to restart the machine. Windows 2000 proved to be a very stable operating system that offered enhanced security and ease of administration.

2001: Windows XP

Microsoft delivered Windows XP as the first NT-based system with a version aimed squarely at the home user. Home users and critics rated XP highly. The system improved Windows appearance with colorful themes and provided a more stable platform. Microsoft virtually ended gaming in DOS with this release. DirectX-enabled features in 3D gaming that OpenGL had difficulties with. XP offered the first Windows support for 64-bit computing, but it was not very well supported, lacking drivers and applications to run.

2006: Windows Vista

Microsoft hyped Windows Vista after the company spent a lot of resources to develop a more polished appearance. Vista had interesting visual effects but the OS was slow to start and run. Vista's flaws -- coupled with the fact that many older computers lacked the resources to run the system -- led to many home and business users staying with XP.

2009: Windows 7

Microsoft built Windows 7 on the Vista kernel. Windows 7 picked up Vista's visual capabilities but featured more stability. To many end users, the biggest changes between Vista and Windows 7 were faster boot times, new user interface and the addition of Internet Explorer 8. With true 64-bit support and more Direct X features, Windows 7 proved to be a popular release for Windows users.

2012: Windows 8

Microsoft released Windows 8 with a number of enhancements and debuted its tilebased Metro user interface. Windows 8 took better advantage of multicore processing, solid-state drives (SSD), touch screens and other alternate input methods.

2015: Windows 10

Microsoft announced Windows 10 in September 2014, skipping Windows 9 and launched on July 2015. Version 10 includes the Start menu, which was absent from Windows 8. A responsive design feature called Continuum adapts the interface depending on whether the user works with a touch screen or a keyboard and mouse for input. New features like an onscreen back button simplified touch input. Microsoft designed the OS to have a consistent interface across devices including PCs, laptops and tablets.

Linux:

Just like Windows, iOS, and Mac OS, Linux is an operating system. In fact, one of the most popular platforms on the planet, Android, is powered by the Linux operating system. An operating system is software that manages all of the hardware resources associated with your desktop or laptop. To put it simply, the operating system manages the communication between your software and your hardware. Without the operating system (OS), the software wouldn?t function.

The Linux operating system comprises several different pieces:

1. **Bootloader** – The software that manages the boot process of your computer. For most users, this will simply be a splash screen that pops up and eventually goes away to boot into the operating system.
2. **Kernel** – This is the one piece of the whole that is actually called ?Linux?. The kernel is the core of the system and manages the CPU, memory, and peripheral devices. The kernel is the lowest level of the OS.

3. **Init system** – This is a sub-system that bootstraps the user space and is charged with controlling daemons. One of the most widely used init systems is systemd? which also happens to be one of the most controversial. It is the init system that manages the boot process, once the initial booting is handed over from the bootloader (i.e., GRUB or GRand Unified Bootloader).

4. **Daemons** – These are background services (printing, sound, scheduling, etc.) that either start up during boot or after you log into the desktop.

5. **Graphical server** – This is the sub-system that displays the graphics on your monitor. It is commonly referred to as the X server or just X.

6. **Desktop environment** – This is the piece that the users actually interact with. There are many desktop environments to choose from (GNOME, Cinnamon, Mate, Pantheon, Enlightenment, KDE, Xfce, etc.). Each desktop environment includes built-in applications (such as file managers, configuration tools, web browsers, and games).

7. **Applications** – Desktop environments do not offer the full array of apps. Just like Windows and macOS, Linux offers thousands upon thousands of high-quality software titles that can be easily found and installed. Most modern Linux distributions (more on this below) include App Store-like tools that centralize and simplify application installation. For example, Ubuntu Linux has the Ubuntu Software Center (a rebrand of GNOME Software? Figure 1) which allows you to quickly search among the thousands of apps and install them from one centralized location.

CHAPTER FORTY-TWO

Unit 6: Windows; Desktop Elements

(**Topics Covered**: Start a programme, Quit a programme, Getting help, Searching files & folders, Changing system settings, Using my computer for browsing disk drives)

The desktop is your workspace on a computer and is always the first thing that you see once you have logged in.

There are several principal components to Windows desktops: The Start menu, the Task bar, and the time, which are all located at the bottom of the screen, and the main workspace, which takes up most of your screen. The workspace is composed of a background, and usually some icons and/ or windows.

Each file, folder or application that you open appears in a window (a sort of container) on the desktop. You can have as many windows open at the same time as you want. Since each window takes up space and there is limited space on your desktop, windows can be placed one on top of another to save space or make room for a new window. You can do this by dragging one window over another.

The most recently opened or used window is always on top (most visible). This is called the active window. When switching between windows or working with multiple windows you should always be aware of which one is the current active window. The easiest way to do this is to look at the Task bar where the button corresponding to the active window is different from the others (for more on the Task bar see section called Task Bar under The Desktop).The frame around an active window will also be darker.

Generally, there are two types of windows, ones that let you view and work with folders and ones that let you work with files using applications.

Start Menu:

When you click on the Start button (which is located in the lower left corner of your screen) a menu appears which should look similar to the one below. This menu gives you quick and easy access to all of the applications and system folders that are available on your computer.

Parts of the Start menu

User name - at the very top of the menu you see the name of the user who is currently logged in on the computer. If the user specified an image when they created their user account, the image is shown next to the name. In the example above, the user *ETI* specified the image of a flower.

Applications that you access most often - this area of the menu shows the applications that you access most often. To open one of those applications, click on its name in the menu. This list of applications is determined automatically by the computer based on your use.

Applications that you accessed recently - the computer keeps track of the applications that you recently used several times and adds them to this list so that you can quickly access them again.

General folders for your personal files - most computers have default folders for different types of personal files such as *My Documents, My Music* and *My Pictures*. This area gives you direct access to these folders, as well as to the *My Computer* and *My Network Places* folders.

Options to configure your computer - this area gives you quick access to ways to change the configuration of your computer such as setting internet and network preferences, specifying printers, and changing the general settings of your computer using the *Control Panel*. The section *Control Panel* under *personalizing your workspace* has more information on this topic.

Search and help options - this area lets you quickly access the search functionality to find files on your computer, or access the help that Windows provides about itself.

Quick access to all of your applications - when you put your mouse over the *All Programs* sub-menu another menu appears which lists all of the applications or application families (Microsoft Office, which contains Microsoft programs such as Word, PowerPoint, Excel and Access is a family of programs) that are installed on your computer. Click on any application in the list to open it.

Searching Files and Folders:

It often happens that you don't remember the exact location of a particular file or folder on your computer, or that you want to be able to see all of the files of a certain type, or ones that you produced on a certain date. One way of doing this is to look through each folder on your computer in turn and note down the relevant information. However, even on computers that have a moderate amount of files and folders this quickly becomes both a time consuming and frustrating task. The easier and more efficient way of doing it is to use the Search options available in Windows.

<u>You can access the search functionality in one of two ways:</u>

- via the Search button in the button bar of a window
- by going to the Start menu and then selecting the Search option, which is shown using the same icon as above. Note: at the ETI, when you select Search, a sub-menu appears. Select the option For Files or Folders.

Getting Help:

Knowing where and how to get help when you get stuck with a computer problem is one of the most important skills you will need to learn. The first step is to clearly identify what the problem is, and then to identify the most appropriate place to look for a solution.

If you are working within an application and are trying to figure out how to do something, you might want to search for a particular topic within the help pages of that application. If you want to know what a particular button does, you might want to search using the alt text for that button (the text that appears when you place your mouse over the button without pressing it) as a keyword within the application's help files. However, if you want more general definitions, or explanations of functionalities that are not directly linked to an application, finding help online might be a better option.

Help within an application:

Almost all applications have a Help menu, located towards the right side of the menu bar. Depending on the application, the options in the Help menu will vary, but one of two options is almost always guaranteed to be there:

- searching local help
- searching online help

When you search local help, you are searching in help files that are contained within the application. This means that you don't need an internet connection to look at them. In most cases, you can search the help by topics or keywords. The other option, to search the online help, usually provides a link to the official help pages for the application which are located online. Online help pages are often more detailed and extensive than the local help.

Note: in some applications the Help menu can be called simply? or Help? rather than Help.

<u>Help online:</u>

The internet can be a very useful resource for finding information about solving computer problems. The help can come in many forms, both official and unofficial - websites, FAQs, forums etc. For example, many applications (or at least the software companies that make the applications) have websites that often contain forums and FAQ sections, or general help. If you're stuck on a problem with a particular application to which you can't find the answer in the local help, the official online help for the application is one of the first places that you should look. If you don't find it there, there is usually a way (email or online form) to contact the customer support service of the company and ask them directly. However, you should only do this if you are sure that you can't find the answer in the other help resources.

Other good resources of information, especially for more general issues that are not related to specific applications are websites such as

- whatis.techtarget.com (technology related definitions in English)
- computer.howstuffworks.com (general info about computers in English)
- www.webopedia.com (in English)
- www.learnthenet.com (info about using the internet in English, French and Spanish)
- www.commentcamarche.net (in French)

which offer general information and definitions on everything related to using a computer, and forums. Simply typing your query into a search engine such as Google will take you to dedicated sites discussing the problem.

Note: when you're constructing your help search, pay close attention to the keywords that you use. If your search doesn't come up with anything the first time around, don't give up. Try using synonyms for the most important words or reformulating your query.

Changing system settings:

Select the **Start** button, then select **Settings** . From there, browse the categories or use search to find what you're looking for.

Turn Off your Computer:

To turn off your computer (shut it down) first select the Start button. At the bottom of the Start menu you will see the option Turn Off Computer.

Using my computer for browsing disk drives:

To start, open a File Explorer window. On the top bar, click the View tab to open that menu, then select the Options icon here to open a new window.

On the resulting dialog box, select the View tab. Here, scroll down and find the Hide empty drives option, which is checked by default. Uncheck this box, which tells Windows to show all possible drives on your PC, even if they don't have any data to read.

You might not see any difference in This PC after making this change if you're using all of your drives. One common scenario that produces a blank drive is a laptop with a built-in SD card slot that doesn't currently have a card inside. This can also happen if you have an SD card reader or docking station connected to your computer without any media connected to the device.

When you tell Windows to show all drives, it simply displays that drive on This PC with the same letter, even when there's nothing to browse on the device.

Unit 7: File management in Windows

(Topics Covered: Using windows explorer, Opening drives & folders, View file details, Copying & moving files use windows explorer, Create a new folder, Rename a file or folder, Delete a file or folder)

File management in Windows:

Even though new technologies are making it increasingly easier to find a specific file or application on your computer, you should never the less have some degree of organization in your files. How you organize your files is your choice - each person has methods and structures that work best for them - but, your files should have some sort of organization. How you name and organize your files and folders is also important since each file/folder is uniquely identified by its name and its location on your computer.

Windows Explorer:

Using *Windows Explorer* is a convenient way to get an overview of the contents of your computer. Although *Windows Explorer* and *My Computer* show similar things, their purposes are quite different. *My Computer* is intended to give you a more comprehensive technical overview, while *Windows Explorer* is intended for browsing and/or modifying the file structure of your computer, and its layout and functionalities are more conducive to performing these tasks than those of *My Computer*.

Also, note that *Windows Explorer* is not the same thing as *Internet Explorer*. *Internet Explorer*, as the name suggests, lets you browse on the Internet, whereas *Windows Explorer* lets you browse your Windows environment (ie the drives, folders and files on your computer).

To launch *Windows Explorer*, go to the *Start* menu, then to *All Programs*, then *Accessories*, and select *Windows Explorer* or right-click on the *Start* menu and select *Explore* from the contextual menu. **Note:** at the ETI you can also open *Windows Explorer* by clicking on the icon located just beside the *Start* button.

The *Windows Explorer* window, show in the example below, is similar to a standard window, with one difference - the *Windows Explorer* window has two panes (sides).

The left pane contains a hierarchical tree that shows all of the drives and folders on your computer. Notice that it only shows folders, and not individual files. Folders that contain sub-folders will have a little + in a box next to them. To see the sub-folders you need to expand that section of the tree by clicking on the little +. When you do this, the + changes to a - and a list of sub-folders, indented slightly from the original parent folder (the parent folder is the folder that contains the sub-folders). To hide the sub-folders again, click on the - symbol.

To see the entire content of a folder (both sub-folders and files), click on the folder in the left pane. The folder is highlighted and its content appears in the pane on the right side. The right pane behaves exactly the same way as any other window view of a folder. You can open a file or see the content of a folder by double-clicking on it. When you open a folder in the right pane, the same folder becomes highlighted in the tree in the left pane.

For efficient file management you should use the left pane to select the folder that you are interested in and the right pane to get an overview of all of the files and folders inside it. In other words, you navigate on the left and look at details on the right.

Rearranging files

By default, files and folders are arranged in alphabetical order. However, you can change the order in which you see the files based on their name, their size, the type of file, or the date on which they were last modified.

The main way to change the sort order is by using the *View* menu of the window, selecting *Arrange Icons by...*, and then choosing one of *Name, Size, Type* and *Modified*. To change the order (ascending/descending) you need to make the exact same selection a second time.

If you are using the *Details* view you can use the headings of the columns (*Name, Size, Type* and *Modified*) to change the order. A little arrow pointing up (ascending) or down (descending) indicates which of the headings is currently being used to sort the files, and the 'direction' in which they are being sorted. To change the sorting, simply click on one of the headings. If you want to change the order within that heading (ie ascending instead of descending) click on the same heading a second time.

Making any window into an Explorer window

You can make any window that gives you a view of a folder into a *Windows Explorer* window at any time. To do this, just click on the *Folders* button in the button bar of the window. Similarly, you can make any *Windows Explorer* window into a normal window by doing the same thing. When moving from a *Windows Explorer* window to a regular window the files and folders that will appear in the regular window are those that were in pane on the right hand side of the *Windows Explorer* window.

<u>Opening Files and Folders:</u>

To open a file that already exists, double-click on it. The file will open in a window using the default application that is specified for opening that type of file. You can also open a file from inside an application by using the *File* menu of the application and then selecting *Open*. When you do this, you will usually see a pop-up window that contains your file structure. Select the file that you want to open from your file structure and then press the *Open* (or *OK*) button.

<u>Creating and saving a file</u>

Files can only be created using an application. When you open an application and start working with it, a file is created. However, in order for you to be able to keep and reuse that file, you need to save it first. Otherwise, when you close the application, the file (and all the content in it) will be lost.

To save a file, go to the *File* menu of the application and select either the *Save* or *Save As* option. If the file you are trying to save is brand new (ie it doesn't already have a name) these two options will let you do the same thing - give the file a name, select the type of file it will be and select where to store it on the computer. Most applications will also let you save using the shortcut Ctrl-S.

Note: you should always pay particular attention to where your file will be stored by checking that the folder or drive that is highlighted in the top center of the *Save* or *Save As* window is the one into which you want to save your file. Be sure to check the whole path, not just the final folder! If the highlighted folder is not the correct folder, you will need to find the correct folder in the hierarchy.

If you try to save a file that already has a name, the *Save* and *Save As* options do different things:

- Save - saves your file with the same name, type and location (no pop-up window appears).
- Save As - lets you change the name, type and location of the file before you save it (using a pop-up window).

Note: when a file already has a name, the shortcut Ctrl-S only lets you save the file (same as *Save* above) but does not let you change the name of the file.

<u>Naming a file</u>

When choosing a name for your file some rules must be followed, and some rules should be followed.

Must be followed:

- certain characters (/ \| : * ? " <>) are not allowed to be part of a file name.

Should be followed:

- file names should not contain blank spaces or accented characters since they can cause problems for certain applications or computers. If you want to add a space into a name, use the _ character (ie My_File.doc)
- file names should be short and meaningful. This makes them easier to find, and makes it easier for yourself and others to quickly see and understand the organization of your computer.

<u>Folders:</u>

A folder acts like a container to let you group items together. For example, you can group files about a certain topic together in a folder to keep them separate from files on other topics. Or, you can group files of a certain type together in a folder - for example, you can group all of your photos in a folder called *MyPhotos*. You can also group folders together inside another folder. For example, if you have photos of your vacations in Paris, Barcelona and Zurich, you can create a separate folder for each city, put the photos from Paris in the *Paris* folder etc., and then put the folders *Paris*, *Barcelona* and *Zurich* in your *MyPhotos* folder. A folder that is located inside another folder is called a sub-folder. In our example, the folders *Zurich*, *Barcelona* and *Paris* are sub-folders of the *MyPhotos* folder. Using folders and sub-folders gives you an easy way to organize your files.

<u>Opening a folder</u>

To open a folder that already exists, double-click on it. You'll see the content of the folder appear in a window.

<u>Creating a folder</u>

There are three different ways to create a folder when working in a window.

- **Using the *File* menu**: Go to the *File* menu in the top left corner of the window, select *New*, then *New Folder*. You can specify the name of the new folder by immediately typing it.

- **Using a contextual menu**: right-click with your mouse on an empty part of the window. You will see a contextual menu appear. Go to the *New* option and then from the menu that appears select *Folder*. You will see a new folder icon appear. You can specify a name for the new folder by immediately typing it.

- **Using the Common Tasks pane**: In the Common Tasks pane on the left side of the window you will see several categories - *File and Folder Tasks*, *Other Places* and *Details*. In the *File and Folder Tasks* section, click on the *Make a New Folder* option. You can specify a name for the new folder by immediately typing it.

In each of these cases, if you've already clicked somewhere else before you name the folder, the folder is given the default name of *New Folder*. You can change it in the standard way of changing folder names - right-click on the folder and select the option *Rename*.

<u>Naming folders</u>

The name of a folder should first and foremost be short and meaningful. Ideally, the name should describe in some way the content of the folder. This makes the folder (or its content) easier to find, and makes it easier for yourself and others to quickly see and understand the organization of folders/ files on your computer just by looking at the folder names.

Note: Since folders are not directly used by other programs, you can use any character in the name of the folder. But, keep in mind that if you plan to share a folder with others, you should avoid using special or accented characters since their computer might not recognize them. If the other person's computer does not recognize an accented character, it will insert random characters in its place, which will make the folder name look strange, or even unreadable to the other person.

<u>Renaming folders</u>

There are several ways to rename a folder.

If you are viewing the folder in a window, select the folder and then do one of the following:

- go to the *File* menu of the window and then select *Rename*
- right-click on the folder and select *Rename* from the contextual menu
- click on the folder name (not the icon)
- select the *Rename* option from the Common Tasks pane of the window

Choosing any one of these options will have the same effect - a little box will appear around the name of the folder, with the current name highlighted. To change the name completely, just start typing the new name. To modify the existing name, place the cursor on the part of the name that you want to modify and click once. You will see that the highlighting disappears and the name looks like regular text with the cursor at the position you selected. You can now make any modification, in the same way as you would if you were modifying text. In both cases, once you have the name that you want, you can either press the enter key or click somewhere outside of the name to save the new name.

<u>Moving, copying and deleting folders</u>

Folders can be moved, copied or deleted, just like files can.

Moving a folder

Moving a folder means putting the folder in a different location on your computer. This can be done in one of two ways. In both cases you first need to select the folder and then do one of the following:

- go to the *Edit* menu of the window and select *Move to folder*
- select the *Move this folder* option in the Common Tasks pane of the window

In both cases you next see a window which shows you an overview of the organization of your computer and lets you select the location to which you want to move the folder. Move through the hierarchy to find the location that you want and then press the *Move* button.

Copying a folder

When you copy a folder, you create an exact duplicate of the original folder, including the subfolders and files that it contains. These two folders (the original and the duplicate) are not linked in any way, so changes that you make in one folder will not affect the other folder. This also means that you can move the copy anywhere you like, rename it etc without affecting the original.

To copy a folder, select the folder and then do one of:

- go to the *Edit* menu of the window and then select *Copy*
- right-click on the folder and select *Copy* from the contextual menu
- use the shortcut Ctrl-C

When you use any of these options, the folder is copied and the computer stores it in its memory. To actually see the copy, you have to paste it, which mean that you have to put it somewhere. To do this, choose a location in your file structure, and then paste it by either using the shortcut Ctrl-V or selecting *Paste* from the *Edit* menu of the window or the contextual (right-click) menu. You will see the folder appear in the location you selected.

Another way to create a copy is to drag the folder directly to another location.

Note: if you paste the copied folder in the same location as the original folder, it will automatically be renamed to *Copy of* ... However, if you paste it anywhere else, the copy will have the same name as the original folder.

Deleting a folder

To delete a folder, select the folder and then:

- press the delete key on your keyboard
- go to the *File* menu of the window and select *Delete*
- right-click on the folder and then select *Delete* from the contextual menu
- drag the folder into the *Recycle Bin* on your desktop
- select *Delete this folder* from the Common Tasks pane of the window

All of these options will place the folder you selected in the *Recycle Bin*.

CHAPTER FORTY-FOUR

Unit 8: Computer Security

(Topics Covered: Views and threats, Protecting computer system using antivirus, Precautions to be taken against viruses.)

Computer Security:

These days you will find that you spend a lot of time with your computer connected to a network, or the internet, or being used in public places. While this gives you a lot of flexibility in how and where you work, it also exposes your computer to more hazards such as malicious applications that can damage its content, or to people using your computer for their own purposes without your knowledge. In this section we go through the basics of how to protect your computer from such problems.

Views and threats:

When you are in a public place (or working with sensitive documents) and you will be away from your computer for a while and don't want others to be able to see what is on your screen or use your computer, it is useful to be able to lock your computer before going away. **Note:** To be able to lock your computer, you must have a password enabled user account (this means that you need to enter a password when you first log on to your computer).

On a keyboard equipped with a Windows logo key press the Windows logo key (a key that has the same symbol on it as the symbol on the *Start* menu) and the L key at the same time. This will enable the password protection.

The other way to lock your computer is using the password protected screen saver as discussed in the section *Changing the screen saver* under *Personalizing your workspace*.

Protecting computer system using antivirus:

A computer virus is a malicious application that installs itself on your computer and can damage its content. A virus can arrive on your computer in several ways, but most commonly it attaches itself to a file that you load on your computer. When you open the file, the virus is released. Some common ways of catching a computer virus are:

- through local area networks
- by loading and opening files from a disk, CD/DVD or memory key
- by downloading files from the internet
- through email attachments
- by accepting file transfers in instant messaging applications
- through file sharing

There are many different types of computer viruses, which can do varying degrees of harm. Some of the common things that a virus can do to your computer are:

- damage existing applications
- delete files
- present text, video and audio messages randomly or continuously (while this does not damage the files on your computer it disrupts work and is generally annoying)
- can cause your computer to behave erratically or crash

Although not technically considered viruses, Trojan horses and worms can also harm your computer.

- **Trojan horse:** an application that appears to do one thing, but actually does something else. A common use of Trojan horses is to create a back door on your computer - a way for external people or software to access your computer when it is connected to a network or the Internet. The danger of this is that people can see personal files on your computer, or use your computer to do malicious things such as sending spam.
- **Worm:** unlike Trojan horses or viruses which need a user to move them between computers or open a file for them to be released, worms can send copies of themselves to other computers on a network without the user knowing about it or having done anything. While they are generally not harmful in the way that Trojans horses or viruses can be, worms tend to slow down the computer and cause erratic behaviour or crashes.

<u>Internet Security:</u>

While the internet can provide a lot of opportunities to meet new people, share media and do practical things such as shopping online, you should be aware of some of the problems that might come up in these situations, and how to protect yourself.

There are many points that fall into this category, but we will concentrate on the 4 most common:

- personal information and the web
- making purchases online
- email scams
- browser security settings

Personal information and the web:

The web is a public space. If you put up a personal website, or MySpace page, anyone in the world can access it and see the information that you provide. This means that if you include a photo, anyone will be able to see it, the same thing for phone numbers, email addresses, postal addresses etc. Unless it is an office number or address, it is usually not a good idea to put your personal phone number or postal address on the web. It is much safer to put an email where you can be reached.

Also, be careful to whom you give your personal information. People who you meet online, especially through social networking sites or instant messaging, may not be who they claim to be. Anyone can say something about themselves or put any photo they want online as their personal photo, but that doesn't mean that the information is true. All of this isn't to say that you shouldn't use these sites and services, lots of people do without having any problems. But, you should be conscious of the fact that while most people are honest, not everyone is, and you should exert the same amount of caution as you would when meeting people in real life.

Note: never give out your personal passwords, PIN numbers etc to other people.

Precautions to be taken against viruses:

There are several ways to protect your computer from viruses

- Install and activate an anti-virus application. **Note:** since viruses change over time and new viruses are constantly appearing, it is important to regularly update your anti-virus application.

- ALWAYS scan any new files that you load onto your computer with anti-virus software BEFORE you open them (and ideally before you load them).
- make sure to automatically download and install any software updates for Windows/Apple OS X or other applications that you might be using. Often, these updates include security updates that will make your computer less vulnerable to the spread of worms, Trojan horses and viruses.
- beware of attachments and files that are sent to you by people you don't know. Always scan such files, and when in doubt, do NOT download or install them. This is especially true of files that you download from the web or receive via sources such as email, instant messaging and file sharing. If you know the source of the file, for example a big company such as Microsoft or Apple, you can generally be quite sure that the files are not infected, but from most other sources, you should always scan the files

There are many commercial and free anti-virus applications on the market. Among the most common commercial anti-virus applications are McAfee and Norton, and among those that are free is Avast.

Author

Dr Anshumali Pandey, PhD, Author.

<u>About the Author:</u>

Dr. Anshumali Pandey, is a renowned & reliable name in the field of Education, Hospitality, Tourism and Tribal Food. He is a Teacher and Chef by profession, and also an Author, a Business Auditor, and an avid culinary traveller to the Indian Sub continental hinterlands. Dr. Anshumali Pandey is a Hospitality Educator (PhD) who specialises in Higher Education, Office Administration, Pay roll, HR, Labour Laws, Audit, and Procurement & Tender Process. He is an Author with 39 Publications consisting of 24 Books.

The books written by Dr Anshumali Pandey are essentially a banquet arising from an experience of over 25 years of Professional life and have boiled down to crisp and accurate writing on his favourite subjects. Hospitality Sector champion requires to be a specialist in many fields and Dr Pandey is one of them. His knowledge is evident from the spectrum of subjects which he has chosen for his books so far, which ranges from being a specialist chef, to Master of Human resources, to Education and to love for children, and topped with Spirituality.

Books written by the Author are –

1. Theory of Indian Cookery
2. Beauty and Irony of Silvassa Tourism
3. A Short Indian Food Story
4. Be Your Own Guide to Indian Cuisine
5. Cookery Fundamentals
6. History of Indian Food
7. The Great Indian Story Book for Children
8. Personal Budget: Easy Work Book
9. Online Classes Log Book
10. Dictionary Making Work Book for School Children
11. The Lazy Bed
12. Hindu Dharm (In Hindi Language)
13. Where is my coffee?
14. Your First Job is Never your Last (Volume 1)
15. You are Almost There (Quick Fix Resume and Interview Hacks)
16. Working for the Enemy? - A lesson in Career Management
17. Public Speaking for the Young
18. A Date With Coffee
19. How to be The Best Hotel Front Office Employee
20. Diploma in Food Production, The complete Syllabus
21. Diploma in F&B Service, The Complete Syllabus
22. Diploma in Front Office, The Complete Syllabus
23. The Time to Speak is Now
24. Munshi Premchand (Short Stories in English)

Connect with me: anshumali.pandey@gmail.com
https://notionpress.com/author/337004

Scan the QR Code to connect with other Books online

www.ingramcontent.com/pod-product-compliance
Lightning Source LLC
Chambersburg PA
CBHW071455140726
47997CB00005B/1730